Proceedings of the 1979 Clinic on Library Applications of Data Processing

Papers presented at the
1979 Clinic on Library Applications
of Data Processing, April 22-25, 1979

The Role of the Library in an Electronic Society

F. WILFRID LANCASTER

Editor

University of Illinois
Graduate School of Library Science
Urbana-Champaign, Illinois

Clinic on Library Applications of Data Processing,
    University of Illinois at Urbana-Champaign, 1980.
    The role of the library in an electronic society.

    (Proceedings of the 1979 Clinic on Library Applications of Data Processing)
    Title on spine: Library applications of data processing, 1979.
    "Papers presented at the 1979 Clinic on Library Applications of Data Processing, April 22-25, 1979."
    Includes index.
    1. Libraries—Automation—Congresses.   2. Library Science—Data processing—Congresses.   I. Lancaster, Frederick Wilfrid, 1933-   II. Title: Library applications of data processing, 1979.   IV. Series: Clinic on Library Applications of Data Processing. Proceedings; 1979.

Z678.A1C5   1979   021'.0028'54s   [025'.02'02854]
ISBN 0-87845-053-X   79-19449

CONTENTS

CONTENTS — *Continued*

Introduction

The sixteenth annual Clinic on Library Applications of Data Processing was held at the Illini Union, University of Illinois, April 22-25, 1979. This conference differed somewhat from its predecessors. Instead of focusing on library automation per se, we chose to look at various manifestations of electronic communication in the world around us (including electronic publication, computer conferencing and electronic mail), to consider present and probable future capabilities of electronic processing and, most importantly, to study the implications of these developments for libraries and librarians. The altered character of this particular conference caused it to differ from its predecessors in another way: most of the papers in 1979 were presented by leaders in fields outside of librarianship itself.

There is a third way in which the 1979 meeting differed from those that went before it. It was planned to dovetail with, and to form an integral part of, an ongoing research project relating to the impact of a "paperless society" on the research library of the future. This project, funded by the National Science Foundation, Division of Information Science and Technology, was conducted by the Library Research Center of the Graduate School of Library Science in the period September 1978 to February 1980. The scenario incorporated within the final paper of these proceedings was distributed to the conference participants in order to gain their reactions and inputs.

Although other conferences have dealt with the future of the library, this may be the first to focus on the library within the context of technological developments in publishing and related facets of human communication. I hope that the papers presented stimulate further thought, within the profession and beyond, on the implications for libraries of the evolution from a largely paper-based society to a society whose communication channels will be largely electronics-based.

I would like to thank Laura Drasgow, Ellen Marks, and Richard Blue for serving on the planning committee for the 1979 clinic.

F. WILFRID LANCASTER
Editor

DEREK DE SOLLA PRICE
Avalon Professor of the History of Science
Yale University
New Haven, Connecticut

Happiness is a Warm Librarian

The title of my talk is drawn from a pleasantly silly button which I wore to the first Library of Congress Conference on Library Automation about fifteen years ago. It was worn partly as the reaction of a humanist who loves both books *and* computers against the peculiar sort of computer macho that seemed to be evolving. There should, of course, be a rider on this perversion of "Happiness is a Warm Puppy." I'm not insinuating that librarians are like puppies, and I'm using *warm*, of course, not in the sense of temperature or even of emotion, but merely of being human, and not steel and silicon. I must say at the outset that I am no male chauvinist pig, but perhaps the full title of this paper ought to be "Happiness is a Warm Librarian—He'll Understand." There is an interesting chauvinist problem here in the trade: the societal typecasting of librarianship as one of the compassionate and nurturing occupations, rather like nursing and clerical, and therefore female. It is interesting that the *compassionate* is always set in contradistinction to the *dispassionate* which characterizes scholarly, innovative leadership. This is, of course, simply societal typecasting, and I want to emphasize the likelihood of enormous change in the course of adapting to the new technologies. These technologies will give rise to quite a new and essentially human need from librarians and information scientists, particularly for the gift of the peculiarly human pattern of thinking. In this little discourse I would like to set forth views which are those of a person who is only a hobbyist of information science...trying to balance the internal and external patterns of development of science and technology.

My real trade is understanding the progress of the evolution of science and technology, and I would like to apply some fairly well known principles to the particular and very strategic technology which is the subject of this conference. The social history of libraries is governed by very long periods of remarkably stable, almost fossilized existence separated by very short periods of remarkably rapid metamorphosis. It has been this way since the beginning. Consider some aspects of this evolution. From the invention of writing, probably about 3000 B.C., until the invention of printing (ca. A.D. 1500), libraries were very tiny. The great library of Ashurbanipal of Babylonia, which is now partially excavated, and the much better known Museum of Alexandria were *very* small collections. The great library of Alexandria (which, by the way, was probably never burned by the Arabs, but just wore out and got thrown away) could have been contained in about two ordinary, small faculty offices, according to the reasonable estimate of E.A. Parsons, who looked into the matter and threw out the mythology. That is a very tiny collection.

During the Renaissance and the Reformation, when libraries and knowledge flourished, the archive of learning grew from a tiny collection to fill a large room. It was not until the late eighteenth and early nineteenth centuries that the library essentially became a building in itself, and then in the late nineteenth and twentieth centuries the library became a whole complex of buildings and related industries and national institutions. Probably now it is in the course of becoming a totally international network that is not completely housed anywhere. Another way of looking at this might be in terms of the scale. Libraries and knowledge are the "growingest" things that we have. Certainly since the seventeenth century there has been a doubling in exponential (compound interest) growth about every ten years.

There were fixed intervals when the technology of knowledge changed grossly. The book very suddenly came into maturity in A.D. 1500. Remember that one generation, the lifetime of one individual, spanned the beginning of printing to the very sudden transformation of the book into a major force. Following was the equally sudden emergence in about 1660 of the operation that was to become the scholarly journal. This happened so quickly that it was simultaneously effected by the English and the French. After that came the rise, also sudden, of the secondary literature, around 1820, just after Napoleon; and lastly, the fairly rapid emergence of computers, which I have seen not just in my lifetime, but in my shorter stay in this country. Those stages are each separated by about 100-150 years. During the time that separates each stage from the next, knowledge measured by any reasonable yardstick grew by something like a factor of 1000-3000, and we are on the way through yet another, and obviously by no means the last, of these transformations.

Roughly speaking, every time knowledge increases a thousand times, something has to change in the knowledge system, and this is the implementation of an innovative, ambient technology. Each stage of the knowledge growth has looked extremely stable. The institutionalization that goes with libraries and the knowledge system at each stage looked extremely static. A look at the structure of the Library of Congress building will reveal that there was a room for everything and it was all nicely arranged for a certain number of people. There was no allowance for the fact that the institution had to become a thousand times bigger. When Yale's library (or any other institutional library) was built, it was planned for near-perfect occupancy. I've never seen a library built with a vacancy factor of more than one-half, even when it's known that a factor of one-half is only going to last ten years if the current rate of growth continues. We don't build libraries for 0.1 percent occupancy. We build them for conditions that we think are going to go on, if not forever, for a very long time. The next generation can make another building.

But change happens much faster than that. The changes have always been extremely rapid and unlike any reasonable projection that could have been made with a technological assessment using the best facts available at the moment. If, for example, Mr. Gutenberg and company had been asked what it was they were doing and what they were planning for and why they were inventing books, they would probably not have been able to admit to much more than the fact that they had gone from a sort of automated production of playing cards to making artificial manuscripts. If someone found an error, it could then be corrected in all copies, and that was a very neat trick. It wasn't really until half a generation later that the new technique suddenly found a totally different market, and the book became the force that produced the Reformation. It wasn't planned that the craftspeople adjacent to the printer—the engravers of scientific instruments and the other urban bourgeois craftspeople then emerging in the late fifteenth and early sixteenth centuries—would latch on to the new technique. As soon as the printers had finished printing the Bible and a few classics, they had to amortize that press and keep it busy, because the press was the next machine (after the windmill) that had to be fed after such a lot of capital had been poured into it. They didn't plan for it, but they took on the friendly neighborhood craftspeople and said, "Couldn't you write a book?" They produced a lot of how-to-do-it books on surveying, and the engraver of instruments engraved first blocks and then plates for the books. This made them much prettier and got them a much wider audience. That such a thing would happen could never have been predicted.

In a way, the system of writing books wasn't aided by printing technologies *replacing* the manuscript tradition. A new system of writing books, which had not been planned, grew up to utilize the available technology. The books that came off the presses were essentially different books from those that had been produced in the eras of manuscript publication. The old technology was not just displaced by the new one doing a better job with the same thing: the new technology did a different job. Similarly, the scientific journals that erupted about 1660 were produced as artifacts of a new stage in the evolution of the press. Ephemeral publications had come into use with sermons and broadsheets, and this led to the newspaper. Again, the available technology was utilized in doing a job that had not been done before. Of course, there had been scholarly letter-writing before, but the new form of communication, that came when a journal could be entrepreneured and sold, was something quite different. The scientific paper is not contained within the new technology; it was the new technology that gave birth to the journal. Similarly, at a later stage, when scientific journals had multiplied by a factor of 1000, everybody could see the embarrassment of so much knowledge that one couldn't keep up with it. Galileo, about 1600, was the first to be enormously surprised at having to read books by people who were still alive. It was something awfully new. Sixty years later, people were at the stage where they had things to read that were not even books yet, but were available because of the technology of ephemeral publications, stuff that came of a current-awareness type of printing rather than printing out of an archive.

With the embarrassment of too much knowledge, one attempt after another was made to solve the problem of this hideously exploding universe. First it was the encyclopedist who tried to make knowledge available without let or hindrance to the people of the time of the French and American revolutions. The encyclopedist produced the well-known *Grande Encyclopedie*. In its day, it cost the equivalent of something like $20,000 a copy. It was a huge price, a huge job of production, and an obvious failure in its direct purpose, but it did a great job politically. The encyclopedia had the greatest effect on those who wrote it, for there was hardly anybody to read it. It did start a fashion in encyclopedias that has lasted, but in a way it has been a failure, because the original object was that the encyclopedia would contain *all* knowledge, not just the sort of quintessence of that knowledge for ready reference in the home. It could not be used at the research front for it couldn't keep up with exponential growth. Ten years later half of all knowledge was not contained in it; it was too new.

The next attempt was that by librarians trying to master universal knowledge by perfect indexing systems. In the beginning, in the early nineteenth century, they really did try to make a card index of all the articles in the journals; they did not simply file volumes under *"Philosophical Transactions of the Royal Society*, Volume I," *"Philosophical Transactions...*, Volume II," and so on. They indexed all of the articles in all of the world's periodical literature, and began the brave and noble attempt called the *Catalogue of Scientific Papers* (a 19-volume compilation by the Royal Society of London of all papers published during the nineteenth century). It was carried on and on, with the ancient technology of handwritten cards in shoe boxes, until it was transferred to other hands and continued as *The International Catalogue of Scientific Literature*, covering the years 1901-16—but there it died. The librarians gave up, and so the secondary literature was spawned as a way of attacking the problem—and I need not say that it didn't really solve things. The mastery of periodical literature is still an open matter.

Presently, we are, it would appear, in a new period of rapid change. Computer technology, both the hardware and software, is not merely a very high technology. It is a technology that is changing as rapidly as any technology in the history of humanity. It shows every sign of continuing with no perceivable limits in rapid innovation of new technologies, both in hardware and software, for at least another generation. Reasonable estimates by people in the business lead us to suppose that there will continue to be radical new advances, for this is one of the very few growing tips where we have hardly begun to master the potential of the technology. So, we are in for not just a period of rapid change, but perhaps for the longest period of rapid change in the knowledge industry that there has ever been.

Another consideration is that though this is an age in which the rest of the world is catching up with the United States, and consequently this country has less and less of its investment in brainpower and high technology to export in exchange for the things it still imports, this is the one area in which the United States has more of a monopoly than in any other product. I remember an age when quite a lot of the world's motorcars and nearly all the nylon stockings came from the United States. Now every country in the world can make them. They are no longer exportable commodities. If this country wishes to maintain anything of its present quality of life, it had better have some good exportables. Some of the countries in Western Europe have a computer industry, but they are very much outclassed by the industry in the United States. It seems reasonable to expect that the expertise of the U.S. computerized knowledge industry may for a whole generation remain virtually a generation in advance of that of the rest of the world. Therefore, my first major point is that we must not predict that there will be stasis—that there will be any stationary equilibrium of the computerized knowledge industry. The syndrome that "it will be a beautiful data system when we get it finished" will not answer. We're not going to have a finished system in our lifetime or for some time beyond. We are going to have a rapidly evolving, changing system in which everybody in the industry must necessarily be on the research front, perceiving a generation of adjustment and quite new social forces. Therefore, for that reason alone, I think we must predict that what is going to evolve is not an old-fashioned library with fancy electronic indexes, nor even merely a computerized something-or-other. We are going to see a continuous series of updates. I would say that if the younger people at this conference are going to do something wonderful, remarkable and beautiful in library and information science, it probably hasn't been invented yet.

Another point about high technology is that it does not work, as I tried to illustrate, by doing an old job better. New products imply the generation of new markets that have not yet been perceived. Look at the recent history of digital watches and hand calculators. I haven't yet worn out an item of either of these, but I have changed the model that I use at least three times since they were first introduced, not because the new one does the old job better, but because the new one does jobs that could not be done before. As a historian of technology, I want to point out that no one could have imagined, even had they been in on the invention, that typewriters (which seemed would only mechanize writing) would invent secretaries; or that the automobile, in the act of replacing horses, would invent suburbs (let alone what its back seat would do to the intimate life of America). In my lifetime I have seen the advent of photocopying and it certainly has had more effect on me than making copying easier and better than I was used to, because copying used to be a relatively trivial activity for very special purposes. Nobody could have predicted that we academic faculty would use it as a way of *not* reading papers; now we just make copies. Librarians should just sit and analyze what the advent of the paperback did to people's reading habits. It did not only make the old books more readily available, but it induced new habits of "bookmanship." I used to spend a lot of my life searching antiquarian bookstores to find copies of the great classics which I absolutely had to have. One of the investments a scholar made was the building of such a library. I now have students who know that if it is not in their friendly neighborhood paperback bookstore it is not literature. I cannot as a teacher recommend books for reading that are not in the paperback bookstore.

One thing that the changing habits did was to destroy this old target of completeness that I had in dealing with the classical literature; completeness, in a way, becomes a rather irrelevant oddity. We tend to assume that the books that have survived are the books that are really wanted. (When you get old and gray, if you happen to find one of your old favorites that isn't "facsimiled" already, you mention it to one of your friends and, before you know it, it is reprinted.) With the junking of the old doctrine of completeness which formerly ruled many a scholar and librarian (but does not any more and ought to be reexamined), I think the librarian syndrome that goes something like, "It's in there somewhere, the trick is to find it," must die. Librarians do not need to take the attitude that "it" is in there somewhere; "if it's not visible it's probably not in there," is the new sort of attitude. Nevertheless, the question "It's in there somewhere, how am I going to find it?" is the central problem of indexing.

There are all sorts of other events one can see coming. One of my favorite observations of the changing technology is that of the demise of the motorcar and the junking of the dormitory suburbs. We are going to use terminals to change dormitory suburbs into service and knowledge industries—suburbs where one can decentralize all of those industries that work with knowledge on terminals. There is no reason to herd office workers into a single building.

Another old syndrome may be passing away; I mentioned the invention of the journal which caught on like wildfire because of something that was not predicted. It started as a formalized newsletter reporting what had gone on in all the other science "clubs," and what was being published in the scientific news of the day. It began as a "current-awareness" newsletter. It was then realized that if one simply took the stack of newsletters, bound them, and then every ten years or so made collections of them with indexes and summaries, automatically the journal would compact current awareness into an eternal archive. It was this attractive quality that generated the new attitude toward the journal: in the very act of communicating (or so one thought) would be generated a permanent archive of knowledge that could then be compressed until all knowledge, right up to the present, was there on the shelves. With all those indexes, of course, everything could be retrieved. I wonder if we still need that job done under the new computer technologies which do a better job of recording all that has been than is done by laying papers on top of each other. It's a difficult question. That job of packing down current awareness into a permanent archive implies a very linear sequential, and therefore probably false, model of knowledge. All sorts of things could be done to improve it. One of my favorite ideas at the moment, coming from a sort of cumulative advantage theory, is that if journals were published in ink that faded rapidly, and every time an article was used it automatically revised the ink back to fresh and stored the revision, then only useful knowledge would be left and it would really work rather well. It's rather like the idea I have heard proposed that every time a library book is used, an extra copy should be bought and put on the shelf at random. Then if someone came in and wanted thirty books, thirty books could be taken from the shelves at random and they probably would be the right ones, simply because the sampling would be on the basis of prior use.

Our habits are a result of the available technology and not the other way around. What happens in the history of technology is *not* that we generate a technology we need for doing something which we then do and do better. That has never been the way it works. We are presented with a new technique without reference to its eventual use. As mentioned already, the most unsatisfactory nodal point in the evolution of libraries was that which came between the beginning of journals and the present day; that is, the generation of a secondary literature. The secondary literature effected much change and evolved a lot, including a few failed attempts along the way with encyclopedias, handbooks and other devices that couldn't keep up; but it still obviously is not satisfactory, even with massive production of abstract services. I suggest that perhaps we will see an extermination of the secondary literature because the job it used to do can probably be done better, once primary literature is managed in a computerized form. There will then be no reason to adopt this intermediate device to combine in an agonizing way the different jobs of current awareness and the creation and maintenance of an archive. These are obviously things that we once wanted to do and we seized upon a technique of journal publication that happened to do both together; they have since become an uneasy and inefficient combination.

It must be remembered that scientific papers or, more generally, scholarly papers are not designed for *communication*. That is only about 20 percent of their function. We publish scholarly papers because that 20 percent packs down very neatly into what used to be an efficient archive. Many scholarly papers today are designed for current awareness only. Some are designed for archive only. Some are designed for neither. Probably the majority of scholarly papers are designed for the simple reason that they are the only known way of finishing one job and taking on another. It is the only way that a scholar can get out of a piece of research that he or she has done in order to start on something different. It is the conventional consequence, and we think we are communicating, but this is not necessarily so. An indication that we do not communicate very well can be seen in the citations or peer rankings of a person's own papers. The citations and peer rankings will agree very well. They'll show which are that person's best works and which are lesser works, and the oddity is that they'll be in very good but negative correlation with the person's own estimate of the value of their work. More frequently than not we regard our most acclaimed works as somewhat slight and of poor quality, and feel much more proud of some paper that is disregarded by our peers. Everybody seems to have a Mendel chip on their shoulder, knowing that their very best work lies virtually unknown and unsung. This is obviously because we are not particularly good at communicating, and of course the worst communicators of all, as may be supposed, are the specialists in communication! The literature of communication is a mess.

The problem of the human place in a linear sequential system is intriguing to a historian because it dates from the very dawn of history. In fact, the people that, not accidentally, invented writing had a very peculiar way of thinking. The Babylonians had, so far as we can see from their mathematics and astronomy, a completely linear sequential mode of thought. Our modern way of thinking and comprehending is not the Babylonian way. At roughly the time of Alexander the Great, the world got mixed up. Babylonian culture combined with the Mediterranean Greeks and their mode of thought. The people who produced the Parthenon were visual comprehenders. When they understood something they said, "I see"; they worked by Gestalt. I am not trying to pretend that such animals as completely left-hemisphered or right-hemisphered people exist. I think that this is a gimmick, but interestingly enough, from the dawn of civilization, there existed people with this peculiarly one-way mode of thought. Babylonian mathematics and astronomy displayed an elegant mathematical complexity, as advanced as the Greeks' or even more so. We've been able to put their complete theory into a single intricate computer program. Their idea of understanding, their concept of a "theory," was an algorithm. Given the algorithm, the entire theory can be comprehended. Every astronomical Babylonian tablet that has been found can be read somewhere on that computer printout. It was a marvelous and accurate system. They thought like a computer and were hopeless at visual Gestalt. The thinking of Greeks was the other way around. They knew almost nothing about numbers and calculations until the Babylonians taught them. Strangely, that peculiar human capability which existed from 3000 B.C. to the time of Christ has only just been revived and utilized afresh. All that genius was floating around with nowhere to go until we invented the computer to use it, and now we find there exist many computer freaks and they all have this peculiar Babylonian mode of thought.

I want to insist, however, on the simple point that Babylonian-style thinking with combinations of linear sequential elements is not the way we customarily proceed. We have a patterned way of thinking. I can go back to books that I read thirty years ago or collections that I searched earlier than that, and know things about them that could not be found using any index. Half the time we use a stored memory item, we use it for reasons other than could be covered by any plausible descriptors. There must be some other way and that is why old-style browsing was important. Linear sequential thought is perfectly good if we have all the necessary bibliographical information or if we want to find somebody's phone number. If, however, a person is in Copenhagen and wants to call his friend Hans Jensen, he must know that the friend is Architect Hans Jensen, because he is listed under "Architect." It is weird how things like that mess up our system.

By and large, we think in a way other than any possible system of linear sequential indexing. We think in a sort of Gestalt pattern and it turns out that knowledge itself probably has patterns other than those expressible in algorithm fashion. It is thus very odd that books are automatically linear and sequential, just like a computer. It is a peculiar artifact of our technology that books stack into rows—maybe it is an unfortunate accident because it has recently been shown that the best way to store books is not in nice, neat rows, but lying all over tables, spread out all over the library.

What I am referring to is perhaps the most momentous discovery or set of discoveries to come out of information science in recent years. A set of papers has been published by Belver Griffith and Henry Small on the mapping of scientific papers by citation clustering.[1] It hasn't been widely regarded as revolutionary because people think that it has something to do with citations,which are peculiar and special. I believe that citations are only an accidental diagnostic, and researchers are now finding out the most peculiar thing: knowledge can be represented by points or areas on a map.

One would think that knowledge is so multidimensional that this would be useless. As it happens, the mapping is almost perfectly two-dimensional and the simple, geographical simile works much better than any linear sequential, book-like Dewey Decimal Classification system. Instead of a series of indexing terms, all of which are linear sequential, one should use a pair of coordinates for the proper representation of knowledge. The representation of a sort of road map then generates itself rather than having order inflicted upon it. The proper representation of knowledge becomes a sort of atlas, or maybe even a globe, in which each item is placed relative to other ones with which it is associated. As knowledge continues to increase, one automatically bends and strains this former system a little by relating things in different ways. We have, in fact, been able to make elementary "maps" and I believe that probably within the decade, as an additional technology, we will be able to get visual representations on a computer screen. The relational algorithms will produce this type of Gestalt phenomenon yielding a representation of the way that knowledge *is*. It should show the way that human beings think, relating all similar things. That gives us the possibility of data systems that are ill-adapted to linear sequential indexing, and a much greater versatility.

Another curious finding of the Griffith-Small discovery is that knowledge exists at a single level of aggregation. Let us use the word *atom* for the units in which knowledge is encapsulated—some big, some small. The average unit is probably something like a year's work because that is a common period of reference. We do one job of work a year and write it up. But there are some trades, like systematic natural history and organic and biochemistry, in which the atoms of knowledge are about two weeks' work, so you get many such atoms and they are very little atoms compared with astrophysics (where the units are probably about two years of work), history (about five years), or philosophy (about ten years). These atoms of knowledge are then aggregated, and interestingly there is a single level of aggregation. Atoms are formed into molecules, and above molecules there is nothing.

A molecule of knowledge corresponds to the work of about 300 people—what we would call a *subfield*. A subfield is made up of entities like plate tectonics, or insulin chemistry, or Cuban economics—specialties in which a few hundred people work. It is not constantly the same people; there is probably a core of a hundred or so, and every year a large number of others flow through. For example, when we encounter a name in a library file, we have probably never seen that name before and will probably never see it again. Most people who float into the knowledge sphere are transients, but upon retrieval we usually get the same names over and over again, and they form a small, stable group. This derives from the cumulative advantage mechanism of scholarly authorship which is a natural birth-and-death process. Knowledge is apparently organized in subdisciplines and subspecialties and at no other level. If we think there is such a thing as physics or physiology or information science, we do so only because it provides a mode of social organization which permits us to have institutes, schools, students, and doctorates in a subject. It does not mean that all of the fields that we teach cohere. People are usually involved in some major specialty plus a number of minor ones, and are waiting in line in case the major field thins out.

Why do these subspecialties contain about 300 people? This magic number implies that there must be something like 3000 specialties in the world, since 3000 specialties multiplied by 300 people gives us the million-odd authors who form the invisible colleges. These colleges are the size they are because 300 represents the ratio between the input and the output of the individual. When a group of individuals live by taking in each other's washing (I thought we only did that in England)—that is to say, live by reading each other's papers—each reads, roughly speaking, a paper a day and writes a paper a year. The ratio is thus 300:1. It is obvious we cannot read ten papers a day with the same intensity that we write one. It is also obvious that we have to read more than one every day, otherwise we are not keeping up with the others. Therefore, if the ratio is less than 300:1, we're not getting enough to read; as a result, we are involved in a lot of different fields. And if we have more than 300 people in a field there is too much to read, and we therefore fission off a section of it. For that reason, the subspecialties, these invisible colleges, reproduce by budding or fission roughly every ten years.

Invisible colleges seem to be the same size now that they were in the seventeenth century and presumably will remain so. When computerized journals are discussed later in the institute, remember that what we really want to do is produce a "taking in of each other's washing mechanism" for roughly 300 people. If there are more than that, too many papers are being collected (merely to make the field commercial or perhaps to give it a higher status); and if there are fewer than that, not enough can be gained to make it worthwhile.

I believe it should be possible for a computer to organize this sort of thing with the coming technology of memory. We will get much larger memories very soon, and we will need them. The big foreseeable bottlenecks will be getting everything we want into machine-readable form, and having memory readily available everywhere with minimal equipment. When all that is done, what we do *not* get is any simple-minded indexing. I think we will move over to some sort of new encyclopedism produced by an *automatic organization of knowledge*. Let's call it AOK—it sounds good. AOK is a way of doing the same sort of thinking that human beings do—simply translated into a different form. For mapping we use this sort of associative indexing extended to its limit, and that is the way knowledge itself wants to go. I do not think that there will be any replacement of the old methods. They will survive even as handwriting survives the typewriter or the terminal. I still happen to love books and believe that they will survive. People still ride horses! I think we will have the convenience of what is being called the *built-in orderly organized knowledge system* (perhaps known better by its acronym BOOKS), and clearly we will preserve it for recreation and for a very neat form of portable learning. What I am against is the mentality of wanting and trying to throw out the old because we think we have a new way of doing the old thing. A new technology never just replaces the old method—it enables quite different styles of life to come into being. Furthermore, it is the very indirect results of a technology that are its most interesting and sometimes its most significant consequences.

With the computer, and especially with the mapping possibility I have suggested, we have a new sort of capability, not just the old job done better or more cheaply or more massively. The consequences must be far from straightforward, far beyond the possibility of technological assessment. When the library computer deals with knowledge itself rather than with those mere skeletons of knowledge that can be cut and dried into algorithmic indexing, we will need librarians who are more than mere mediators. We will need people who are better than simultaneous translators, for the new technology will require a very rare sort of talent that has not been utilized for a long time. We will need people who can think in both Babylonian and Greek modes. Most people who can talk very well to computers are not particularly good at talking to people, and vice versa. We need the rare sort of person who can talk to people and tell them of the possibilities of this new technology, which will be different from the technology that is taught to students at library schools. We will need terminal people who can talk to nonterminal people, and that's what I really mean by saying that far into the terminal future, Happiness is going to be a Warm Librarian.

REFERENCE

1. Small, Henry, and Griffith, Belver C. "The Structure of Scientific Literatures I: Identifying and Graphing Specialties," *Science Studies* 4:17-40, Jan. 1974; Griffith, Belver C., et al. "The Structure of Scientific Literatures II: Toward a Macro- and Microstructure for Science," *Science Studies* 4:339-65, Oct. 1974; Small, Henry G. "A Co-Citation Model of a Scientific Specialty: A Longitudinal Study of Collagen Research," *Social Studies of Science* 7:139-66, May 1977; and _____, and Greenlee, Edwin. "Citation Context Analysis of a Co-Citation Cluster: Recombinant-DNA." (In process.)

RICHARD C. ROISTACHER
Research Associate
Bureau of Social Science Research
Washington, D.C.

The Virtual Journal: Reaching the Reader

In 1978 I described an organization for on-line scholarly journals.[1] Such journals can be maintained in information systems much like those used for bibliographic data and which are equipped with extensive indexing and retrieving facilities. In addition to the usual paraphernalia of information retrieval, virtual journals would also have editorial boards and referees. Since the virtual journal is exempt from page limits, everything submitted can be published.

However, it was suggested that one of the search terms for each article be a quality score given by the referees. Such a system would allow for all of the present diversity in point of view and quality. An author could publish in any journal desired, but might have to accept a poor referee score from a "better" journal.

An additional feature of a virtual journal would be the inclusion of a system of readership counts and scores of articles. This system would allow authors a chance at the beatific vision of vindication in the form of high readership counts and high reader ratings following publication of an article with low referee ratings.

The major problems inhibiting establishment of a virtual journal are not computing capacity, information retrieval technology or storage costs, but rather the cost and speed of data communication. My earlier paper used cost figures for communication taken from 1977, when it cost approximately $7.33 to store the average-sized article on-line for a year. It was estimated that transmission costs over Telenet for the average-sized article would have been about $2.40. Since that time, storage costs have fallen to $5.29, but actual experience with Telenet has shown transmission costs to be about $3.55 (without adjusting for inflation).

Experiences with Teleconferencing

Since writing the 1978 article, I have become heavily involved in teleconferencing, using Robert Parnes's CONFER program on the Michigan Terminal System (MTS). CONFER is a powerful, easy-to-use teleconferencing system which has gained a high degree of acceptance among its users. MTS offers many inducements for use, including a large variety of text processing, graphics, statistical, scientific and information retrieval software.

A Failure

My colleague, Albert Biderman, has used CONFER to organize a consortium of people engaged in writing a joint grant proposal. Each participant wrote a part of the proposal at his or her own institution, using CONFER only for coordination.

During the course of the conference, the University of Michigan stopped operating MTS for a week in order to replace the computer with a larger one. The week prior to the replacement was marked by extremely high computer usage as people rushed to complete tasks before losing computing services. Consequently, it was often difficult for conference participants to gain access to one of the seven Telenet ports. The result of the experience was that the participants soured on computer conferencing, and abandoned the project. (It is no excuse to say that computers are not replaced very often. There is always something happening which does not happen very often.)

A Mixed Case

I have been utilizing CONFER as a discussion and consulting medium for users in state statistical agencies who are doing substantive data analysis on MTS. One of these agencies decided to transfer all of its operational data from its local machine to our Amdahl V470 in Ann Arbor. The agency has been an active user of our system for almost a year, despite the many vagaries of telecommunication. Other agencies, which did not transfer their data to our computer, found that they had nothing to discuss with each other, and that it was not worth the trouble to look for messages.

A Success

A group of people without prior computing experience used CONFER to plan an annual professional meeting. Since the organization concerned was in acute danger of disintegrating for lack of a meeting, the participants were highly motivated to learn to use the system.

The Lesson for Virtual Journals

I believe that our mixed record of success and failure in these endeavors is indicative of what must be done to ensure for virtual journals a significant level of readership. Our failures have involved people possessing all degrees of computer skill who did not feel it worthwhile to fight their way onto the system in order to compute or exchange information. The factors influencing our teleconferencing successes and failures were (1) availability of a communication line, (2) experience of the user, (3) the degree to which the user desired to do substantive work on our computers, and (4) the need for several users to work cooperatively.

Our major difficulty has not been in teaching people to use our computing system or our teleconferencing program, but rather in providing them with terminals and reliable connections to the machines. Our two Amdahl 470s can handle about 500 simultaneous on-line users. However, these computers are connected to the Telenet common carrier network through a total of seven low-speed connections. Since the machines have a national clientele, it is often quite difficult for a remote user to obtain a connection.

The Communications Environment

Our teleconferencing trials and tribulations lead me to conclude that while we have achieved the necessary sophistication in central facilities for a virtual journal, we have not yet achieved a satisfactory telecommunications or local user environment. I think that technology is rapidly making available the tools for telecommunications and a local environment, but we must know which tools to use. I regret that this discussion must delve into some of the grittier details of data communications.

Communications Line Capacity

Our present remote client uses a 30-characters-per-second (CPS) upper-/lower-case terminal connected by an acoustic coupler to the local port of a data communications network. This setup allows the client to receive a 60-character line in two seconds and a page of text in a nominal two minutes. In fact, the buffering delays in Telenet mean that a page takes somewhat more than two minutes to print. The user must have a computer terminal, be familiar with Telenet and the remote host, and be willing to sit and wait while the text is printed out at a leisurely pace.

While 30 CPS is the most common speed for remote data terminals, there are other line speeds in use. At 30 CPS, the printing of text lags somewhat behind a slow human reader. At 120 CPS, the next increment in line speed, a screen of 60 lines fills in 30 seconds, which is about as fast as a fast reader can scan it. At 480 CPS, the next increment of speed, a 60-line screen will fill in 7½ seconds, which is faster than anyone can read. At 960 CPS, a page-size screen fills with text in a flash, and the reader is free to go from page to page at will.

Higher Transmission Speeds

At present, speeds higher than 120 CPS require a direct connection between the terminal and the telephone line, something not commonly available to remote users. However, it is clear that new technology will find ways of bringing ever-higher transmission speeds to the individual user. Thus, my first design consideration for the local user environment for a virtual journal is that the line speed be as high as possible, preferably 480 CPS, but no less than 120 CPS. The 120-CPS connections are presently available from several data common carrier networks in large cities, and I expect that such connections will become standard over the next three to five years.

However, new technology will allow users access to much higher speeds. Recently Xerox Corporation introduced a communications system called XTEN which combines a laser communication channel between buildings with a sophisticated high-speed data network within buildings. XTEN is designed to be entirely independent of the telephone system and will furnish extremely high transmission speed.

While at some point such circuits will probably exist in every house and office, it may be that in the near future they will require special distribution points. One possibility would be to have libraries serve as the distribution points for these exotic, high-speed communication circuits. The retailing of communication facilities, however, is only part of the problem of providing a local environment.

The Local Environment

One of the paradoxes of successful remote computing is that it seldom looks like remote computing. The remote computer user is not likely to be alone at a terminal, but is usually one of a group of users in the same location. As a result, such users have access not only to on-line documentation, but to large stacks of paper manuals; and not only to on-line consultants, but to experts in the next office. If this is necessarily true for case-hardened computerniks, it will be all the more true for journal readers in general.

The natural agency for maintaining the local environment for virtual journals is the research library. The library should be responsible for consulting, and possibly for the retailing of communications. Research libraries could invest in a subscription to a virtual journal or information retrieval system as well as a high-speed data line. The high-speed line could be shared among local users in any of several ways.

Multiplexing

The most common way of sharing a line is multiplexing, in which several users make concurrent use of the data line. A multiplexed line capable of 240 CPS may be split locally into eight 30-CPS lines. However, multiplexing is probably not an appropriate role for the library, as it competes directly with general providers of communications.

Staging

A better way libraries could use such an arrangement of high-speed, long-distance lines and lower-speed, local lines would be by staging. In staging, the library would retrieve information *en bloc* and then make that information available to the local users. For instance, if a user wished to retrieve an article from a virtual journal, he could ask to see the current table of contents for the journal. If the current files for the journal were available in the library's local computer, the user would be given imme- diate access to them. If, as would usually be the case, the local file was not current, the computer would retrieve an update from the journal's archive via the high-speed connection. The user's wait, however, would be only a few seconds.

Staging has advantages far beyond those of line-sharing. In particular, staging allows the local user to learn a single set of file manipulation and information retrieval commands. While there are many different com- mand languages for computers and information systems, there are a rela- tively limited number of file designs for text information retrieval. The local computer could have available facilities which would allow sup- ported files to be manipulated by its data base software. Thus, in most cases, the user could utilize a single command language for manipulating a wide variety of data files from diverse sources. Staging not only makes life easier for the local users, but is a logical extension of library services and library automation.

Terminals as Furniture

We have now given our local journal reader a reliable high-speed connection to the journal, as well as local consulting and a uniform command language. The reader can sit in an office or reading room looking at text on the screen just as if it were a friendly, local microfiche reader. Unfortunately, most people do not regard these readers as either friendly or local. Rather, they are a necessary tool for which one leaves one's comfortable office or study for a drafty library reading room. How then are we to take the virtual journal the final steps to the readers?

Our experience with teleconferencing has shown that successful users have had either high rewards for using the system or high penalties for failing to use it. In both cases they have had to make investments in learning to use the system so that there were relatively few barriers for its continued use. The most successful users were those doing substantive work in graphics, statistical analysis or document processing. Since these people spent many hours at the terminal in the course of their work, the receiving and sending of messages and participation in conferences were not an isolated activity but were part of a routine. People who used the computer only for teleconferencing rapidly found that the rewards of participation did not exceed the problems of having to find a connection and of learning to use the command language.

It thus remains to make the virtual journal terminate in some object more friendly to the average scholar than a computer terminal. The answer is probably the communicating word processor. The present trend of sharp decreases in the price of hardware should continue to the point where the average office typewriter is nothing but a computer terminal minus communication facilities. Increasingly more office typewriters will include memory and intelligence, thus transforming them into word processors. Scholars will use such machines for the writing of papers either directly, or indirectly through secretaries. In this way, they will become familiar with the machine's operations and will regard its use for communications as a welcome extension of their capabilities, rather than as a foray into *terra incognita.*

Using word processors as terminals has the added advantage of making virtual journals accessible to those who cannot or will not type. The nontypist can ask a secretary to produce the latest table of contents of a virtual journal. After indicating either a choice of articles or a search strategy, the scholar can wait while the secretary produces the desired articles on the word processor to be read later at leisure. Thus, the journal reader is allowed to treat the word processor as either an on-line inactive system or a traditional, published journal.

Conclusions

The local environment for a virtual journal should be marked by three characteristics:

1. a data line capable of producing text at higher-than-demand speeds;
2. a single retrieval and command language independent of the particular journal or data base being accessed; and

3. a terminal which has uses deeply imbedded in the working life of readers.

We presently have available computing and information retrieval facilities necessary to a virtual journal. We are still evolving the communications and local terminal facilities necessary to ensure a wide readership.

REFERENCE

1. Roistacher, Richard C. "The Virtual Journal," *Computer Networks* 2:18-24, 1978.

The Impact of Technology on the
Production and Distribution of the News

MARY S. MANDER
Visiting Lecturer
Department of Journalism
University of Illinois
at Urbana-Champaign

Part I: Computerized Newsrooms

When the computer first was introduced to postwar America, it was portrayed as a friendly robot, a machine capable of vacuuming the floors for the beleaguered housewife, an electronic brain that could play chess and other games requiring highly developed skills. Like its technological predecessor, the telephone, it was thought of as an adult toy. Its practical use in the business world was not at first envisioned.[1] It was termed *artificial intelligence,* just as the printing press in its incunabula period was termed *artificialiter scribere*—artificial writing. Few, if any, persons envisioned the present applications of the computer for booking airline reservations or selecting rookies in the National Football League's annual draft. Least of all was the application of the computer to the newspaper world considered.

Publishers turned to the computer, with varying degrees of success, to solve problems which the industry faced as it entered the decade of the 1960s. Once the new technology arrived in the pressroom, however, it precipitated the reemergence of an age-old problem: man versus the machine—a problem which dates back to times when a civilization based on the pasture and the plough gave way to one based on industry. Besides its impact on the ranks of labor, the computer, once it entered the newsroom itself, transformed the organization of the press. It has made possible the development of small papers which operate as satellites to larger metropolitan dailies. In other words, the future holds the possibility of a growth of electronic newspaper networks.

The task of this article is threefold. First, I will cover the historical circumstances leading to the adaptation of the computer to the newsroom, and give a thumbnail sketch of the uses to which it has been put. Second, I will make note of the impact the computer has had on labor. Finally, I will investigate how the new technology has made possible the development of satellite presses.

Historical Circumstances and Technological Change

As recently as 1965 most newspapers in this country were using equipment largely unchanged since the last decade of the nineteenth century.[2] By 1900 automation had transformed the newspaper into a full-blown industry. The typesetting machine which Ottmar Merganthaler invented in 1886, and the stereotype and the rotary press, all worked together to turn the Fourth Estate into an efficient enterprise capable of producing a large number of papers in a relatively short period of time. The Industrial Revolution, begun in earnest in the United States at the onset of the last century, created dense city populations. At this time the press was transformed to meet the needs of industrial society. Its method of distribution changed. In the 1830s the newsboy appeared on the streets of Boston and New York and peddled his wares to the people. He fitted the lifestyle of a new kind of audience, one composed of mill workers, for instance, who could not afford the price of a subscription payable in advance. With the onset of the twentieth century, the industry experienced a technological hiatus that lasted until the 1950s when small weekly newspapers began to experiment with offset printing.[3]

The news industry has, with a remarkable degree of success (given the short period of time), adapted both computer and satellite to its own ends. What appears at first glance to be a sudden and widespread adoption of computer systems, including electronic editing, was more the gradual and at times painful task of converting the new technologies to solve seemingly overwhelming problems facing newspapers during the 1960s.

At first, publishers blamed their declining revenues during the late 1950s on alternative information sources. The scapegoat, in their eyes, was television.[4] Advertisers, it seemed, were spending their dollars on the medium that would transcend geographical boundaries. Television appealed to advertisers because it appeared to be a better way to organize the consumer market. In reality, the crisis confronting the newspaper industry could not be laid solely on the doorstep of the fledgling television industry. The economic straits newspapers found themselves in were the result of a complicated interweaving of many different forces. For example, the implementation of the postal zip code in 1962 helped advertisers distribute their material via direct mail rather than by way of the newspaper ad.[5]

However, the loss of revenue attributable to the zip code was a secondary tributary to the real crisis: the decline of the central city. For well over a hundred years, since the bawdy days of the penny press, the newspaper had belonged to the city, and the city in the late 1950s and early 1960s had evolved from an exciting, thriving metropolis to a ghetto beset with alarming crime rates and race problems.[6] The era of James Gordon Bennett—an immigrant who had arrived in New York City disillusioned and deep in debt, who at forty thought his life was over and who subsequently became the chief architect of the penny press—had passed away. Gone were the days of cutthroat city competition, the likes of which press notables William Randolph Hearst and Joseph Pulitzer had thrived on.

Editors of today, however, were slow to recognize the changes going on around them. Fundamental and far-reaching transformations had affected the structure of the postwar family and the pattern of the laborer's workaday world. When the 1960s began, the news industry was in trouble: "Everything about the newspaper suddenly began to seem wrong."[7] The cost of newsprint had skyrocketed. Papers were produced in areas distant from their readers and thus required delivery over busy city thoroughfares to suburbs. Also, they depended for their production on organized labor which was becoming increasingly expensive.[8]

The Computer's Adaptation to the Newsroom

In the pioneering stages of computer adaptation to the newspaper, production and business tasks were the target for change. The computerized systems used in the industry, then, were designed not with the editor or reporter in mind, but rather for the people working in the business offices. As such, these operations, because they are common to virtually all businesses, did not require programmers to adapt their "packages" specifically to newspaper use.[9]

The newsroom and the advertising departments, the "front end," were the last to utilize the new technologies. During the pioneering stages of computer experimentation in the early 1960s, individual papers made piecemeal and at times secretive attempts to adapt the computer to the newspaper's special tasks. The early systems were cumbersome and crude, and required elaborate coding. They promised much but delivered little. Their benefits were offset by their primary drawbacks: the need to rekeyboard material and the problems involving on-line storage. The breakthrough came in 1961 when MIT demonstrated the first time-sharing computer. After 1965, when time-sharing became commercially viable, there was a rapid increase in the use of the computer in the newsroom.[10]

As shown in Table 1, the number of video display terminals (VDT) has increased from a modest 23 in 1970 to over 15,000 in 1978. A cautionary note must be introduced into any discussion of numbers of electronic and computer units. Although real numbers are sizable, the actual number of

TABLE 1. Growth in Number of Electronic and
Computer Units in Newspaper Applications

Year	OCR Typewriters	OCR Units	VDT Units	Computers
1978	22,237	712	15,841	1,982
1977	23,538	738	9,867	1,472
1976	21,384	671	7,038	1,206
1975	18,778	543	3,896	971
1974	13,819	377	1,666	800
1973	6,107	186	685	719
1972		87	360	707
1971		16	155	632
1970			23	537
1969				529

Source: Puncekar, Sandra L., ed. "Electronic Applications; O.C.R.—V.D.T.—Computer; ANPA Member Newspapers, 1978." *ANPA R.I. Bulletin,* 1979, p. E-5, Table 1. (Reprinted by courtesy of ANPA Research Institute.)

papers using the computer in the newsroom—as distinct from the pressroom—is about 600, or 3/8 of the total number of papers in the United States.[11] Nevertheless, the trend is not insignificant.

Detailed listings of the numbers and types of equipment used, as well as their functions, were compiled by the American Newspaper Publishers Association (ANPA) Research Institute and are partially reported in Tables 2, 3 and 4. The data in the tables are based on responses to a special questionnaire sent to ANPA member newspapers. The purpose of the questionnaire was to determine the extent to which electronic devices are used throughout newspaper departments.[12] Table 2 indicates that nearly all responding newspapers use electronic devices for editing and reporting purposes. Table 3 arranges the data in terms of circulation figures. Table 4, which lists the number of VDT units per paper, shows that about half of the papers responding use fifteen or fewer units.

Fifteen years ago there was not an electronic editing system around. Today a significant number of newspapers in this country use them. In fact, there are currently some journalists who have never handled copy in any other way.[13] With the aid of portable terminals small enough to fit under an airplane seat, the journalist is able to submit his copy directly from a political convention, the sports arena, or the scene of the crime. In using the computer to write his story, the reporter can revise, add or delete instantaneously. If a sentence or paragraph is no longer needed, it can be made to disappear with the press of a button. The result is copy that is

TABLE 2. List of Departments Utilizing VDT
Units, Number of Newspaper Offices Using Them,
and Number of Units Used

Functions and Departments Reported Using VDT Units	Number of Newspaper Offices	Number of VDT Units
Editing	423*	5,632
Classified department	273	2,313
Reporters	239	3,188
Composing room ad makeup	194	659
Composing classified ads	150	377
Composing text keyboarding	138	587
Business and accounting	130	540
Bureau	76	482
Business and circulation	68	608
Portable	64	317
Composing room	44	169
Display advertising department	36	105
Composing ad makeup	18	43
Composing proofreading	16	48
Newsroom	12	98
Data processing	11	69
Composing room page makeup	11	52
Computer room	9	21
Library	8	47
Remote advertiser	8	15
Programming	7	20
System monitor	6	9
System management—classified or display advertising	5	30
Service department	4	9
Composing typesetter control	3	6
System management—news	3	3
Production control	3	3
Sports and Sunday	2	11
Commercial work	2	7
Business power control	2	4
Remote advertising areas	2	2
Power consumption panels	1	50
Building security	1	13
Journalism lab	1	12
Display ad lines	1	10
Reader insurance	1	4
Press totalizer	1	4
Credit	1	2
Editor's page makeup	1	1
Composing ad makeup	1	1
Business circulation	1	1
Unknown—not identified	27	189
Totals	517	15,761

*Includes newspapers that use VDT units for editors and reporters (depending on copy flow).
Source: Puncekar, Sandra L., ed. "Electronic Applications; O.C.R.—V.D.T.—Computer; ANPA Member Newspapers, 1978." *ANPA R.I. Bulletin*, 1979, p. E-8, Table 5. (Reprinted by courtesy of ANPA Research Institute.)

TABLE 3. NUMBER OF NEWSPAPERS REPORTING
USE OF OCR AND VDT UNITS ACCORDING
TO CIRCULATION RANGES

Circulation Range	Newspapers Using OCR Units	Newspapers Using VDT Units
Up to 5,000	-	10
5,000 - 10,000	12	37
10,000 - 15,000	18	50
15,000 - 20,000	23	45
20,000 - 25,000	17	39
25,000 - 50,000	98	148
50,000 - 75,000	45	69
75,000 - 100,000	17	20
100,000 - 150,000	22	32
150,000 - 200,000	17	22
200,000 - 500,000	22	29
500,000 - 1,000,000	4	7
More than 1,000,000	-	-
Totals	295	508

TABLE 4. NUMBER OF VDT UNITS
PER NEWSPAPER

Number of VDT Units per Newspaper	Number of Newspapers
1 - 5	82
5 - 10	79
10 - 15	70
15 - 20	49
20 - 25	49
25 - 30	23
30 - 35	22
35 - 40	21
40 - 45	19
45 - 50	15
50 - 60	10
60 - 70	14
70 - 80	9
80 - 90	9
90 - 100	4
100 - 150	20
150 - 200	6
More than 200	7
Total	508

Source for Tables 2 and 3: Puncekar, Sandra L., ed. "Electronic Applications; O.C.R.—V.D.T.—Computer; ANPA Member Newspapers, 1978." *ANPA R.I. Bulletin*, 1979, p. E-7, Tables 3 and 4. (Reprinted by courtesy of ANPA Research Institute.)

always "clean." Depending on the policy of the individual paper and the extent of its computerization, reporters can use computerized data banks to do background research for their stories. Journalists have instant access to wire service news, stories written by colleagues, abstracts of articles on related subjects, and an index to the paper's morgue.[14]

Besides reporters, editors utilize VDTs and optical character readers (OCR). Before the advent of cold type,[15] the proofreading of the text was performed in the composing room. Most typographical errors were due to rekeyboarding and the linotype machine. Proofreading today is done in the newsroom and ultimately is the responsibility of the editor.

Advertising

The area in which the computer has been used with a good deal of success is classified advertising.[16] VDTs can be programmed with a standard form. By the time the operator has filled out the form, the computer will have done such tedious editing steps as hyphenation and justification. The screen will display the cost of the ad; it will indicate whether the advertiser is a poor credit risk; and finally, it will display the total number of ad lines slated for that particular edition. The computer has the added advantage of being able to handle ads for different papers, and for different editions and zones of the same newspaper.

The electronic classified system of advertising minimizes paper-handling—ideally at least—and produces output with a minimum of human intervention. Display advertising, on the other hand, is a totally different story. Display copy is the result of the efforts of several people, including many who do not work for the newspaper. Most often the copy is made up days or even weeks in advance, a factor which makes on-line storage expensive and almost impossible. A small number of electronic layout systems are available to newspapers today. Contrary to classified ads, which can be automatically processed by computer, display ads require much more proficient operators.

Those few layout systems which do exist position display ads in a newspaper edition. They operate quickly and with some versatility. Always, however, the operator is able to modify computer-made decisions. The full-page composition and makeup terminal is usually a stand-alone unit, the input and output of which is paper tape or magnetic tape. The operator at a typical work station is able to perform the standard composition, layout and editing functions—specifying type face and size, line length and spacing. In addition to its use in advertising departments, the computer has been successfully adapted to the major wire service operations.

Wire Services

United Press International (UPI), The Associated Press (AP) and others provide their subscriber newspapers with low- and high-speed wire service transmission. UPI began its relationship with the computer in 1965 when it switched from radiocast transmission to Transatlantic Pictures Plus News Communications System. At the time, the new system gave UPI a transmission capacity equivalent to ten two-way telephone channels operating at sixty words a minute—a remarkable expansion over the previous system. In July 1975, however, UPI switched to an Information Storage and Retrieval System (IS&R) that made the earlier developments look like a crude and clumsy attempt to increase the flow of worldwide news. With well over 450 terminals tied to IS&R, UPI had the distinction of being the first news agency in history to use a completely electronic system for writing, editing and distributing its news services. The electronic system made possible the development of DataNews, UPI's high-speed wire service. DataNews and AP's DataStream service offer direct input into subscriber computers. The subscriber computer then monitors the wires and selects, with the help of a standardized coding system, the stories suitable to its needs.[17]

Gradually, then, publishers have turned to the computer to solve economic problems facing the industry in the 1950s and 1960s. Once the computer entered the pressroom, however, it precipitated an age-old struggle: laborer versus employer.

The Reemergence of Man vs. Machine

Charles Babbage, who in 1833 constructed the first computer, an analytical engine, refers to the problems between management and labor in his treatise, *On the Economy of Machinery and Manufactures*. Workmen long have thought that their interests and those of their employers were mutually exclusive. The difficulty, Babbage thought, that the man-versus-machine contest gave birth to was a neglect of valuable machinery, and, in consequence, an almost certain neglect of improvements in production.[18] When the computer was finally adapted to newspaper use, however, the winner of the man-versus-technology struggle seemed to be the computer—hands down.

The impact of the new technologies on the industry was first and most painfully felt in the ranks of labor. The plain fact of the matter is that the computer does not require as many hands or as much skill to operate as the linotype. For publishers, the computerized production was a reassuring step toward freeing the industry from one of its most troubling characteristics: the newspaper was a "labour-intensive medium at a time when skilled labour was becoming well organised and very expensive."[19] What was seen by publishers as a promise was viewed by labor as a threat. Their job security was at stake.

In the United States, the most recent and widely publicized confrontation between labor and publisher took place in New York. The principals in the drama were the Printing Pressman's Union #2 and the Publishers' Association of New York City, representing the *Times*, the *News*, and the *Post*. The Printing Pressman's Union had not struck since 1923, the last time manning agreements had been reached. During the technological adaptations in the 1970s, publishers had made it clear that the manning levels agreed to in 1923 were no longer viable. In 1976 the *Times* announced that manpower reduction would be its major objective in the coming year. In April 1977 Arthur Ochs Sulzberger, chairperson and president of the company, told stockholders that manning was the most serious and pressing problem facing New York's leading newspaper.[20] The upshot was that in August 1978 publishers proposed terms which gave management the authority to determine the size of crews. The pressmen walked out of the negotiations and publishers predicted a long strike. The president of the Allied Printing Trades Council declared that New York was a union town and that there would be no *Washington Post* scene in the nation's largest city.[21] What ensued was a strike which lasted eighty-eight days and ultimately kept the city in a veritable news limbo.

At no time during the lengthy strike were wages an issue or stumbling block. Job security lay at the heart of the issue. When a tentative 6-year agreement was reached between parties, both sides called it a victory.[22] The pressmen received job guarantees, but conceded manning reductions, through attrition, of 20-30 percent.[23]

The Rise of Computer Networks and Satellite Papers

Besides effecting changes in the ranks of labor, the computer has enabled the editor to come to terms with the news demands of changing demographics. With the great population shifts from the city to the suburb during the 1950s and 1960s, the newspaper industry found that it had to reorganize itself to meet the needs of its suburban audience.[24] The expansion of the great metropolitan dailies into the suburbs generally took the form of zoning, with news bureaus established in outlying population centers. A certain number of pages in each edition were assigned to regional news produced by these bureaus, and one or more suburban editions were distributed in the area. The *Los Angeles Times* recently went a step further and set up a bureau in San Diego.[25]

Besides zoning, the computer has made other visible alterations in the organization of the newspaper. It makes possible the establishment of newspapers which are satellites to larger, metropolitan journals. A case in point is the *New Jersey Bulletin* which serves the New Jersey market but is published by the Philadelphia *Bulletin*. Replete with editorial staff, a classified and display advertising crew, a mailroom operation for handling preprints and a circulation department, the headquarters of the satellite paper is located in Pennsauken, New Jersey. However, it is tied by computer to and uses the composing and pressroom of the Philadelphia plant.[26]

The philosophy underlying the formation of the satellite newspaper is that a newspaper must be responsive to the local needs of the readers. It is only with the aid of the computer that operation of a network of editorial staffs is at all possible. The network of computers used in Pennsauken and Philadelphia allows the satellite paper immediate access to the Philadelphia facilities. At the same time, the New Jersey operation produces a paper entirely different from the one produced in Philadelphia. The New Jersey newsroom has eleven editorial terminals which editors and reporters use to write, dispatch, correct, edit and file their stories. In addition, each terminal has a memory system capable of storing the equivalent of 125 column inches of news copy. All terminals are linked to computers in Philadelphia via telephone lines. Through this linkage, the satellite paper has access to any story, directory or listing in the system which is available to the Philadelphia staff.

After stories are written and edited, the news editor retrieves them, decides where they should go, and then advises copy editors about copy length, headline size and other miscellanies. When copy editors are finished with their work, the stories are released to phototypesetters. Page dummies (of a color different from that of the Philadelphia paper) are sent to the composing room where an entirely separate set of plates is made. The finished product of this computerized editorial and production system is a newspaper that is substantially different from *The Bulletin*.

Another kind of network newspaper is the San Diego edition of the *Los Angeles Times*. While it is an attempt to participate in the growing market San Diego offers, the *Los Angeles Times* edition specializes in regional, national and international news. It is somewhat less strong in the area of local news and sports.[27] The point is that there are two distinct possibilities for the future of the newspaper. On the one hand, computerized production of the news may encourage the further development of newspapers aimed at special audiences—much like format radio. Since newspapers, like radio, draw the majority of their revenues from local as opposed to national advertising dollars, this seems a likely development. At the same time, the development of a national newspaper or a number of national newspapers through computerized interconnections is a distinct possibility. At present we are in a period of technological dislocation. Like any period of dislocation, trends are contradictory, chaotic and unclear. No particular development stemming from the use of the computer in the newsroom is absolutely certain.

Least certain is the total demise of the newspaper in its present form. Critics have been predicting the death of the newspaper since the 1930s.[28] Those who maintain that the newspaper of tomorrow will be distributed via the home television set point to the pilot study being conducted by the TV station KSL in Salt Lake City, which is investigating teletext delivery of information to the home TV viewer. Although the electronic newspaper is currently a popular topic, critics who predict that the paperless world is just around the corner do not take into account present-day trends in the production of newsprint. To be sure, the primary drawback of offset printing is newsprint waste, and newsprint costs have doubled in the last ten years. They are second in magnitude to the cost of labor.[29] However, the computer is being used in the newsprint industry to help publishers pinpoint factors contributing to waste. Likewise, other methods of keeping costs down—such as newsprint recycling—are being utilized.[30]

Conclusion

Once we successfully muzzle the technological optimists who predict that Ceefax will do away with the news*paper,* we still have to contend with the technological pessimists. These are the ones who associate the computer with the dehumanization of humankind. They link the use of computer-based information systems to a poverty-stricken notion of knowledge and an ever-diminishing store of cultural products—such as great literary works.[31] As for its application in the Fourth Estate, critics of the computer lament the possibility of a completely electronic newspaper. The world without a morning paper to read over the first cup of coffee is a drab and dreary one indeed. Nothing we can say will completely assuage the fears of technological pessimists. However, it might be beneficial to point out that Socrates once decried the invention of writing because he thought it wrought havoc with the memory. Abbot Trithemius once warned against too much reliance on the printing press, for it would never be as good as handwriting. Although writing transformed the human memory system and the printing press altered the uses of handwriting, neither was completely done in by the new inventions. In the same way, it is doubtful that the computer will transform beyond recognition or undermine the importance of the newspaper in our everyday lives.

ACKNOWLEDGMENTS

Thanks are due to F. Wilfrid Lancaster for inviting me to participate in the 1979 Clinic on Library Applications of Data Processing; to Carolyn Marvin for her suggestions regarding this paper; and to Kathryn Brown for typing the manuscript.

REFERENCES

1. Cherry, Colin. "The Telephone System: Creator of Mobility and Social Change." *In* Ithiel de Sola Pool, ed. *The Social Impact of the Telephone.* Cambridge, Mass., MIT Press, 1977, p. 113.

2. Changes in the first half of this century most often involved speeding up rather than actually altering production techniques. *See* Udell, Jon G. *The Economics of the American Newspaper.* New York, Hastings House, 1978, p. 88.

3. Although the offset press was first used successfully in California in 1936, it was not until the late 1960s that offset printing became a commercially viable alternative to letterpress. *See* Moghdam, Dineh. *Computers in Newspaper Publishing: User-Oriented Systems.* New York, Marcel Dekker, 1978, p. 24.

4. Biggers, George. "Newspapers in a Television Age," *ANPA Mechanical Bulletin,* no. 484, June 30, 1953.

5. Smith, Anthony. "The Future of the Newspaper: The Waning of the Fourth Estate," *Intermedia* 6:10, Aug. 1978.

6. Ibid., pp. 7, 9-10.

7. Ibid., p. 7.

8. Ibid.

9. Moghdam, op. cit., p. 27.

10. Ibid., pp. 46-47.

11. For these figures I am indebted to Richard J. Cichelli, Research Manager, Computer Applications, ANPA Research Institute.

12. Puncekar, Sandra L., ed. "Electronic Applications; O.C.R.—V.D.T.—Computer; ANPA Member Newspapers, 1978." *ANPA R.I. Bulletin,* 1979.

13. Beaton, Roderick W. "Wire Services in Your Future: Don't Take Anything for Granted." Speech delivered to the Ohio Newspaper Association Convention, Columbus, Ohio, Feb. 9, 1978, p. 9.

14. Moghdam, op. cit., pp. 80-81, 84-85.

15. "'Cold type' is used as a descriptive phrase in the newspaper business because 'hot' molten lead is not used in this process; instead print images of copy and illustrations are produced and copied photographically on paper." Udell, op. cit., p. 98.

16. All descriptions of computer use in newspaper advertising are taken from Moghdam, op. cit., pp. 94-98, 111-21.

17. Beaton, op. cit., p. 8. *See also* Moghdam, op. cit., pp. 93, 104-06.

18. Babbage, Charles. *On the Economy of Machinery and Manufactures.* 4th ed. London, Charles Knight, 1835, pp. 250-59. For an assessment of Babbage, *see* Beales, H.L. *The Industrial Revolution, 1750-1850: An Introductory Essay.* New York, Augustus M. Kelley, 1967, pp. 14-16.

19. Smith, op. cit., p. 7.

20. "New York in Limbo: The Story Thus Far," *Columbia Journalism Review* 17:5, Nov./Dec. 1978.

21. The pressmen's strike against the *Washington Post* in 1975 resulted in the union's ouster from that paper. *See* ibid., p. 9.

22. "Tentative Long Term Pact Reached with N.Y. Pressmen," *Editor & Publisher* 111:12, Nov. 4, 1978.

23. Consoli, John. "Times and Daily News Publish Again in N.Y.," *Editor & Publisher* 111:12, Nov. 11, 1978.

24. Smith, op. cit., p. 9.

25. "N.J. Satellite Newspaper Uses Phila. Press/Composing Rooms," *Editor & Publisher* 111:35, Dec. 9, 1978.

26. Ibid., pp. 35-38.

27. Stein, M.L. "How is L.A. Times Doing with San Diego Edition?" *Editor & Publisher* 112:14, May 19, 1979.

28. Udell, op. cit., p. 144.

29. Ibid., p. 124.

30. *See* Wilken, Earl. "Newspaper Production Problems '78-1979," *Editor & Publisher* 112:26, 28, Jan. 6, 1979.

31. *See* Weizenbaum, J. "Once More—A Computer Revolution," *The Bulletin of the Atomic Scientists* 34:14, Sept. 1978.

The Impact of Technology on the
Production and Distribution of the News

CAROLYN MARVIN
Lecturer
Institute of Communications Research
University of Illinois
at Urbana-Champaign

Part II: Delivering the News of the Future

When people find themselves in the midst of rapid technological change, its most significant dimensions often elude them. The apparent impact of computers, satellites and lasers on the production and distribution of news is a case in point.

During the last two decades newspapers have made increasing use of new electronic technologies to perform their familiar functions more easily: to handle increasing information flows, to select the content and construct the appearance of the final news product in a more flexible way, to print and distribute newspapers faster and more cheaply, and not least of all, to keep track of the cost of doing business. Original expectations for greater facility in the performance of all the old jobs have been handsomely met by the new technologies, and for all the public knows (since these transformations have taken place behind the scenes), newspapers are the same as they ever were. These appearances are very deceptive.

For the newspaper of the future, the heart of the significant technological change is the computer's transformation of print production, since the same digital signal which prints a newspaper can be converted to other final formats as well—such as teletext, or text displayed on a video screen. Because of the great variety of possibilities for print and teletext, in combination or separately, the forms and procedures through which each of us will receive news in the future, if there is a single future, is not yet fixed. But possibilities that have been only speculative for decades are now beginning to take form in public and commercial information systems both here and abroad. The challenge these developments pose to the printed newspaper could very well transform it.

The electronification of the newspaper, which we traditionally regard as the achievement of print technology alone, did not begin with the computer. The newspaper ceased forever to be solely a print medium with the organization of wire services more than a century ago. The telephone was a second important addition to the electrified apparatus of news gathering, and electric presses in the late nineteenth century made the newspaper a more efficient nervous system for expanding metropolises. In spite of the essential contribution of electricity and electronics to newspaper operation, newspaper people have continued to regard themselves almost exclusively as printers or print journalists, even though these labels have been inadequate for more than a hundred years. The habit of thinking of the newspaper solely as a print product may help explain why it took the industry so long to recognize that computers would transform it as surely as they are transforming so many other traditional information institutions.

The computer first came to work for the newspaper as a more efficient accountant, but it soon demonstrated that it could perform other tasks—such as printing the paper—better than these tasks had ever been performed before. Currently, in addition to their composing and printing functions, computers are helping metropolitan papers caught in the central-city squeeze pursue their audiences out of the city with suburban branch printing facilities that simplify distribution. The *Los Angeles Times*, with a circulation of more than a million, and the largest daily consumer of newsprint in the country, has established a remote printing plant south of Los Angeles in Costa Mesa and intends to establish one north of Los Angeles in the San Fernando Valley.[1] The *New York Times* is very cautiously contemplating a national daily edition printed at computer-controlled remote printing plants connected to the editorial operation by microwave links.[2]

The most spectacular possibilities of this kind of organization are being developed on a much larger scale. Electronic newspaper facsimile transmission by microwave, landline or orbital satellite to geographically remote printing plants makes it possible to have a newspaper as national or as international in its distribution as a network television show. This is the achievement the *Wall Street Journal* has been working toward for several years. Each day the *Journal* beams an electronic facsimile of its newspaper from a composing plant in Chicopee, Massachusetts, to Western Union's WESTAR I satellite.[3] Each digitally coded page is read off the satellite at ground stations located in seven different states and equipped with automated printing facilities. More than half the *Wall Street Journals* sold daily are printed by these plants from two satellite feeds; eventually there will be just one feed for all copies of the *Journal*—wireless printing, if you prefer. By the end of 1982, the *Journal* plans to build seventeen ground stations which will print the signal beamed by a single satellite.[4] This is an ambitious undertaking, but the *Journal* recently estimated that the cost of buying satellite bandwidth to transmit coded facsimile to its remote printing plants is roughly thirty-five times less than the cost of equivalent bandwidth on telephone lines.[5] Satellite printing makes a national *Wall Street Journal* exceedingly profitable to produce because the cost of long-distance facsimile transmission remains the same no matter how many receiving stations there are to read the signal. By shortening the delivery distance from plant to consumer, each new ground station also reduces the costs of delivery.

The *Wall Street Journal* has more in mind than transmitting newspapers to its seventeen ground stations. The *Journal* already has the machinery to send other kinds of information products by satellite, either its own products or someone else's, and it is building more machinery of the same kind. By 1982 it expects to have the largest private communications network in the country.

The real significance of the experiments of the *Wall Street Journal* and other newspapers with assorted forms of long-distance electronic transmission is that:

1. At virtually every newspaper which uses computers for editing and printing, because it is economically advantageous to do so, the basic machinery to convert news into digital impulses is in place.
2. While this digital signal now almost always ends up in a print-on-paper format, the same signal could also be tansmitted by landline, microwave, satellite, or other, more exotic communications link to wire services, broadcast antennas, or directly to homes and businesses. Information held in a versatile electronic form, in other words, can be reconstituted in a variety of formats, of which only one is printed paper.
3. Some publishers already regard the electronic potential of their newspapers to produce other kinds of news and information formats as insurance. They believe electronic systems increase their options in case of a shift in consumer demand away from the printed page, a severe escalation in the price of newsprint, or a number of other possibilities. Some of these publishers are examining opportunities to market electronically generated information products besides their own newspapers. *The New York Times*, the *Wall Street Journal* and the *Los Angeles Times,* among others, are now forthrightly discussing how long the printed paper will be their primary information product. While none of them expects it to vanish, all are entertaining the possibility that the familiar printed paper will be one of several packaging options in

electronic home information systems sometime after 1990. They also are spending a great deal of money on this sort of speculation with future investment decisions in mind.

Representatives of the American Newspaper Publishers Association, Associated Press (AP) and United Press International (UPI) have, for example, organized a task force to explore not only the possibility of a satellite delivery system for newspapers, but also to identify "future newspaper...applications for satellite communications."[6] And a group of major newspaper publishers, broadcasting companies, newsprint companies and electronics manufacturers recently spent more than half a million dollars to commission an Arthur D. Little study called "The Impact of Electronic Systems on News Publishing," which attempts to look as far ahead as 1992.[7] According to the trade press, the major conclusion of the study, which sells for $25,000 a copy, is that home electronic information systems will not pose a serious threat to conventional news publishing for at least a decade. After that, it predicts, print-on-paper news may be in for a fight unless newspaper publishers themselves try to satisfy new consumer tastes.

The factors that will shape the future of the printed page, whatever it may be, are basically three: (1) the costs of the newsprint, labor and gasoline required to manufacture and deliver the printed page, compared to the costs of electronic software and hardware alternatives; (2) consumer preferences shaped by what other information entrepreneurs do; and (3) regulatory change.

Economics

The most obvious factors are economic. Newsprint prices have doubled in the past decade, and tripled since 1950.[8] Well over half of American newsprint consumption depends on Canadian supplies and is subject to the special vagaries of price hikes, mill and railroad strikes, and transportation difficulties in a foreign country. Conservationist concerns about forest destruction are increasing. All these factors point to future newsprint shortages and steeper prices. Experimental efforts to substitute new substances like kenaf fibers for wood pulp, or to process wood pulp in new ways to yield more and lighter-weight paper from poorer grades of wood, may eventually help to stabilize newsprint costs, but are unlikely to reduce them permanently in the long run.[9] Petroleum-based fuels for trains and trucks that carry newsprint from mill to printing plant and ultimately to the subscriber, also make the price of newsprint and newspapers highly vulnerable to oil politics and supplies.

The only thing that costs most newspapers more than newsprint is labor, both in rising wage contracts and in losses incurred by strikes among newspaper production workers, and in transportation and newsprint production. Thirty strikes took place in the newspaper industry alone last year.[10] Labor costs are also going up at the post office, one of the traditional delivery systems for newspapers. Those costs are now a major factor in postal rate hikes.[11] Newspaper publishers must balance all these costs against those of electronic news delivery formats. Hardware costs, which are primarily engineering costs, are declining, but software costs, representing brains rather than machined parts, are more complicated. The more flexible and complex software is, generally speaking, the more expensive it is. And not only newspaper entrepreneurs are considering electronic alternatives from an economic perspective. Since the revenue to meet newspaper production costs comes mostly from advertising, the future of the printed page rests in part with advertisers who must decide whether to buy space on the printed page or its electronic counterpart.

Consumer Preferences

Any economic advantage in electronic news formatting is of little importance if the habits of generations of newspaper readers cannot be budged. The litany of benefits of the little black box in every living room—a convenient shorthand which takes in a vast literature of dreams for home information systems—has often been publicly rehearsed. The variety of information functions imagined for these systems includes novel ways of presenting the news which are simply impossible in a printed newspaper. For example, a householder would be able to access information which now ends up on the newsroom floor because there is no space for it in the next edition, even though that information might interest him or her more than what does get into the paper. By means of electronic information retrieval he could also select from a vast data base of constantly updated news at his own convenience, since electronic information retrieval operates on demand and not on fixed or infrequent distribution schedules as newspaper editions and broadcast news programs do.

The question, however, is whether such novelty can displace the comfortable routines of newspaper reading. Not all newspaper aficionados will want to give up browsing the generalist newspaper for the specialist and narrow efficiency of a dial-up newsscreen, and the modest price and great portability of the newspaper that gets on the subway with its reader will be hard to beat in any electronic form. If, in an increasingly energy-conservative world, more and more people give up private driving, for example, reading the newspaper aboard public transportation might be an option of increasing preference. It is a mistake, however, to imagine that consumers will suddenly be asked to choose between newsscreens and newspapers. People who use computerized information services on VDTs at work soon begin to imagine ways they could be put to use at home. Houses and apartments with built-in microwave ovens can have built-in cable and information service connections as well, especially when these are linked to temperature control and home security functions. When such facilities are available as a matter of course, people will learn to use them. A shift in the kinds of information consumers want is less likely to be initiated directly by electronic news than by other kinds of information services which, in achieving acceptance, absorb or reshape those of the traditional newspaper. Consumer preferences, in other words, will be shaped by the entire range of available information options as well as by the features of any single one.

However conventional newspapers choose to develop in the meantime, telephone- and television-based information services are already entering private living rooms in Western Europe. At least two European-based commercial services are surveying market possibilities in California and New York.[12] Since 1977 the British Broadcasting Corporation has offered a service called Ceefax which brings subscribing British television viewers news and weather data, travel and financial reports, consumer affairs and entertainment information, airline schedules, job listings, and stock exchange indexes.[13] A similar service, Oracle, is operated by independent commercial television. Ceefax is free; its costs are covered in the mandatory license fee all British television set owners pay yearly. Oracle is financed by advertising in the form of sponsored pages and classified advertising. On June 1, 1978, the British Post Office inaugurated an interactive wired-teletext service called Viewdata, now renamed Prestel, which offers electronic mail services between subscribers. In addition, more than one hundred third parties, including the Stock Exchange, Reuters, the Consumer Association, local newspapers, chains of shops, the Meteorological Office, travel agents, the Sports Council, and special electronic publishing companies set up expressly to exploit the new medium, market a wide variety of information services. The Prestel combination of telephone, broadcasting and computer technologies in a single home information system is a portent of things to come. Prestel counted 1500 subscribers last December, and the post office hopes for 50,000 by the end of this year.[14]

France is at work on a similar interactive system called Antiope, and Canada, West Germany and Japan are experimenting with systems of their own. Tama New Town, a Tokyo suburb, has become a test community for cable news and information services provided free by the government and fifty corporations, including banks, broadcasters, publishers and electronics manufacturers.[15]

By comparison, development in the United States has been more cautious. Equipment manufacturers are jockeying for position at every level—with cable systems, with cassette and video recording equipment, with intelligent terminals or minicomputers, with satellite dishes to receive information services on rooftops, and with decoders for over-the-air broadcast services like Ceefax. (Texas Instruments manufactured the original decoders used in British systems, and is now working on a decoder which will meet the technical specifications of American broadcasting systems.[16])

In spite of the activity of equipment manufacturers, information services vendors who aim directly at households instead of at large firms or government agencies have been slower to move in the marketplace. A broadcast teletext news service is now being tested by KSL-TV in Salt Lake City. Ceefax-like information is carried piggyback on the normal broadcast signal, and may be called up for display on a television screen with a special decoder. The only regular viewers of the service in its present testing stage are KSL-TV personnel who describe its capacity in the following terms:

> Station officials say the number of "pages" that can be transmitted is virtually endless....A computer takes about two minutes to send out...800 pages, then repeats them in sequence, so that depending on when in the cycle you punch a page number, the wait for it to appear on the screen could vary from 1 to 120 seconds.
>
> Each page can display about 120 words, so the total capacity of the 800 pages is more than 100,000 words....That is the equivalent of a 50-page newspaper, not counting the advertising.[17]

The vertical scanning interval of the broadcast signal on which teletext travels is a subject of contention, however. Other uses could be made of the same spectrum space, like transmitting captions for the deaf, or monitoring viewer channel selection and television use. Such requests have already been filed with the Federal Communications Commission (FCC), which must resolve this allocation question before deciding whether to grant final permission for the KSL-TV service. KMOX-TV in St. Louis, which is owned by CBS, has also been experimenting with teletext by comparing advantages and disadvantages of a Ceefax-type signal and an Antiope-type signal. And a committee of the Electronics Industry Association has been meeting regularly to work out agreements on technical standards and specifications for teletext which it will soon recommend to the FCC.

Other information vendors are also moving into place. AP offers an abbreviated news wire formatted for video display to a number of operating cable systems, and UPI will soon market world news reports to home computer owners through an arrangement with Telecomputing Corporation of America, whose computers will provide the access point for customers of that service.[18] QUBE, a much-publicized interactive cable television station operating since December 1977 in Columbus, Ohio, is well set up to distribute news and information services, but it has so far made only primitive use of its capabilities, mainly by extending game show participation beyond the production studio to the viewing audience.[19] In 1980 one of the very largest newspaper chains in the country, Knight-Ridder, will begin testing Viewtron, a video news and information service modeled on Prestel, in about 200 homes in the Miami area. Cox Cable, the distributor of the service, also plans to make an entire channel available to the University of Florida College of Journalism and Communications for an experimental cable "newspaper."[20]

Regulatory Changes

Regulatory uncertainty is an important factor in the slower willingness of electronic information vendors to tackle the home market. The rules which govern the different parts of the telecommunications industry are under intensive review as a congressional subcommittee works out a long-overdue replacement of the Communications Act of 1934. Several mammoth antitrust suits are also testing current industry practices and alignments. Until information entrepreneurs know the outcome of the battle for marketing territory between cable television and broadcasting, and of similar territorial struggles among unregulated data processors like IBM and Xerox, specialized common carriers like Satellite Business Systems, and regulated common carriers like the telephone company and the United States Postal Service, they are sensibly biding their time. Whether conducted within the framework of regulation, legislation or litigation, these are all battles about who shall be permitted by law, and in what markets, to provide various communications and information services.[21] Much of the confusion has occurred because digital electronic technology has played havoc with traditional legal divisions between telecommunications and data processing. This is the line the new Communications Act is trying to redraw, and along which the courts will distribute victory and defeat.

The newspaper is an interested party in all these rearrangements. Its future product, print, teletext or both, will compete with some emerging electronic information services and make customers of others. Some newspapers and wire services may even seek to set up their own electronic communications channels to distribute information products directly to individual subscribers. This is clearly what the *Wall Street Journal* has in mind.

In order to be ready for anything—in order not to become paper dinosaurs—many newspaper publishers are also rapidly diversifying into as many different kinds of media and media products as they can. In so doing, newspapers not only make larger regulatory targets of themselves, but their identities and concerns as publishers are no longer necessarily paramount. Otis Chandler, publisher of the *Los Angeles Times* and chairman of the board of the Times-Mirror Company, which owns a variety of publishing, broadcasting and newspaper interests, foresees a day when there may be a half-dozen media companies (and nonmedia companies like Gulf and Western as well) dividing not only ownership of all newspapers among themselves, but large chunks of other media also, including magazines, books, periodicals, films, the allowable number of radio and television licenses, cable franchises, data banks, and information retrieval services.[22]

Cross-media ownership and concentration are facts of life with which we have lived for years. Is it therefore really true that in the future different media will simply be the different packages in which relatively few vendors sell the different kinds of information that interest us? The prediction that all development in communications technologies will come to nought but greater concentrations of media ownership and less and less information diversity is as classic as the alternative prediction that new communications technologies will inaugurate an era of perfect democracy and well-being. So predictable a prediction deserves to be regarded a little skeptically.

A future of ever-contracting media control extrapolates trends that do exist in the present, but in communications history, the future has not always been just more of the present. The printed book, for example, seemed at first to be only an extension of the manuscript, but it created completely new information structures and infrastructures.[23] Although it seems quite likely that new information technologies will accelerate concentration, it is equally possible that they will create distinctively new media formats which will not fit into and which will undermine the old monopolies of information. If they are truly revolutionary technologies, this is exactly what they will do. (Of course, nothing in history suggests that revolutionary change does not produce new forms of monopoly in its own good time.)

The capital requirements of profitably operating the new communications technologies suggest that we do face greater concentration of media ownership in the short run. Imagine the likely outcome, for example, of the contest for a local audience between a small, independent newspaper and a communications conglomerate with the electronic resources to deliver area news and advertising in either electronic or paper form through the modified living room television set. Besides doing everything the small newspaper could do with greater flexibility, efficiency and resources of talent, the conglomerate could do more as well, with information services the newspaper could not possibly provide. The embodiment of "localism" which is often thought to be the unique strength of the independent newspaper may affect such contests decisively, but just as often will prove unequal to the struggle. On the other hand, an accessible, computer-linked cable television system could strengthen the small, independent newspaper—truly a dying breed in the present newspaper world— by providing it with an economical delivery alternative, a cable channel, to rid it of the albatrosses of gasoline, newsprint and labor costs. But whether or not this is salvation depends on who owns the cable franchise. It could be the Times-Mirror Company.

All of which brings us to an aspect of the newspaper press that everyone hopes will survive and prosper in any electronic evolution of the newspaper format. That aspect is the *freedom* of the press. The issue can be simply sketched. Our government does not directly regulate printed media like books, periodicals and newspapers. It does regulate some electronic media, such as broadcasting, telephones and satellites. If newspapers begin to distribute their news messages over the electromagnetic spectrum, the traditional distinctions which have kept them safe from regulation are in danger of being blurred. It is very hard for governments to regulate media without interfering in some way with the message. To the extent that newspapers do come to resemble their electronic media counterparts, it will be more difficult for them to maintain their separateness in law, and their traditional independence from government may become more and more fragile.

One of the concerns behind current legislative efforts to deregulate electronic media is the belief in some quarters that newspapers must eventually bow to the same pressures.[24] The traditional rationale for regulating broadcast and not newspaper outlets has been the relative scarcity of radio and television stations. Today, however, there are nearly as many broadcast outlets in the United States as there are daily and weekly newspapers, and cable technology promises greater electronic abundance still. Why newspapers should be exempt from regulation under these circumstances is not clear, and any movement of the newspaper toward electronic distribution will be closely scrutinized by regulators. The gradual convergence of electronic and print media technologies, the dependence of newspapers on a variety of electronic information sources, and the belief, widely subscribed to, that Big Media have much too powerful an impact to be left to go their own way, all point to a coming reconsideration of the traditional privileged status of the newspaper.

New electronic news and information formats may engineer completely new social and political roles for themselves, but they must do so in an electronic environment that has rarely seen a true diversity of cultural and political viewpoints, and which has been hampered in this by both private concentration and government regulation. Perhaps this aspect of our future is most difficult to foresee. It is not too hard, after all, to rearrange our imagination to trace the logical processes by which the newspaper industry is developing. It is much harder to imagine just what the eventual social significance of technological rearrangement in the production and distribution of news will be.

REFERENCES

1. Hausman, Robert. "Bottom Line: Rosy Outlook at LA Times," *Editor & Publisher* 112:35, April 14, 1979.
2. "New York Times May Publish National Daily," *Editor & Publisher* 112: 15, Jan. 13, 1979.
3. "The Wall Street Journal by Satellite." Dow-Jones promotional literature, 1975, pp. 1-2.
4. Telephone interview with Tom Frost, Asst. Satellite Operation Manager, *Wall Street Journal,* April 19, 1979.
5. Ibid.
6. "Satellite Task Force Retains Research Firm," *ANPA General Bulletin,* no. 6, pp. 48-49, Feb. 14, 1979.
7. "Home TV Centers to Upset Print Media in 1990s," *Editor & Publisher* 112:9, 40, Feb. 24, 1979.
8. Udell, Jon G. *The Economics of the American Newspaper.* New York, Hastings House, 1978, pp. 124-25.
9. Wood, J. Howard. "Newsprint Developments in the U.S." (Address to 31st Féderation Internationale des Éditeurs des Journaux et Publications Congress, The Hague, Netherlands). May 26, 1978. *See also* Compaine, Benjamin M. *Future Directions of the Newspaper Industry: The 1980s and Beyond.* White Plains, N.Y., Knowledge Industry, 1977, vol. 2, p. 251.
10. The most conspiratorial view of the new satellite technology suggests the possible use of that medium as a strikebreaker because it provides a means of bypassing work stoppages by strikers at one location or even at one company.
11. *See* Postal Service Staff Study for the Committee on Post Office and Civil Service. House of Representatives, 94th Congress. *The Necessity for Change.* Washington, D.C., USGPO, 1976, pp. 9-11.
12. Holmes, Edith. "Viewdata, Teletext Storm Europe; Does U.S. Market Exist?" *Information World,* Winter 1978, p. 2.
13. Ibid. For additional useful background information, *see* Lunin, Lois F. "Data Bases + Television + Telephone = Viewdata," *Bulletin of the American Society for Information Science* 5:22-23, Oct. 1978; Hawkes, Nigel. "Science in Europe: British May Use Telephones, TV's, to Tap Data Bank," *Science* 201:33-34,

July 1978; and Winsbury, Rex. "Newspapers' Tactics for Teletext," *Intermedia* 6:10-12, Feb. 1978.

14. Holmes, op. cit.

15. Vedin, Bengt-Arne. *Media Japan.* Stockholm, Nord-Video, 1977, pp. 51-58.

16. *See, for example,* "Scientific-Atlanta Plans TV Reception Direct from Satellite," *Wall Street Journal,* April 19, 1979, p. 13, cols. 2-3; "Toshiba Introduces Five-Hour Capacity Home TV Recorder," *Wall Street Journal,* April 16, 1979, p. 25, col. 3; and Dwyer, John. "Home Nerve Centre for the 1980s," *Electronics Weekly,* Oct. 11, 1978, pp. 8-10.

17. "All the News Just as Easy as Tuning the Pages," *Chicago Sun-Times,* April 8, 1979, p. A20. *See also* Edwards, Kenneth. "Teletext Broadcasting in U.S. Endorsed by FCC," *Editor & Publisher* 111:11-12, Nov. 18, 1978.

18. "UPI's World News Report Planned for Home Computers," *Editor & Publisher* 112:117, April 21, 1979.

19. *See* Wicklein, John. "Wired City, U.S.A.: The Charms and Dangers of Two-Way TV," *Atlantic* 243:35-42, Feb. 1979.

20. "K-R Plans 1980 Pilot Test for Viewtron," *Editor & Publisher* 112:117, April 21, 1979.

21. For an overview, *see* Sirbu, Marvin A., Jr. "Automating Office Communications: The Policy Dilemmas," *Technology Review* 81:50-57, Oct. 1978; and Killingsworth, Vivienne. "Corporate Star Wars; AT&T vs. IBM," *Atlantic* 243:68-75, May 1979.

22. "Chandler to Newspapers: 'Must Continue to Evolve,' " *Editor & Publisher* 112:18, 47, Feb. 3, 1979.

23. Eisenstein, Elizabeth. *The Printing Press as an Agent of Change.* 2 vols. Cambridge, Cambridge University Press, 1979.

24. *See* White, Margita. Address to Chief Executives Forum Convention, Scottsdale, Ariz., March 28, 1979. These were former FCC Commissioner White's first public remarks after leaving the FCC on Feb. 28.

MICHAEL GORMAN
Director
Technical Services Department
University of Illinois Library
at Urbana-Champaign

Technical Services in an Automated Library

The context in which this paper is set is that of the research library. The automation of technical processes in those libraries is already underway, is increasing and should be encouraged. I shall not here address the topic of the organization of technical processing in the future "paperless library"; rather, it is my belief that in the medium-term future, technical processing, as outlined in this paper, will provide a structure not only to meet medium-term future needs and exigencies but also to be responsive to the drastic changes in our communication systems that are implied by the terms "electronic" or "paperless" society.

Before giving my views on the future of technical processes and their organization, it is necessary to outline where technical services are now and to indicate the forces and pressures which will change those processes. It is fundamentally important that we make a clear distinction between the *processes* and the *methods of organization* of those processes. For example, libraries in the foreseeable future will have the extensive and complex problems associated with the control of serials in one form or another, but this fact does not by any means imply the need for a serials department or division in libraries, or even for a person dedicated exclusively to the control of serials. We must engage in some form of cataloging but we need not have a single, comprehensive cataloging unit.

Where are we now? I have over the last year visited a number of large and medium-sized academic libraries in North America. Without exception they have had a major division concerned with technical services or technical processing. From this point of agreement one finds a considerable range of divergence. A major difference lies between those libraries which have a strictly centralized technical processing operation and those which have decentralized technical processing in that, for example, there are separate technical services departments in their law or music libraries, or in major autonomous libraries within their system (such as Stanford University's Hoover Institution on War, Revolution and Peace). Commonly, there is a combination of centralization and decentralization.

Another major difference between technical processing departments lies in what they contain. Most technical services operations cover the ordering, claiming and receipt of materials; the cataloging and classification of materials; and serials control. Outside this common core one finds that some technical services operations contain some or all of the following functions: circulation, documents, foreign language and special collections, and bibliographic instruction in technical services areas. This leads me to believe that the distinction between technical services and public or reader services in individual libraries is based on custom and tradition arising out of incidental circumstances, rather than on fundamental principle.

The next major difference lies in the basic organization of technical processes. Broadly speaking, technical services departments can be organized by *function* (ordering, cataloging, etc.) or by *types of material* (serials, monographs, audiovisuals, foreign language, etc.) or by a combination of these. The decision on this fundamental organization was, in many cases, made years ago for reasons which may then have been cogent but are now almost certainly forgotten or irrelevant. The future of technical services departments will involve a basic reconsideration of their organization.

In summary, we have an idea of present-day technical services as being centralized or decentralized to some degree, as containing certain core activities and a number of other activities, and as being organized around types of material or functions. What, then, are the forces exerting pressure to change? I believe they are three in number, and will examine each of these forces and attempt to predict their impact on the future of technical services.

Automation

The first of the major forces is automation. Within a 20-year career in different types of libraries I have seen a number of changes. Without exception the most striking have resulted directly or indirectly from the application of computer technology to library activities. This has been especially marked in technical processing. Although I have found one (not especially distinguished) academic library which denies that automation will play any role in its present or future technical processing, the overwhelming majority of libraries are already at the stage where automation is a reality and an essential part of their forward planning. Libraries are in a transitional stage in their use of automation, a period full of signs and portents which though they embody contradictions in detail which make understanding difficult, they nevertheless show a markedly progressive tendency. To take one obvious example, the use of central data bases (the "utilities") to prolong the life of the card catalog is clearly a transitional phenomenon. It is unfortunate that automation has been used in this way but it is important to note that at the same time substantial reserves for the future—in the shape of massive, centralized machine-readable data bases and individual library machine-readable records—have been created. It is virtually certain that the use of automation to shore up card catalogs and to produce microform catalogs will be a minor feature in the future. Within the next decade, the main use of centralized data bases in the technical processing activities of research libraries will be for the production and maintenance of the integrated bibliographic tool which will replace the numerous and inconsistent bibliographic processes based on ineffective paper files. Concurrently, we shall see a degree of cooperation and resource-sharing unprecedented in the history of academic libraries. I believe this period of resource-sharing will bring the end of the self-contained library and the "fortress library" mentality which has prevented progress for so long. Indeed, we may see the day when the calf and the lion shall lie down together in the shape of true cooperation between academic and public libraries within a region. (As a cautionary note, it is vital to remember the philosopher Allen's dictum that the "calf shall lie down with the lion, but the calf won't get much sleep.") As a result of cooperation and resource-sharing, we will see the better use of library resources (financial and bibliographic) to serve the wider community.

What then are the specific effects of automation on libraries' future organization? First is the enormous impact of shared cataloging networks, notably OCLC. When one compares libraries today with those of a decade ago, the most striking difference is that the use of centralized cataloging—which chiefly revolved around the emendation of LC cards—has been replaced by a degree of use of OCLC (and, to a much lesser extent, the other "utilities"). This use is phenomenally high, varying between 70-99 percent. Such a reliance on externally produced records is unprecedented in library history and has led to profound changes in attitudes and organization within libraries. Where is the library using OCLC's services that could survive the withdrawal of those services? Where is the library with an organization that has remained unaffected by such a massive switch from homemade cataloging to the cataloging of others? The use of OCLC in my own library at the University of Illinois at Urbana-Champaign—one of the largest libraries in the world—has had a profound impact both in terms of cataloging efficiency and organization. We have gone from having a huge and growing backlog of cataloging to being the largest current user of

OCLC, and to having a negligible backlog of cataloging. We are presently cataloging over 10,000 titles a month. This is approximately 20 percent more than our current intake, and will inevitably clear our backlog in less than two years. This has been achieved through major changes in organization.

The most important organizational impact of the use of centralized data bases via terminals is that it implies the centralization of automated cataloging. Typically, the library starts its flirtation with automation by acquiring terminals connected to OCLC and then trying to fit the use of those terminals into its previous procedures. This first tentative advance is generally a failure. The successful use of OCLC and the other "utilities" demands a reconsideration of the workflow and, more importantly, of the level of staff (clerical or professional) performing that work. Such a reconsideration inevitably leads to the conclusions that, first, automated processing must be centralized and integrated in order to avoid the dissipation of resources which scattered and intermittent use of terminals produces; and, second, a sharply decreasing level of professional involvement is necessary in order to achieve speed and cost-effectiveness in the cataloging process. In the library of today, where 80 percent or more of all cataloging is done by staffs largely composed of nonprofessionals and paraprofessionals, it is impossible to justify maintaining the large staffs of professional catalogers which have been necessary in the past.

The centralization and automation of the bulk of technical processing also implies integrating those processes. In the premachine era there may have been good and sufficient reasons to have separate operations for the processing of monographs, serials, documents, maps, music, nonprint materials, and materials in nonroman languages. This situation is no longer tolerable if the library is to achieve efficiency, speed and financial savings by means of automated processing. Such dispersion of activities also leads to inconsistencies in the handling of materials and disparities in the allocation of human resources. It is necessary for each library hoping to use automation effectively to consider each of the divisions by types of material with the idea that, unless there is some strong reason to the contrary, those divisions will be eliminated. The ideal is a single sequence of activities (ordering, claiming, receiving, copy cataloging, etc.) which would be applied to all materials. Some materials demanding special expertise, such as those in foreign languages and perhaps government documents, may continue to demand special treatment, but such separations should be kept to a minimum.

Automation within one library should be built on a single data base which contains bibliographic records for all the library's holdings and records of all the activities surrounding those materials (ordering, circulation, binding, etc.). Thus, all the hitherto-dispersed information about the library's collection will be brought together and made available to all. The bulk of the work involved in building and maintaining this central, integrated library tool will be done centrally by largely nonprofessional staffs.

However, the centralized data base can and should allow decentralized input in some instances. Two potential uses of decentralized input are of particular significance: decentralized serial check-in and decentralized original cataloging. In many libraries with a departmental or branch structure, serial check-in is performed twice; once centrally in maintaining a central serial record and once at the branch library which maintains its own files. This is clearly inefficient and wastes money. In the automated library it will be possible for each branch or service point to receive its serials directly and to record their receipt via a local terminal linked to the central data base. In this way the maintenance of a central (and universally available) record will be carried out in a decentralized manner without the wasteful duplication of effort demanded by our present system. As far as original cataloging is concerned, decentralized input will allow subject and language specialists to catalog materials within their area of specialty as only one among a number of professional tasks. Thus, the elimination of the physically discrete central cataloging department, containing professionals who do cataloging exclusively, is foreshadowed by the ability to contribute data to a central data base from any location within the library system.

Automation and its concomitant centralization and cooperation demand a different approach to standardization. Too often in the past, "quality" in technical processing has meant the perpetuation of local practice regardless of its utility, the proliferation of meaningless and petty regional variation, and the blind adherence to the letter of rules without regard to their spirit or intention. In automated processing an adherence to agreed standards (in descriptive cataloging, subject cataloging and content designation) is needed. Foolish consistency is neither required by the new systems nor called for by the users of those systems. Standards there must be, however, and the mechanisms for agreeing on those standards and on achieving their common use will be an important part of the emerging bibliographic environment.

In sum, automation is a powerful force operating on the library as a whole, bringing predictable and unpredictable changes in the nature of library processes, and implying a reconsideration of all our traditional ideas on how the library should be run and how work should be allocated. In particular, automation inevitably implies a deprofessionalizing of all ordering and claiming procedures, of the bulk of cataloging procedures, and of all procedures involved in maintaining the central record of the library's holdings and activities.

Financial Constraints

The second major force exerting pressure for change is money. The politician's cliche is that we live in an age of diminished expectations. The money that seemed so plentiful only a decade ago has gone. Unfortunately, in even the most enlightened societies libraries and other superficially "inessential" social services are the first to suffer in a climate of economic austerity. We who believe in the overriding social and cultural value of libraries must adjust to this austerity, not just by opposing the proponents of Proposition 13, but by creative and profound thinking on the necessities and priorities of today's libraries and what we must do to preserve those libraries for today and posterity. We have to make sure that none of the money we have is wasted, and we have to search constantly for cost-effective replacements for our traditional library procedures.

In technical processing this search for acceptable economy leads to a number of conclusions. First, no library can survive without the direct or indirect use of cataloging data from other libraries made available in machine-readable form. In our present situation this means that the library must search for access to high-quality, large data bases which supply as high a percentage as possible of records which match the library's acquisitions. This question of maximum correspondence between data bases and the library's collection is crucial and overrides almost any other consideration in the relationship between libraries and "utilities." No library can afford an unacceptably high proportion of original cataloging. Second, the library must strive to increase its use of machines in place of human labor, and to increase the efficient use of nonprofessional labor. No library can afford to pay persons to do work which is better done by a machine, nor can any library afford the luxury of underemployed or inappropriately employed professional labor. This means an inevitable concentration of the professional quotient of the work presently done by professional staff, so that overall the library will have fewer professional staff but those professionals will be doing more professional work. Third, our economic realities demand that all libraries share resources—human, financial and bibliographical. We have the economic imperative to cooperate more, the means (in automation) to cooperate more effectively, and the incentive in the established fact that cooperation provides better service to our library users.

The major impact of financial constraints will be in the necessity for libraries to examine their processes very closely. As far as technical processes are concerned, this analysis will be directed toward the elimination of duplication and waste. As I have stated earlier, the answers to these problems lie in centralization and organization by function rather than by type of material. A searching analysis of the relative roles and strengths of professionals, paraprofessionals and nonprofessionals in performing processing tasks will also be necessary in order to lower or to contain the ever-increasing expenditure on labor. Connected with this last is the necessity to transfer tasks from human beings to machines whenever this is possible and desirable. Another important area of analysis is the preparation for the transfer from manual or semiautomated systems to fully automated systems. In technical services it is vitally necessary to be aware that change from premachine processing to machine-era processing is not just a change in the direction of more speed and less wastefulness. It is a true change which will alter the substance of what is done as well as the methods of doing it. It is a fundamental error to automate what one has. Rather, one should automate in the direction of what can be. In order to achieve this, it is necessary to analyze the purpose of a task as well as the method of performing it.

Beyond the problems of technical processing departments, financial constraints will certainly bring about a reconsideration of the overall organization of the library. It is impossible to imagine a major restructuring of technical services which does not imply a rethinking of all the library's processes and services. In particular, it is evident that the strict division between technical and public services will be eroded in the near future. That distinction has undoubtedly wasted money and human resources because the specialization implied by two types of librarians within one library has not allowed either category to reach full efficiency, nor has it allowed the library to make the best use of its employees.

The Search for Professionalism

The third force exerting pressures for change lies in the nature of professional librarianship. Because it is evident to every thinking librarian that the library of the future will be radically different from that of the past, we have started to revise our ideas of the role, the nature and the purposes of professional librarianship. In library education and in the practice of librarianship one can sense a questioning arising from changed circumstances. This questioning focuses especially upon the achievement of a well-rounded and satisfying work experience. Few young librarians are willing to dedicate themselves (or perhaps confine themselves) to being a "technical services person" or a "public services person." Many librarians feel that a choice made early in their career has proven to be a restriction on their professional experience. This limitation of people to particular facets of librarianship is not only perceived as inimical to their full professional development but also inhibiting to the efficiency of the library. There seems to be little doubt that the division between the two types of librarian will be done away with in the next decade, partly because the division itself is harmful and partly because of the dissatisfaction of librarians themselves.

It is easy to see how the technical/public service division has wasted good people. Who does not know a specialist cataloger with vast knowledge of her or his subject and its bibliography who is seldom if ever called upon to use that knowledge in the direct service of the library's patrons? Who does not know a reference librarian whose deliberate ignorance of cataloging and technical service matters has inhibited her or his effectiveness in serving the public? Who has not seen important initiatives in a library thwarted by mutual incomprehension and failure to communicate on the part of both "factions"? The time has come to end this divisiveness, to use all librarians more effectively, and to plan for a new structure for the library of tomorrow.

In academic libraries in particular a new challenge has arisen, one which causes librarians to reconsider the nature of their profession. The increasing importance of "faculty status" to academic librarians and the increasing pressure on those librarians who carry that status to conform to, and be judged by, normal academic criteria have meant that in many academic libraries the nature of the librarian's calling and the respective duties of academic and nonacademic library workers have come under close scrutiny. In academic libraries the "publish and flourish" philosophy means that the days of the professional librarian as high-level clerk are either over or at least numbered.

The effects of this move toward more professionalism in librarianship can be stated simply. They are that the search for better-rounded professional experience will contribute to the end of the technical/public service dichotomy and that the rethinking of the role of the professional librarian will lead to the fundamental rethinking of the organization of libraries.

Future Prospects

I have described the three forces (automation, money and the drive toward professionalism) which I see as affecting the organization of technical processing activities. I will now describe the short (1- to 5-year) and medium (6- to 15-year) term prospects for the accomplishment of technical processing which I believe will result from the action of those forces upon our present situation. In the short term, I believe that technical processing will be carried out by an administratively distinct element of the library. However, I discern certain inevitable developments which will change technical processing in libraries over the next five years. First, organization by function rather than by type of material will come to be seen as the most efficient response to the use of "utilities" and other developments in automation. Therefore, the typical technical processing operation will bring together all ordering and receipt operations, all bibliographic operations, all operations connected with the use and maintenance of automated data bases, and all professional cataloging operations. Such functional organization will undoubtedly pay in dividends in terms of productivity and the most efficient use of personnel. Second, this functional organization will demand the centralizing of activities, especially those of a clerical nature and those intimately connected with automated procedures. Third, technical processing departments will increasingly concentrate on the "core" activities described early in this paper and will have a tendency to shed some of the "fringe" activities (special collections, book selection, etc.) which have accrued to technical services departments by happenstance or tradition over the years. These activities will be dispersed throughout other library departments or will be gathered together in a "third force" between technical and public services. Thus, in the short term we can see technical processing as functionally organized, centralized and concentrating on "core" activities. This will provide a good basis for processing in the transitional period between the post-paper file library and the fully automated library. In the fully automated library one will need another solution.

The most striking feature of technical processing in the fully automated library will be the abolition of technical services as a major administrative subdivision of the library. This will coincide with the abolition of public services as a separate administrative subdivision of the library. Although this major reorganization will go far beyond nomenclature, it is significant that both units are named restrictively—"technical" service with its overtones of technological elitism and "behind the scenes" secrecy, and "public" service with its implication of exclusive rights to serve the library's patrons. We will be better off without both terms.

Once we have done away with this basic division, we will be free to apportion work correctly and to see the library as a functional rather than traditional organization. I believe that libraries at the end of the 1980s will be organized along the following three basic groupings:

1. a centralized automated processing operation, staffed primarily by nonprofessional and paraprofessional library workers;
2. professional groups organized around special subjects and services; and
3. a centralized library management operation.

The centralized processing operation will be based on the construction and maintenance of the integrated, automated system which will replace our presently scattered paper files. This system will use a single data base in which is recorded the existence and current status of all the materials which the library holds. The single, automated multipurpose tool will revolutionize the service which the library is able to offer its patrons and, more germane to the subject of this paper, will necessitate the creation of a new structure within the library. The tasks which the central processing unit will perform are:

1. the ordering, claiming, receipt and routing of library materials;
2. automated/rapid cataloging based on the use of OCLC or another "utility";
3. the maintenance of data base records (including order records, circulation records, bibliographic monograph and serial records, etc.) relating to the library's materials;
4. the addition to the central data base of newly created machine records; and
5. accounting, bookkeeping and other "housekeeping" activities.

The central processing operation will be staffed almost entirely by nonprofessional and paraprofessional staff. Professional involvement will be restricted to policy-making and a limited amount of supervision. In fact, there is no proven reason why any professionals need be involved in this kind of library activity. There would seem to be a role for the paraprofessional supervisor that already exists in many large libraries.

If one were being fanciful one might have an image of the central processing operation of the future as the engine which drives a large machine. Such an engine is central to the working of the machine but it is not essentially what the machine is about. Pursuing the analogy of the library as a machine, we can see the purpose of the machine as delivering materials and services to the library users. This purpose will primarily be carried out by the second element to which I have referred: the groups (or "clusters") of professional librarians organized to carry out services to the library's users in connection with subjects, particular services or special types of material. These clusters will probably be relatively small in number (one eminent modern librarian believes strongly that twelve is the maximum number for effectiveness in administration; history abounds in instances which support his view) and will carry out all professional duties associated with their subject area (sciences, social sciences, etc.), services (undergraduate services, domiciliary services, etc.), or special materials (audiovisuals, nonroman languages, etc.). These professional duties will include:

1. the selection of library materials,
2. the original cataloging of all materials for which copy is not available (the results of this cataloging will be processed by the central processing unit),

3. reader and reference services,
4. bibliographic instruction, and
5. professional bibliographic services.

It is evident that these groups will overlap in some particulars (e.g., science materials in an undergraduate library), but it is also true that such overlaps occur in our present premachine libraries and that professionalism implies a willingness and an ability to cooperate. Besides, these groups are not intended to be hermetically sealed and may be visualized as overlapping circles. Such an arrangement will be advantageous to the professional librarian in that it will offer him or her a thorough professional training and a satisfying and well-rounded professional experience. It will benefit the users of the library in that the best use of professional talent best serves the library user, and also in that the concentration of professional librarians in particular areas of expertise (subject or otherwise) will ensure a depth of service that our present systems rarely achieve.

The third element of the future library's structure is administrative. Anyone viewing modern libraries dispassionately will grant that administrative excellence is rarely encountered and that even an adequate (or commonsense) level of administration is often lacking. It is essential that the differently structured large library of the future be managed well. This does not imply that rigid hierarchical doctrines or business pseudo-expertise should be imported into libraries. In fact, such archaic administrative ideas (rightly despised by librarians for years) are no longer found even in the most cynically exploitative business enterprises. What we need in libraries, now and in the future, is responsive, human and intelligent management and coordination. The tasks of this third element will include:

1. general administration,
2. personnel and career services,
3. quality control,
4. coordination of library services,
5. budget allocation and control,
6. policy formulation and coordination, and
7. coordination with other libraries and library agencies.

The administrative element should not be seen as the highest of the three elements. On the contrary, this future library organization should abandon hierarchical and elitist concepts, allowing everyone—nonprofessional, paraprofessional, professional librarian, administrator and librarian/administrator—to find a fulfilling role in a cooperative and multidimensional environment.

For the reasons outlined earlier in this paper, I believe that the library of the medium-term future—the post-machine but pre-electronic library—will have a different structure from that of the library of today. Because of the forces molding libraries at this time, such change is inevitable. The pressures of automation, finance and the search for professionalism in librarianship will shape a new kind of library. That library will be geared administratively to the post-machine age, will allow well-rounded professionalism to flourish, will make the best use of automation, and will be effective in terms of cost, in terms of the use of library personnel, and in terms of service to its local, regional and national community.

GERARD SALTON

Professor
Department of Computer Science
Cornell University
Ithaca, New York

Toward a Dynamic Library

The library world has been forced to exist under troublesome conditions for many years. The difficulties are due to a variety of causes, including constantly increasing service demands, the great variety of library material that must be processed (tapes, cards and microforms, in addition to the normal printed materials) and, most important of all, the severity of the budget crisis. It is an unfortunate fact that library support levels have been shrinking at the very time when the cost of library services and materials is reaching a record high.

It was, perhaps, natural in these circumstances that library administrations should turn to the use of computing equipment as a means for coping with the increasing transactions and the cost explosion. Two main approaches were followed in the 1960s. The first, termed *piecemeal mechanization*, denotes the conversion of library operations to computer processing, one application at a time. Thus, one library would create an automated circulation system, while another concentrated on automating the acquisitions process.

It became clear very early that the piecemeal mechanization approach was fraught with difficulty. The files to be processed were often very large and subject to continual changes and updates, and a great many different processes had to be considered. An additional problem was the desire to maintain real-time control over all library items, that is, the status and whereabouts of each library item were to be ascertainable at any time. It is easy to understand, therefore, that a conversion to an automated processing system would not be simple and straightforward. This situation produced substantial disenchantment with the use of computers in the library, and some observers even claimed that computing equipment could not viably be incorporated into a library environment.[1]

The second main effort in library automation in the 1960s produced a number of prototypes for *integrated library management systems* which dealt with the complete library operation as a unit. Several complete management systems were designed by IBM, University of Chicago, Stanford University and others; some of these systems are most impressive in their conceptions and relatively easy to use. However, the recent trend in the direction of cooperative ventures among libraries has somewhat dampened the enthusiasm for the integrated stand-alone systems, and the feeling now seems to be that they are too costly to be supported by single library organizations without substantial outside aid.[2]

Presently, the library crisis remains undiminished; indeed, the budget situation may be more unfavorable now than it was ten or fifteen years ago. However, two fundamental changes have occurred in recent years. First, many librarians feel that the technical library processing tasks are becoming too big and too costly to be borne by an individual library. As a result, the opposition to the formation of compacts between libraries and library networks has substantially decreased, and some library administrators are reconciled to a small loss of autonomy in return for the benefits obtainable from cooperative endeavors.

In addition, a number of advances have taken place in the computer art that may be of substantial benefit in library processing. First, the increased storage capacity of the modern computing equipment has considerably simplified the processing of large library files. Recently, console terminals have also been developed which provide a friendly environment for user/system interaction, and these on-line systems have proved to be not only commercially successful, but essential for many types of applications, such as airline reservations, banking transactions, point-of-sale terminal processing, and so on. Later in this paper it will be shown that interactive processing methods can provide great benefits in library application. Finally, there has been progress in the design of computer networks and in the use of "distributive" computing, in which a process is separated into several pieces to be handled by different computers with interaction between processors to insure that the final product conforms to the initial specifications.

The combination of large memory capacities, intelligent front-end devices for user/system interaction, and distributive computing methodologies have changed the outlook for the mechanization of library processes. Accordingly, the current plans for the design of the library of the future differ from the earlier versions. The piecemeal mechanization efforts and the integration of library processes into a single management system are being replaced by the construction of cooperative library networks and by tentative plans toward a paperless library system which would operate at some future time in a totally new environment.

The main considerations in the design of library networks and paperless library systems are outlined in the next section. Some concepts are then introduced which may be utilized in the implementation of an alternative, so-called dynamic library. Finally, a number of specific processes are examined which may be incorporated into the proposed dynamic library system of the future.[3]

LIBRARY COOPERATION AND THE PAPERLESS FUTURE LIBRARY

Library Networks

It is generally recognized that a great deal of similarity exists among the technical processing cycles that form the basis for monograph and serials processing in libraries of comparable size and scope. Thus, the basic book-ordering, bill-paying and acquisitions operations are more or less similar; so is the cataloging process, and—possibly with somewhat greater variation—the circulation system. The basic tool for all these operations is a comprehensive library catalog which includes descriptive information for all library items. Such a catalog is consulted during the acquisitions process to determine whether an item on order may already exist in the collections. Furthermore, when a catalog description exists for a given item, it serves again for the creation of a more complete record during cataloging. Finally, the catalog entry is used repeatedly for charging and discharging materials during the circulation process.

From these basic facts it follows that a comprehensive machine-readable library catalog accessible from a variety of geographic locations would be useful in controlling the technical processing performed by a number of different library organizations. Appropriate console entry devices must exist in each participating library to be used to access the common machine-readable catalog. This type of machine-readable union catalog forms the basis for the well-known catalog card ordering system managed by OCLC.[4] An automated system in which a variety of different library organizations are hooked to one or more common mechanized catalogs is known as a *library network*.[5]

It is clear that a great many different network configurations are possible in principle. Normally, a single centralized catalog is used to control the operations originating in various remote libraries; alternatively, each participating library in the network could manage its own mechanized catalog in such a way that the local user population is given access not only to the local catalog, but also to the remote catalogs of other libraries in the network. Such a system makes it possible to share library resources and to reduce the burden of technical processing for any one organization. The following possibilities are immediately apparent:

1. Technical processing costs can be saved by sharing the burden of the operations; for example, a given library item might be cataloged once and other participating organizations would use the already-established cataloging record. This kind of argument was used in creating service organizations such as OCLC.
2. A shared mechanized catalog could support more sophisticated subject-acessing procedures than a conventional manual card catalog if additional types of content identifiers or a greater variety of conventional subject indicators were included.
3. The shared catalog constitutes a resource-sharing tool in the sense that the user population can be given access to the pooled resources of a number of different libraries; the network organization could then lead to a broad system of interlibrary loan procedures and cooperation.
4. The system could be used for shared collection development if each participating library were to orient its acquisitions policy toward particular subject areas; this would save resources by avoiding multiple acquisitions of rarely used materials.

While a resource-sharing library network could certainly provide a variety of actual and potential advantages to participating organizations, substantial difficulties still exist before such networks can actually fulfill the previously mentioned promises. There are problems of a nontechnical as well as of a technical nature. The nontechnical questions relate to the differing interpretations of aims and responsibilities of participating libraries: many libraries currently maintain different standards of growth and retirement policies; there may be user groups who deserve or expect specialized services of various kinds; in addition, administrative and other constraints imposed on the participating organizations may hamper the cooperative effort. The financial arrangements among the network participants would necessarily be difficult to manage because of the fundamentally uneven standing of the component libraries. Clearly, much of the service would be rendered by the wealthier units endowed with the best collections, and the weaker units may function mostly as recipients of the services. The question then arises of who pays how much to whom.

Whenever a number of user organizations share a common set of files, questions of privacy arise because it becomes necessary to preserve data confidentiality for items with restricted circulation characteristics. Finally, the effect of a library network system on outside organizations, such as the publishing industry, must be considered. Obviously, when fewer published items are bought by libraries, and most items circulate freely without royalty payment, the publishing industry, and by extension authors, are liable to suffer. Many of these social and legal problems have not yet been considered in detail. One may hope that with goodwill on everyone's part, appropriate accommodations may, in time, be found.

Among the more technical problems of library and computer network organizations are those relating to the actual technical implementation. What, for example, should be the role of minicomputers in the network? What are the comparisons of communications costs, storage costs and data accessibility when each item is stored in a single, central location as opposed to data duplication at several points in the network? What are the software and hardware requirements implied by the latter, a distributed data base design, compared with the more normal centralized data base system? What problems are likely to arise when it becomes necessary to merge different technologies, such as computing equipment, communications lines and photographic technology?

The question of formal standardization and bibliographic control may also be expected to cause grief in a network situation. The current perception on the part of many librarians is that increasingly stringent controls are necessary as one moves from the level of a single-library item to the level of a complete institution, and from there to a larger system comprising several institutions, and finally to a comprehensive library network. Their idea is that a catalog item admitted into the network must conform to specific rules of description, formatting and control, and that these rules must be standardized. Such requirements would make it possible to use standardized query and search protocols to access any item, no matter where it is located:

> There is growing realization that the authority file (which specifies established forms of headings and other bibliographic descriptions) is the foundation and basic building block of the automated library system.[6]
>
> Protocols must be carefully formulated and followed; otherwise the network users will require a variety of manuals...and need to reformulate search requests each time a network component using a nonstandard form of indexing is accessed.[7]

If these precepts are to be followed, it is clear that substantial difficulties may arise in (1) deciding about appropriate standards, (2) converting nonstandard items to the common format, (3) deciding what items to admit into the network, and (4) exercising the quality control necessary for upgrading the items.

In a mechanized library situation, it is likely, however, that storage space restrictions will be much less confining than has been customary for a normal catalog using three-by-five-inch cards. It is not clear in these circumstances why a multiplicity of different indexing systems could not coexist quite peacefully. This possibility is examined in more detail later in this paper.

The Library of the Future

In addition to implementing plans for the construction of cooperative library systems and networking arrangements, a certain amount of attention is also given in some library circles to the role of the library in the society of the future. A number of blueprints are in existence which postulate the storage of all existing knowledge in machine-readable form. A huge, mechanized storage system would replace the normal library, and effective console-driven information retrieval protocols operating in an on-line mode would be used to locate stored items of interest to individual users. Conventional books and journals in the form of printed information on paper could be dispensed with in such a situation: "Any concept of a library that begins with books on shelves is sure to encounter trouble....We should be prepared to reject the schema of the physical library—the arrangement of shelves, card indexes, check-out desks, reading rooms, and so forth."[8]

In fact, the replacement of the current labor-intensive, constant-productivity library setup with a remotely accessible, machine-readable data store, and the elimination of paper products exhibit substantial attractions:

1. a paperless, comprehensive machine-readable data store would eliminate the existing fragmentation of materials in a given subject over many different journals and books;
2. the large volume of material which necessarily will have to be processed and stored in the future would become much more manageable in a paperless system;
3. since the cost of standard (paper) publications is continually increasing, in part because of the labor-intensive nature of the publishing industry, substantial savings may be produced with respect to publishing in a paperless situation; and
4. the delays currently built into the standard publication system could largely be eliminated, and the dissemination of research results could be speeded by abandoning the conventional publishing chain producing paper products.[9]

In a paperless society, many individuals would own personal computer terminal devices which could be used for a variety of purposes, such as maintenance of private files, composition of letters and articles, recording of incoming messages and text and, incidentally, for library search and retrieval purposes. The role of the traditional library in such an environment is unclear; almost certainly the "library" would provide search services for users without personal on-line access. Printout services for bulky materials that could not economically be handled by the personal terminals might also be provided by a library center. Items of purely local interest might be collected and cataloged, and specialized search services could be provided for certain classes of customers.

It is not possible in the present context to go into a detailed examination of the merits and disadvantages of a completely automated, paperless communications system, or to assess the technical feasibility questions. Suffice it to say that a complete abandonment of books and journals as we know them would certainly produce inconveniences to large classes of the population: many people now use library materials in out-of-the-way places—on the beach, in bed, in buses and on airplanes—where computer access may not be immediately available. In any case, the use of computers to obtain on-line access to library materials (which may be expected in the foreseeable future) certainly does not imply the immediate elimination of printed materials. Furthermore, quite a few of the claims made in favor of the paperless library are almost certainly exaggerated: that a paperless on-line system is more "democratic" because everyone will have equal access to the vital information which is now confined to a few selected experts; that the library of the future could store items which under current conditions never make it through the publication process (as if it were advantageous to be able to access the bulk of materials that have never been subjected to quality control); that on-line communications systems would prevent the duplication of research and development efforts by making it easy to discover prior work; that a good deal of work now performed in offices and factories could be done at home using the computer console, thereby reviving the cottage industry and decreasing work alienation; and that the preparation of reports and articles from a computer console will help people improve their writing style and spelling ability.

In the next few paragraphs an alternate concept of the library of the future is outlined in which computer access plays a role in identifying pertinent materials, but where printed materials are maintained whenever possible. Whether this alternative future library has a greater chance of being implemented than the proposed paperless system remains to be seen.

CONCEPTS OF THE DYNAMIC LIBRARY

The main idea behind the dynamic library is flexibility, and the use of customer/system interaction to control library operations.[10] The description of a particular library item can be made to vary with the environment in which it is placed, and also with the judgments obtained from the user population about the usefulness and importance of the item. The classification system used to organize the library collection is similarly adjustable as the interests of the users change. Thus, when particular subject areas become of special interest, a more refined classification system can be used for them than for the remainder of the collection. This implies that the search system itself can also be adjusted with changes in classification. Finally, since the retrieval system operates in an on-line mode, information about previously retrieved items can be used to adjust the original query formulations in such a way that improved output may be retrieved from the collections.

The idea, then, is to avoid the imposition of outside rules in the form of authority lists, special indexing conventions and preestablished classification systems, and to treat the library like the dynamic environment it is, where the file contents as well as the user population are subject to continuous change. To give a brief example before turning to the technical details, suppose a document ostensibly dealing with the use of computers in medicine is to be indexed. How appropriate would it be to choose the term *computers* as a subject indicator? The answer is that no one knows. If this item is placed in an environment of medical documents to be accessed by medical people, the term *computer* may be precisely right, because it will help in distinguishing this particular document from other medical items in the collection. If, on the other hand, the document winds up in a computer science collection where it is accessed by computer experts, then the term would probably be inappropriate, because all the other documents deal with computers and the special nature of the item will not be recognized.

This example suggests that no one particular content analysis or cataloging system will be adequate for all purposes, but that the subject description must depend on the collection environment and the user population. In a computer environment where console access to the stored collection is available, there is no virtue in insisting on fully controlled, static indexing, classification and search procedures. Instead, each item can be described in many different ways, and each user can access the items in accordance with his own viewpoint.

The following main characteristics are important in the design of the dynamic library.

1. The operations are software procedures which facilitate access to the collections and retrieval of useful information; there is no intention to tamper with the storage and dissemination of printed materials.

2. Machine-readable information, consisting of at least abstract-length excerpts, is used to generate content identifications for each item, and the content analysis will depend on the general collection environment within which a given item is placed.

3. The files are interrogated remotely by the user population, and the relevance assessments obtained from the users about specific items are used to improve the available content descriptions. The same relevance assessments are also used for query reformulation purposes to enable the improved queries to retrieve more relevant and fewer nonrelevant items than the original formulations.

4. Dynamic classification systems, which consist of broad, general classes of related items for use by the casual client, as well as smaller, more refined classes to serve the experts in particular subject areas, are used to organize the stored collections.

5. The eventual value of a particular term for indexing purposes, or of a particular document in retrieval is dependent on the accrued experiences of the user population with that document, and on the total collection environment.

In order to understand the dynamic operations in detail, it is necessary to introduce the concept of *similarity between items*. It is obvious that similarities exist between library items; library personnel use this fact to arrange related items in adjacent places on library shelves. Unfortunately, the relationships between items are not recognized operationally in conventional library environments. In the dynamic library, the computation of similarities or distances between library items, or between terms, lies at the root of the operations.

Consider a collection of documents, and assume that each document is identified by a set of terms, or content identifiers. The identifiers might be words or phrases extracted from the documents, or entries found in a thesaurus. The collection may then be represented in matrix form:

$$
\begin{array}{c}
D_1 \\
D_2 \\
\vdots \\
D_n
\end{array}
\left[
\begin{array}{cccc}
d_{11} & d_{12} & \ldots & d_{1t} \\
d_{21} & d_{22} & \ldots & d_{2t} \\
 & & & \\
 & & & \\
d_{n1} & d_{n2} & \ldots & d_{nt}
\end{array}
\right]
$$

$$
\begin{array}{ccccc}
Q & \quad q_1 & q_2 & \ldots & q_t
\end{array}
$$

As shown above, each row of the matrix represents a document (D), and a given entity d_{ij} represents the weight, or value, of the jth identifier attached to document i. A query (Q) is similarly represented by a term vector; q_j represents the value of the *j*th identifier in query Q.

Whereas the rows of the matrix are used to represent the documents, a particular column of the matrix identifies the assignment of a specific term to the items of the collection. This is indicated by the respective vector forms:

Document $\quad$ D_i $=$ $(d_{i1}, d_{i2},...d_{it})$
Term $\quad\quad\;$ T_k $=$ $(t_{1k}, t_{2k},...t_{nk})$
Query $\quad\quad$ Q_j $=$ $(q_{j1}, q_{j2},...q_{jt})$

Where row D_i identifies the *i*th document, column T_k represents the *k*th term, and Q_j the *j*th query.

A similarity measure (s) may be computed between pairs of items as a function of the global similarity between items. The use of a global similarity measure makes it unnecessary to insist on the presence or absence of a particular identifier, because the eventual similarity value depends on the values of the complete collection of identifiers. Typical similarity measures between the two vectors

$$X_i = (x_{i1}, x_{i2},...x_{in}) \text{ and } X_j = (x_{j1}, x_{j2},...x_{jn})$$

might be expressed by the following formulas.

$$s_1(X_i,X_j) = \sum_{k=1}^{n} x_{ik} x_{jk}$$

$$s_2(X_i,X_j) = \frac{\sum\limits_{k=1}^{n} x_{ik} x_{jk}}{\sum\limits_{k=1}^{n}(x_{ik})^2 + \sum\limits_{k=1}^{n}(x_{jk})^2 - \sum\limits_{k=1}^{n} x_{ik}x_{jk}}$$

The similarity computations between pairs of document vectors and pairs of term vectors, and between a document and a particular query, are illustrated as follows:

$s(D_i,D_j)$ $\quad$ Similarity computation between documents D_i and D_j

$s(T_k,T_l)$ $\quad$ Similarity computation between terms T_k and T_l

$s(Q_j,D_i)$ $\quad$ Similarity computation between query Q_j and document D_i

It is possible to represent a collection of items on a two-dimensional map in such a way that the similarity between items is inversely related to the distance between them in the space. This is shown in Figure 1 for three items, where the similarity between items A and B is clearly much greater than between A and C.

These preliminaries are used in the remainder of this study for the description of the dynamic library operations.

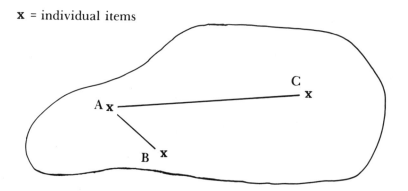

x = individual items

FIGURE 1. SPACE REPRESENTATION OF SIMILARITY MEASUREMENTS
Similarity inversely related to distance
s(A,B)>>s(A,C)

Dynamic Classification

In a conventional library environment, a classification system serves to group into common classes items exhibiting certain similarities. When documents are represented by sets of content identifiers, it is possible in principle to compute a similarity coefficient between all pairs of documents, and to group into a common class all items with sufficient similarity (i.e., sufficiently small distance between them). This produces a clustered arrangement of documents such as that shown in Figure 2a, where each "x" represents a document, the large circular structures are the classes, and the small squares at the center of each circle are dummy documents, called centroids, which represent the given classes.

It should be noted that the classification process outlined above represents a *global* vector processing operation involving all document vectors. In an automatic retrieval environment, it is desirable to replace global operations by local ones involving only small subsets of items. For classification purposes, global operations are required; however, comparatively inexpensive automatic classification systems can be used in practice.[11]

The classification system of Figure 2a is similar to conventional library classifications, except that the classes are automatically constructed, and that overlap may exist because some items appear in several classes. To search a classified or clustered file, it is convenient first to compare a given query with the class centroids—by computing the similarity coefficients $s(A_i, C_j)$—and next to consider for individual comparison with the query all those documents located in classes with sufficiently high query-centroid similarity.

As indicated earlier, it is possible to tailor the classification system to the interests of the user population by altering the threshold in the similarity measure needed to enter a given item into a given class. Thus, a small number of large classes, obtained by using fairly low threshold values in the required similarity computations between items, may be adequate for casual, nonexpert users. When it becomes necessary to perform more directed searches in a particular subject area, each large class may be broken into a number of smaller classes by raising the magnitude of the similarities needed to group items into common classes. The effect of this operation is illustrated in Figure 2b in which two large initial classes are broken down into five smaller ones.

In principle, the cluster refinement operations can, of course, be repeated by constructing still smaller and more homogeneous classes in subsequent iterations. Just as it is possible to use a variety of content description or indexing systems which allow the user to choose query formulations tailored to his own background and experience, so can several different classification systems be stored simultaneously in an automatic environment, thereby accommodating many different user interests. A standard search would use the broadest or least-refined classes. As the user became more interested in a given subject area, refined classes could be used in subsequent searches. This makes it possible successively to reject more and more extraneous items, and to concentrate the search in the few specific areas that are actually of interest.

Dynamic Query Reformulation

One of the major advantages of an on-line information search-and-retrieval environment is the ability to assess the usefulness of the retrieved items as soon as a given search operation is terminated. This enables immediate query reformulations when the initial search output is unsatisfactory, followed by reassessment and reformulation processes until a satisfactory search output is obtained. All on-line retrieval systems make

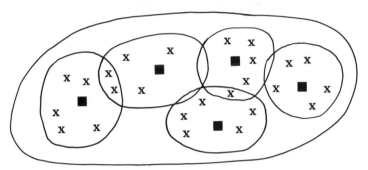

FIGURE 2a. DYNAMIC CLASSIFICATION:
CLUSTERED DOCUMENT COLLECTION

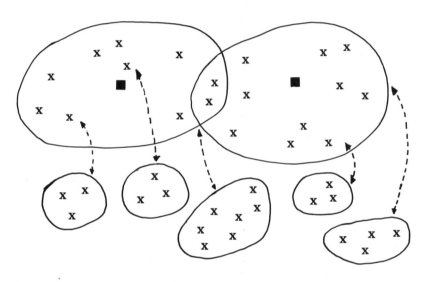

FIGURE 2b. DYNAMIC CLASSIFICATION: REFINEMENT

provisions for query reformulation; normally, vocabulary displays are
provided, consisting of terms similar to those used in the original query
formulation, and the user is required to choose the new query terms that
may help improve the search results.

Instead of giving a detailed description of the existing query reformulation procedures, it may be more useful to provide a model for query
improvement based on the vector space processing previously discussed.
Consider a typical document space, and assume that a number of items

located in a given region of the space have been retrieved in response to a search request. The user may then be asked to provide assessments of relevance for some of the retrieved items. This normally identifies some relevant and some nonrelevant items, and makes it possible to construct an improved query which is closer to the relevant and further from the nonrelevant than the original query. In other words, the query/document similarity coefficient for the new query should be large for the relevant items and small for the nonrelevant ones.

The well-known *relevance feedback* process is an automatic query reformulation process based on relevance assessments supplied by the user population. The query transformation is executed in two steps:

1. the new query is moved close to the items identified as relevant by the addition of terms taken from the relevant items, or alternatively, by increasing the weight of those original query terms that are present in the relevant items; and

2. at the same time, the new query is moved away from the nonrelevant items by subtracting from the original query those terms also present in the nonrelevant items, or alternatively, by decreasing the corresponding query term weights.[12]

A typical document space with added relevance assessments is shown in Figure 3a, and the relevance feedback operation is illustrated in Figure 3b. It is clear that the query transformation process can be iterated several times by constructing new query vectors based in each case on relevance assessments for items retrieved by a previous query formulation. Strong experimental evidence indicates that such a feedback operation can provide substantial improvements in retrieval effectiveness.[13]

Relevance judgments can also be used as a basis for query reformulation in conventional environments where Boolean query statements are used to retrieve documents manually indexed by keywords. The user feedback process devised for the retrieval service of the Commission on the European Communities consists of the following main steps.

1. Relevance assessments are obtained for some of the documents retrieved in response to an initial search request.

2. The set of terms used to index some of the items known as relevant is examined; for example, (A *and* B *and* C *and* D) and also (E *and* F *and* G).

3. Some terms from the query statements chosen in (2) are removed in order to broaden the resulting search statements; for example, statements (A *and* B *and* D) and also (E *and* F) are constructed.

4. These shortened queries are used as new search statements to retrieve additional documents; the relevance of some of these newly retrieved documents is then assessed.

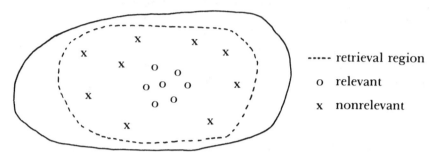

FIGURE 3a. QUERY IMPROVEMENT USING RELEVANCE FEEDBACK:
DOCUMENT SPACE WITH RELEVANCE ASSESSMENTS

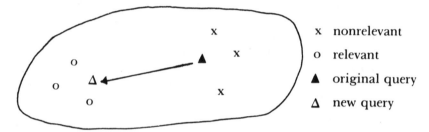

FIGURE 3b. QUERY IMPROVEMENT USING RELEVANCE FEEDBACK:
RELEVANCE FEEDBACK OPERATION

5. For each of the new query statements a "query quality factor" is computed as the ratio of the new relevant items retrieved to the new non-relevant items retrieved.
6. Those partial queries with sufficiently high query quality factors are chosen and a final feedback query is constructed by inserting *or* connectives between the corresponding partial query formulations; for example, the new statement used could be [(A *and* B *and* D) or (E *and* F)].
7. The newly constructed query is used for search purposes and the process is repeated if desired.[14]

Additional feedback techniques incorporating slight variations of such a process can easily be devised.

One of the virtues of the relevance feedback and related query reformulation methods is the *local* nature of the operations; normally, only the previously retrieved documents are used, rather than the whole document set. Such consideration lies at the root of a number of local clustering systems designed to improve the final search output. It is thus possible to use the automatic classification procedure previously mentioned to cluster the (local) set of documents retrieved in response to a particular search. The corresponding document classes can then be used to determine a specific ranking order in which the output items can be brought to the user's attention. By displaying whole groups of related documents, and bringing them to the user's attention simultaneously, the choice of new terms to be incorporated in a feedback query may be simplified.

A somewhat more formal process of this kind has been used experimentally with apparently good results:

1. documents obtained in response to an initial search request are retrieved as before, and relevance assessments are obtained;
2. the similarity coefficients between pairs of terms extracted from the relevant retrieved documents are computed by comparing pairs of columns of the reduced term assignment array (see matrix, p. 68);
3. clusters are constructed of similar terms by using as cluster centroids the original query terms, and grouping around them the sets of related terms identified in step (2); and
4. the clusters of related terms are then used for query reformulation purposes.[15]

Again, related methods are easy to construct. In each case, the dynamic nature of the process is evident, because all methodologies involve user relevance assessments obtained by user/system interaction, and all processes are based on local rather than global vector operations.

Dynamic Generation of Term Values

The document vector model discussed earlier is based on a knowledge of the value (or weight) of each term incorporated in a given document vector. In the absence of information about the appropriateness of a particular term for content identification purposes, it is always possible to assign initially a neutral weight of 1 to all terms present in a given vector, and a weight of 0 to terms absent from the vector. In general, however, it is preferable to discriminate further by distinguishing terms that are particularly important in describing a given item from terms that are less important; this can be done by assigning higher weights to the former than to the latter. As mentioned earlier, it is preferable to use the collection environment to determine appropriate values of terms than to proceed by hunch or fiat, as is now often done in conventional retrieval situations.

Two main considerations must be made: first, the environment in which a given document is placed exerts an important influence on term value (the term *computer* may be fine in a collection of medical items, but not in a collection in computer science); second, user assessments of document relevance should also be taken into account when available, because terms that congregate in documents judged relevant in a given subject area may be expected to be more important than terms found mostly in the nonrelevant items.

When user relevance assessments are not available, the value of the individual terms or content identifiers may be determined by considering only the context of the given collection. Consider the situation in which a document collection has already been indexed, that is, in which term vectors of the kind shown previously are already available, and assume that a new term k is to be assigned to the document collection. It is interesting to examine the expected effect of assignment of a new term on the complete document space configuration. Under normal conditions, a dual effect will be noticed:

1. the items to which term k will have been assigned may be expected to resemble each other more than before, because all these items will now exhibit an additional term in common; hence the similarity coefficient between any pair of such items will increase, and the distance between them will correspondingly diminish; and
2. at the same time, the average distance between the set of items with term k and those without term k will become larger, since the corresponding similarities between pairs will become smaller after the new term assignment than before.

This effect is illustrated in Figure 4, where the documents inside the dotted area are those to which term k is to be assigned. In Figure 4, items changing position as a result of the term assignment are transferred from the original "x" position to a new "o" position. It should be noted that the dual operation of compressing certain items (by reducing the distance between them) and increasing their distance from the remainder of the collection is precisely what is needed to enhance retrieval effectiveness, under the assumption that the compressed items can be identified with the relevant document set. Indeed, when the relevant set of items appears clustered tightly in the space, the corresponding documents can easily be retrieved together; hence the *recall* will be high. When these same items are simultaneously removed from the remaining items, the search *precision* will also be high, because extraneous, nonrelevant items are then easily rejected. (*Recall* is the proportion of relevant items retrieved, and *precision* is the proportion of retrieved items that are relevant. One normally postulates that the average user desires high recall as well as high precision.)

A question now arises about the frequency characteristics of terms capable of effecting the type of space transformation illustrated in Figure 4.

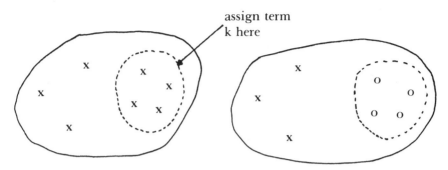

FIGURE 4. Basic Document Space Alteration

Three cases may be considered: first, a high-frequency term k assigned to nearly all documents in the collection; next, a low-frequency term assigned to almost no documents in the collection; and finally, a medium-frequency term assigned to a few documents but not to all. The corresponding space transformations are illustrated in Figures 5a, 5b and 5c, respectively.

1. The high-frequency term assignment will pull all the documents closer together (Figure 5a). A compressed space in which all items appear close together is unfavorable to retrieval, because it then becomes difficult to distinguish the relevant from the nonrelevant items.
2. The low-frequency term assignment will leave the document space more or less unchanged (Figure 5b), because such a term is assigned to very few items; again, the relevant items (assuming there exist more than one or two) are not separated from the nonrelevant.
3. The only favorable situation is produced by the medium-frequency terms assigned to some items (presumably the relevant set) and not to the others (Figure 5c).

Thus, when no information is available about the relevance characteristics of the terms, the medium-frequency terms are the only ones exhibiting favorable space transformation characteristics. If, for example, the space density is measured as the average similarity between pairs of items (or as the sum of the pairwise similarities), it may be seen from Figure 5 that for the high-frequency terms, the overall space density increases, the low-frequency terms leave the density more or less unchanged, while the medium-frequency term assignment may be expected to decrease the space density. The *discrimination value* theory, described elsewhere in the literature, assigns the highest weight to those terms capable of producing the

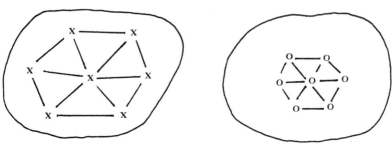

FIGURE 5a. Effect of High-frequency Term
Assignment on Document Space

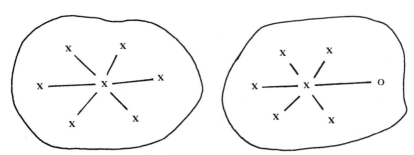

FIGURE 5b. Effect of Low-frequency Term
Assignment on Document Space

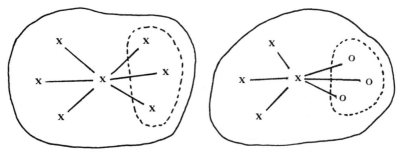

FIGURE 5c. Effect of Medium-frequency Term
Assignment on Document Space

greatest decrease in space density upon assignment to a collection of documents.[16] If the discrimination value of term k (DV_k) is defined as the space density before assignment of term k minus the space density after its assignment, a typical indicator of term value is given by $d_{ik} = f_{ik}.DV_k$

where d_{ik} represents the weight of term k in document i, f_{ik} is the frequency of the term in the document (the number of times the term occurs in the document), and DV_k is the discrimination value of the term k.

Consider the case where user relevance assessments are available for certain documents. In these circumstances it may be possible to compute the values of the probability parameters p_k and q_k, where p_k is the probability that a relevant document contains term k, and q_k is the corresponding probability that a nonrelevant document contains term k. It may be shown that an excellent indicator of term value is given by the ratio of the relevant items containing term k, divided by the ratio of the nonrelevant containing term k, or

$$w_k = \log \left[(p_k/1 - p_k) \div (q_k/1 - q_k) \right] \qquad (1)$$

When binary vectors are used to identify the documents (i.e., term weights are restricted to 0 and 1 only) and the terms are assigned to the documents independently of each other, the term weight assignment w_k can be shown to be optimal.[17]

This development is of no practical use unless actual values can be substituted for the parameters p_k and q_k. Once again, the interactive retrieval environment comes to the rescue. Indeed, after a number of feedback iterations, it is possible to construct for each term k a table of frequency values, as shown in Figure 6. In the figure, r_k represents the number of all documents (N) which are identified as both relevant and containing term k (out of a total of R relevant documents); similarily, $(n_k - r_k)$ represents the number of nonrelevant documents containing term k out of all nonrelevant $(N - R)$ documents. Using the relevance information obtained from the user population in the course of the search operations, approximations can be generated to the term assignment values of Figure 6. This makes it possible to substitute the following actual frequency values for the probability parameters of Expression 1:

$$w_k = \left[(r_k/R - r_k) \div (n_k - r_k/N - R - n_k + r_k) \right] \qquad (2)$$

The more accurate the relevance information obtained from the user population, the closer the values indicated in Expression 2 will be to the theoretically optimal values of Expression 1.

Summary

In light of the foregoing discussion, currently favored plans for a national library network using a completely secure network kernel appear to be the reverse of what is actually needed. When the user becomes part of the system, as he or she necessarily does in an on-line search environment, there is no need to impose strict controls on the input; there is no need for a

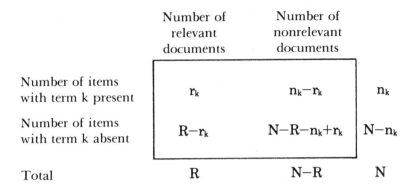

FIGURE 6. ASSIGNMENT OF TERM k TO RELEVANT
AND NONRELEVANT DOCUMENTS

unique, controlled, standardized indexing system; there is no need for a unique, agreed-upon classification system; and there is no need for a static search environment.

Instead, it becomes reasonable to relax the input controls by eliminating to the greatest extent possible authority lists and cataloging rules. Each item can be described by merging the content indicators assigned by a large variety of different procedures, and access can be obtained by the user with respect to a variety of different viewpoints. A range of different classification systems can be used, including broad classes for casual users and narrow ones for experts with specialized needs. Finally, the user population itself can help in selecting useful information search strategies and in adjusting the term weights based on the collection context and on prior experience with the search environment.

REFERENCES

1. Mason, Ellsworth. "Along the Academic Way," *Library Journal* 96:1671-76, May 15, 1971.

2. De Gennaro, Richard. "Austerity, Technology, and Resource Sharing: Research Libraries Face the Future," *Library Journal* 100:917-23, May 15, 1975.

3. This paper is drawn from a study supported in part by the National Science Foundation (DSI 77-04843).

4. Kilgour, Frederick G. "The Ohio College Library Center: A User-Oriented System." *In* E.J. Josey, ed. *New Dimensions for Academic Library Service.* Metuchen, N.J., Scarecrow Press, 1975, pp. 250-55.

5. Martin, Susan K., ed. *Journal of Library Automation,* vol. 10, no. 2, June 1977.

6. Avram, Henriette D. "Introduction." *In* Edwin J. Buchinski. *Initial Considerations for a Nationwide Data Base* (Network Planning Paper No. 3). Washington, D.C., Library of Congress, 1978, p. 1.

7. Buchinski, ibid., p. 39.

8. Licklider, J.C.R. *Libraries of the Future.* Cambridge, Mass., MIT Press, 1965, pp. 5-6.

9. Lancaster, Frederick W. *Toward Paperless Information Systems.* New York, Academic Press, 1978.

10. Salton, Gerard. *Dynamic Information and Library Processing.* Englewood Cliffs, N.J., Prentice-Hall, 1975.

11. _____, and Wong, A. "Generation and Search of Clustered Files," *ACM Transactions on Database Systems* 3:321-46, Dec. 1978.

12. Rocchio, J.J., Jr. "Relevance Feedback in Information Retrieval." *In* Gerard Salton, ed. *The Smart Retrieval System: Experiments in Automatic Document Processing.* Englewood Cliffs, N.J., Prentice-Hall, 1971, pp. 313-23.

13. Ide, E., and Salton, Gerard. "Interactive Search Strategies and Dynamic File Organization in Information Retrieval." *In* Salton, *The Smart Retrieval System,* op. cit., pp. 373-93.

14. Vernimb, Carlo. "Automatic Query Adjustment in Document Retrieval," *Information Processing & Management* 13:339-53, 1977.

15. Attar, R., and Fraenkel, A.S. "Local Feedback in Full-Text Retrieval Systems," *Journal of the Association for Computing Machinery* 24:397-417, July 1977.

16. Salton, Gerard, et al. "A Theory of Term Importance in Automatic Text Analysis," *Journal of the American Society for Information Science* 26:33-44, Jan.-Feb. 1975.

17. Robertson, S.E., and Jones, K. Sparck. "Relevance Weighting of Search Terms," *Journal of the American Society for Information Science* 27:129-46, May-June 1976; and Yu, C.T., and Salton, Gerard. "Precision Weighting—An Effective Automatic Indexing Method," *Journal of the Association for Computing Machinery* 23:76-88, Jan. 1976.

MARTHA E. WILLIAMS
Director
Information Retrieval Research Laboratory
Coordinated Science Laboratory
University of Illinois
at Urbana-Champaign

Future Directions for Machine-Readable Data Bases and Their Use

Prior to discussing my views on the future directions of machine-readable data bases and their use, it is appropriate to indicate the point of departure. The history of the use of machine-readable data bases by the public commenced in the late 1960s and has progressed from a small-scale batch-searching activity, where services were largely restricted to SDI and operators were delighted if a system could be made to be self-supporting, to the current large-scale on-line retrospective and SDI service, where individual organizations are not only "for profit" but are making profits and operating with budgets in the tens of millions of dollars per year.

Data Bases and Their On-line Use

The importance of data bases within this information-oriented society can be measured in terms of their number, size, diversity, and volume of use. Prior to 1970 there were not more than a few dozen publicly available data bases, and combined they contained fewer than 30 million records.[1] Based on data collected for the directory *Computer-Readable Bibliographic Data Bases* and its updates (which contain data for the years 1975 and 1977), there was an increase in the number of bibliographic and natural language data bases, from 301 in 1975 to 362 in 1977, and an increase in the number of records contained in them from 50 million to 71 million. Of even more significance is the fact that the number of on-line searches of those data bases doubled between 1975 and 1977, from 1 million to 2 million.[2] The 1978 data indicate that there are 528 bibliographic and natural language data bases. In 1978 there were 2.67 million on-line searches. Also during 1978, a number of new data bases were brought up on-line. BRS brought up an additional seven, SDC fourteen, and Lockheed twenty-one data bases.[3] The size, number and diversity of data bases are increasing, the use of data bases is increasing, and their use by new and different types of clientele is increasing. And the biggest increase in use will take place when end-users themselves are able to do a significant portion of the on-line searching without the aid of intermediaries.

Problems Due to Variety

Despite all the optimism, there are problems that result from the tremendous variety and variability that one finds in data bases. Data bases vary with respect to content: the subjects are different from data base to data base. There is a tremendous range of subject material in the more than 500 bibliographic and natural language data bases. Data bases vary with respect to format: each data base producer has his own format and very few of them conform to a standard. Data bases vary with respect to chronological coverage: some are less than a year old and some have been in existence more than ten years. Data bases vary with respect to relationships that may exist between them. For example, one data base may contain access keys which link it to one or more other data bases. The CASIA data base of Chemical Abstracts Service, for example, provides links to the CACON data base. One is an index, the other contains citations, and they are linked by CAS numbers. (These two data bases have just recently been combined into a new data base called CA Search.) Among the data bases which contain ties to one another are some of the Predicasts Inc. files and some of the BioScience Information Service files. Data bases vary with respect to vocabularies: some have controlled or semicontrolled vocabularies and most include free language terms. Titles are available for searching in almost all bibliographic data bases.

Data bases vary with respect to the systems used for searching them. There are many different systems available for on-line and batch-searching of data bases. There are also many different services offered through various on-line and batch systems. All of the on-line systems differ from each other with respect to access protocols, command languages, system responses and messages, system features, and even data element labels or tags.

Data bases vary with respect to the way they are loaded in different systems. Different on-line vendors will load the same data base in different ways. Lockheed, SDC, and BRS, for example, do not mount the same data base in the same way. One vendor may combine corporate information terms with subject terms; others will keep them separate. One may combine geographic location information with subject information; others will not. As a result, one cannot search the same data base in exactly the same way in two different systems and get the same results. Data bases vary with respect to the features and functions found in the different systems, and in the techniques one can use for searching them; and they vary regarding output.

A user, or the user's representative (intermediary), has to contend with and accommodate this variability in data bases and systems in doing on-line searching. This leads to a problem. As the number and variety of data bases and systems increase, user confusion increases and the need for intermediaries trained to cope with the variables increases.

The Problem Regarding Retrieval Steps

Overall, there are various levels of retrieval goals. Initially, there is a need to retrieve source information; in other words, to determine what data base has the information the user wants. Following that is the need to retrieve the information or data itself. At a somewhat higher level is the desire to retrieve facts. And even higher than that is the goal to retrieve knowledge, and eventually to eliminate uncertainty.

Parallel with these retrieval goals are several retrieval steps. First it is necessary to identify the source locator or directory that contains pointers to secondary sources. Then it is necessary to identify and locate the secondary system that contains the required information, for example, BIOSIS Previews, CA Search, or COMPENDEX. Following this step, the secondary system must be queried. Finally, it is necessary to locate the primary source, obtain or access the primary document, read the appropriate portions, and assimilate the facts and data needed to satisfy the original purposes of the search and retrieval operation. These steps are all discrete, and most investigators (end-users) find it difficult to carry out all the steps without seeking outside help. However, if information retrieval is ever going to become really widespread, it will be necessary for end-users to do their own searching. And if end-users are to do their own searching, the discreteness of all of these steps must become much less apparent. In other words, what is really needed is a transparent information system, a means of reducing the discreteness of the retrieval steps so that the user can proceed directly from entering a query to the end-point of the search, retrieving the desired information, facts, and data from primary documents, without going through all of the intervening steps.

The Problem Regarding Multiplicity of Names

Another area of confusion for end-users, or even for their intermediaries, is that of distinguishing the various names for the component systems and entities involved in on-line searching. Searchers should be able to recognize the distinctions among various communications networks; parent organizations that may have an on-line search system; information service organizations; the names of the services provided, the software packages, the computer operating systems, and the data bases; and the coded names of the data bases within specific systems (different vendors assign different names to the same data base). The name of an on-line vendor organization is *not* identical with all of these entities. The multiplicity of entities involved in on-line systems and the multiplicity of names for those entities contributes to the confusion in using on-line systems.

The Problems of Subject Access

One of the biggest problem areas of on-line searching is that of subject access. Anyone who produces data bases or is knowledgeable in their use knows what these problems are. The use of both controlled and uncontrolled terms in most of the data bases requires that the user employ both in his query. In addition, within any given data base, vocabularies may change every four to five years or less. Thus, a user searching several years of a data base must know how the vocabulary has changed over the years. The terms one would use today to describe a concept may not retrieve the relevant items from data base issues of ten years ago.

Another subject access problem is that of homography; words that are spelled alike but have different meanings in different contexts will retrieve unwanted items. There is also the problem of synonymy. A user must specify all of the synonyms appropriate for a particular term or concept that might have been used by an author in order to retrieve all the items that relate to the concept. If items in a data base have been well indexed using a controlled vocabulary, the problem of synonym specification can be greatly reduced. Unfortunately, most data bases have natural language titles and abstracts that do not contain highly controlled terms.

Another aspect of the subject access problem is the problem of chemical nomenclature. This is a very significant one because of the large number of chemicals—approximately 5 to 7 million. An individual chemical can be named in many ways, all of which are legitimate and correct. For example, in the course of analyzing chemical data bases we identified 27 different types of nomenclature schemes used in 165 machine-readable chemical data bases.[4] This means that there are *at least* twenty-seven different ways in which a given chemical can be identified. In addition to the controlled ways of naming chemicals, there are many kinds of trivial names or company-assigned names given to chemicals and chemical products to further expand the nomenclature problem. An indication of the extent of the problem can be seen when looking for synonyms in the

Chemline data base of the National Library of Medicine; as many as 110 different names have been found for the same chemical entity.

Another subject access problem results from the fact that terms are used differently in different data bases. A term having the same meaning in different data bases will be assigned different values. For example, a term such as *acid* would occur tens of thousands of times annually in CA Search, and only a few thousand times in BIOSIS Previews. The same term might occur fewer than a hundred times in COMPENDEX. It is obvious, then, that if a question containing the term *acid* is asked of all three data bases, the term cannot be used the same way in each. In one case the query will retrieve too much material, and in another case it may not retrieve enough. In one case the term could stand alone, thereby retrieving every item that contained it. In the case where it is a high-frequency term, it would need to be used in conjunction with other terms to reduce the number of "hits."

Yet another problem related to subject access is that of subject codes. These are found in various data bases and are often data base specific. Thus, a data base-specific code used in one data base certainly cannot be used as a search term in another data base, because the code does not occur in that data base. Consequently, if a question is to be run against multiple data bases, the search terms and strategy must vary to obtain optimal results. Subject codes that do not exist in a data base can be used as search terms with the net effect of wasted machine time and money.

Standards in the On-Line World

It seems that the way to solve the problem of variablity in the on-line data base world would be standardization. Standardization of on-line retrieval services would involve many different components, including data bases, subject access or analysis, the recording media, the systems, command languages, software, communications systems, and hardware. Moreover, each of these components would have to be analyzed at the subcomponent level.

Standards associated with data bases would need to deal with the following:

1. *content*—identifying which data base elements should be included in a particular search service;
2. *data representation* for each element or item within a record—indicating the character code and character set used;
3. the *form* of terms contained in a record—indicating whether they are abbreviated, coded, or fully spelled out;
4. *format*—indicating such things as the spacing and sequencing of data elements within a record;

5. *representation on a recording medium*—including the physical characteristics, physical format, and logical format; and
6. *subject access or subject analysis*—covering such things as classification schemes, natural language (which is obviously not standardized and never will be), key words, etc.

Some data bases have index terms; some do not. Some have controlled terms; some have semicontrolled ones. These all differ from data base to data base and would need to be standardized, if standards are to be used as the solution to the problems we are facing.

There would need to be standards regarding the systems for searching, file-loading techniques, file names, data element identifiers, and system vocabularies. These all differ from system to system. There would have to be standards for software—the software for search and retrieval, command languages, system features, protocols, and system techniques. Both responses and messages from systems would have to be standardized. Communications systems would need to be standardized—including access procedures and protocols, passwords, and system designations. These differ from one communications network to another.

Even if it were possible to develop standards for all the subcomponents mentioned, they would take a long time to develop and once achieved, their implementation is usually voluntary; thus, it is unlikely that development and implementation of standards for all of these items will ever be accomplished to simplify the problems of on-line retrieval. This does not mean that standardization efforts should not be continued. Certainly, wherever standards can be achieved, problems can be alleviated to a certain extent. The goal of achieving standards in all of the necessary areas, however, is unrealistic.

Alternative to Standards—A Transparent System

Since it is unlikely that all of the necessary standards will be developed and since it is even less likely that, if developed, they would be implemented, an alternative to standardization is needed. Such an alternative could be the development of a "transparent system." The likelihood of a single transparent system is remote, because there are too many organizations with vested interests; that is, too many organizations have invested sizable sums of money in developing systems, data bases, etc., and the chances of their changing without a demonstrable economic benefit are unlikely. The possibility of a distributed, integrated transparent system, however, is not unreal.

We at the Information Retrieval Research Laboratory of the University of Illinois are currently conducting a research project, with National

Science Foundation funding, that involves designing a transparent information system. We are determining what the components of a transparent system should be. We are also determining who is doing research and development on various elements that could be involved in such a system. We are considering alternative system architectures by weighing the alternatives of centralization vs. distribution of the various components in light of economic considerations, update requirements, etc.

A transparent system involves a variety of types of users, computers, terminals, operating networks, software, communications networks, and data bases. The various classes of users should include schoolchildren to sophisticated researchers. We must also consider the various classes of computers—maxi, mini, and micro—for various system components; the use of dumb or intelligent terminals for input and output; the operating network; software requirements; communications networks; and data bases of all types, whether they contain references, numeric data, full text or facts. We are also including derivative data bases; that is, data bases that contain descriptive information about other data bases—data bases that include term frequencies and word patterns, etc., or data bases that include quality indicators or value judgments associated with items contained within a data base.

A transparent information system would require directories, and a directory of directories in order to send a user to the appropriate subject-area directory or to gain information about the various files in a particular subject area. A transparent system would contain applications programs of various types—not just search and retrieval software, but statistical packages, modeling packages, and various other kinds of programs needed to manipulate data found within data bases. And it would contain a variety of "transparency aids." These transparency aids consist of converters, selectors, evaluators, analyzers, and routers. In order to provide insight to transparency aids, I will briefly discuss the first two classes of aids—converters and selectors.

Converters

Converters are needed in many areas. They are needed, for example, for access protocols. Currently there are a variety of types of access protocols to gain entrance into various networks and to send a user to the appropriate on-line service. Access protocol converters are needed to convert system A's protocol to system B's and vice versa, or for converting both A and B to a common protocol or standard. This does not mean that system A, which might be Tymshare, and system B, which might be Telenet, would have to make internal changes. Someone outside of those systems could convert both of them to a standard. Thus, neither A nor B would lose the investment they made in their existing system.

Converters are also needed for the *language* of the access protocols; they can be used to convert the native language of the system to a foreign language. This would enable a speaker of German to use an English language-based system in German instead of English. There is a need for command language converters, whether they convert langauge A to language B, vice versa, or both to a standard. And there is a need for converters for the *language* of the command language, again from native language to a foreign language.

Converters are needed for converting the controlled language of one data base to that of another and vice versa. Converters are needed to transform natural language terms in a data base to controlled language terms. There need to be converters for system responses and messages; again, to convert the system messages and responses of system A to those of system B, vice versa, or both to a standard. And again, native to foreign language conversions are needed for system responses and messages. This is not infeasible. Currently, work is being done at the National Bureau of Standards on their network access machine which actually does convert access protocols and even dials up the target system.[5] The native to foreign language conversion problem is being handled in several places right now. The Canada Institute for Scientific and Technical Information (CISTI) permits use of either English or French protocols to access the CAN/OLE system. Similar work is being done by SDC for the use of the ORBIT system in Canada and other French-speaking countries. The command language conversion problem is being worked on by a number of people.[6] MIT began work on a common command language five or six years ago.[7] The language, called CONIT, is operational on four different on-line systems. Euronet is also working on the problem of a common or standard command language for use within the DIANE (Direct Information Access Network for Europe) system over the Euronet communication network.[8] The problem of the language used for commands, system responses, and messages has also been addressed by Euronet in Europe, SDC in the United States, and CISTI in Canada.

The problem of converting a data base's controlled vocabulary to that of another data base is under study at Battelle Columbus Laboratories.[9] The problem of converting a natural language to a controlled language has been worked on by the Robot System. The more difficult problem of converting free native-language text to free foreign-language text is being worked on by the Commission of the European Communities.[10] They are developing an autotranslation system for interconversion of at least four languages. All of these research and development efforts will result in the development of converters that are transparency aids.

Selectors

Another class of transparency aid is that of selectors. Selectors are needed for a variety of purposes. A selector could select classes of data bases appropriate to user characteristics and to the user's query. As the number and types of data bases increase, automatic selectors are needed to help a user determine which data base to use for a particular query. Data base selectors can be based on and include data such as term frequency, relative frequency of terms within a data base, user-assigned values, growth rates of the vocabularies, and variant forms of terms. Work has been done on automatic data base selection at the University of Illinois, at BRS, and at SDC. The University of Illinois work was carried out within the Information Retrieval Research Laboratory of the Coordinated Science Laboratory, with National Science Foundation funding.[11] Our research commenced in 1977 and was intended to determine the feasibility of an automatic data base selector (DBS). The work has been completed and the feasibility proven.

The University of Illinois's DBS includes normalizers for several variables found within the data bases. Procedurally, in order to build a test model selector we used the inverted files for twenty data bases from Lockheed and SDC and merged them, keeping one record for every unique term found in any data base. Within each term record we recorded information about the data base in which it was found, the frequency with which it occurred, and an indication of the kind of term it was—a word from a title, a word from an abstract, a controlled term, or an uncontrolled term.

Two other organizations that have developed aids to data base selection are SDC and BRS. SDC has developed a Data Base Index (DBI) and BRS has developed the CROS data base. DBI is restricted to data bases at SDC, and CROS is restricted to data bases at BRS. SDC's DBI operates on a single term at a time and produces a sequential ranking indicating which data bases contain the term in question; no indication of distance ranking is given; that is, if a given term occurred 1000 times in data base 1, 980 times in data base 2, and only 5 times in data base 3, there is no way of knowing that the distance between data base 2 and 3 is so great that the latter should probably not be searched. If terms are combined, the resulting list of data bases indicates that the combined terms occurred in the same data base— though not necessarily in the same record. Also, when terms are combined in DBI, the resulting list of data bases is unranked, so the user will not know which data base is the most likely candidate for search.

Bibliographic Retrieval Services' CROS operates on single or combined terms, so long as they are contained in a single search statement. The list of data bases produced as a result of a CROS search is alphabetically arranged by BRS data base mnemonic, and the postings value for the statement, including logical combinations, is indicated next to each mnemonic. The user can then select the data bases with the highest numbers of references for the search. The search must then be run against the data bases chosen by the user. A limitation of CROS is that the values provided are for the on-line portion of the data base only; it does not reflect the off-line backfiles that BRS has for a given data base.

DBI and CROS are both operational and usable on publicly available systems. The University of Illinois's DBS is a test system and so is not publicly available (although the algorithms are available as they were developed with public funds). DBS was designed to determine which data bases are most likely to provide references in answer to a user's query and to provide results in the form of a histogram. The resultant list of data bases is in ranked order and the distance between data bases is indicated by the histogram. Neither DBI nor CROS accounts for variable factors associated with data bases; thus, results are based on postings alone. DBS, on the other hand, utilizes a mathematical model that operates on the term records and takes into account the number of years' worth of a data base, relative frequency of the term within the data base, relative frequency of the term across data bases, and the value of a term type (title, abstract, controlled or uncontrolled) within a data base as indicated by the data base producer.

A data base selector, to be of the most value to a user, should include all data bases, whether they are on-line or batch, and it should factor in the variables that account for the different ways in which the same file may be mounted in different systems. Such a selector capability would probably have to exist outside of the on-line systems, as it is unlikely that an individual on-line system would wish to promote data bases that it does not offer.

A data base selector is only one type of selector that should be included in a total transparent retrieval system. Automatic selectors could be developed for selecting search service organizations (on-line vendors or batch-search operators), communications networks, command languages (if users have preferences), terms to be used in query expansion, applications packages for operating on retrieved data, and output formats.

Converters and selectors are two types of transparency aids that would be used in a transparent system. In addition, there would be automatic routers,[12] evaluators, and analyzers. I have discussed only converters and selectors to illustrate what a transparency aid is.

Conclusion

The purpose of this paper has been to explain the current status of data bases, to discuss some of the current limitations in the on-line use of data bases, and to indicate future directions. In the future, we will certainly see the development of systems and components that will simplify the retrieval process. A variety of automated aids are being and will be developed to carry out many of the activities that are now done by search intermediaries. Many of the conversion, translation, selection, evaluation, and analysis activities which are carried out by searchers can be done or assisted through automation. I have referred to these as "transparency aids" and have described some of them in the context of a transparent system. Whether or not a total integrated, distributed transparent system will be developed is uncertain, but the development of many of the separate components is assured. Many of them have already been developed, others are in the research phase, and others are not yet on the drawing boards. Many changes are underway in this dynamic field, but if an integrated transparent system is developed, the changes will not be apparent to the user. What the user will see is a greatly improved and easy-to-use system.

REFERENCES

1. Williams, Martha E., et al. "Data Base Statistics for 1977" (Final report on NSF Grant No. SP 77-0986; Coordinated Science Laboratory Report No. T-76). Urbana-Champaign, University of Illinois, 1979.

2. Williams, Martha E., and Rouse, Sandra H., eds., comps. *Computer-Readable Bibliographic Data Bases: A Directory and Data Sourcebook.* Washington, D.C., American Society for Information Science, 1976. (Looseleaf updates published 1977 and 1978.)

3. Williams, Martha E., ed. *Computer-Readable Data Bases: A Directory and Data Sourcebook.* Washington, D.C., American Society for Information Science, 1979.

4. _____, and MacLaury, Keith. "Mapping of Chemical Data Bases Using a Relational Data Base Structure." *In* Ludena, E.V., et al. *Computers in Chemical Education and Research.* New York, Plenum, 1977, pp. 3-23; and Williams, Martha E., et al. "Data Base Mapping Model and Search Scheme to Facilitate Resource Sharing—Vol. 1. Mapping of Chemical Data Bases and Mapping of Data Base Elements Using a Relational Data Base Structure" (Final report on NSF Grant No. SIS 74-18558; Coordinated Science Laboratory Report No. T-56, Vol. 1). Urbana-Champaign, University of Illinois, March 1978. (PB 283 892/8G1)

5. Rosenthal, Robert. "A Review of Network Access Techniques with a Case Study: The Network Access Machine" (National Bureau of Standards Technical Note 917). Washington, D.C., USGPO, 1976. (PB 256 525/7G1)

6. Iljon, Ariane. "Scientific and Technical Data Bases in a Multilingual Society," *Online Review* 1:133-36, June 1977.

7. Marcus, R.S., and Reintjes, J.F. "Experiments and Analysis on a Computer Interface to an Information-Retrieval Network" (Report on NSF Grant No. IST-76-82117; Laboratory for Information Decision Systems Report No. LIDS-R-900). Cambridge, Mass., MIT Press, 1979.

8. Negus, A.E. *Study to Determine the Feasibility of a Standardised Command Set for EURONET: Final Report on a Study Carried Out for the Commission of the European Communities, DG XIII.* London, INSPEC, Oct. 1976.

9. Niehoff, Robert T., and Kwasny, Stan C. "The Role of Automated Subject Switching in a Distributed Information Network," *Online Review* 3:181-94, June 1979.

10. Rolling, L.N. "The Second Birth of Machine Translation, A Timely Event for Data Base Suppliers and Users" (Paper presented at the Seventh Cranfield International Conference on Mechanised Information Storage and Retrieval Systems). Cranfield, England, July 1979.

11. Williams, Martha E., and Preece, Scott E. "Data Base Selector for Network Use: A Feasibility Study." *In* Bernard M. Fry and Clayton A. Shepherd, comps. *Information Management in the 1980's: Proceedings of the ASIS Annual Meeting.* White Plains, N.Y., Knowledge Industry, 1977, vol. 14, C13-D6, fiche 10; and Williams, Martha E. "Automatic Database Selection and Overlap of Terms Among Major Databases" (Paper presented at the Seventh Cranfield International Conference on Mechanised Information Storage and Retrieval Systems). Cranfield, England, July 1979.

12. Hampel, V., et al. "An Integrated Information System for Energy Storage." Livermore, Calif., Lawrence Livermore Laboratory, 1978. (UCRL-80349); and Goldstein, Charles M., and Ford, William H. "The User-Cordial Interface," *Online Review* 2:269-75, Sept. 1978.

ROBERT S. HOOPER

Chief, Systems Analysis Staff
Office of Central Reference
Central Intelligence Agency
Washington, D.C.

SUSANNE HENDERSON

Librarian, Systems Analysis Staff
Office of Central Reference
Central Intelligence Agency
Washington, D.C.

The Status of "Paperless" Systems in the Intelligence Community

The Central Intelligence Agency (CIA) and the Defense Intelligence Agency (DIA) have consolidated resources to build a "paperless" information system called SAFE (Support for the Analysts' File Environment). The system will provide intelligence analysts from both agencies with a set of tools to assist them in performing their primary mission: to prepare finished intelligence for national-level policy-makers. This paper covers the evolution of CIA's SAFE System and its current status.

It is estimated that in full operation, SAFE will do away with a minimum of 10 million pieces of paper yearly. While paper reduction has been a goal, it has not been the guiding principle in system development. We recognize that the computer is not always the best way to handle information. Sometimes information is handled most efficiently on paper or microform. In designing SAFE, we have tried to strike a balance and take into consideration the best features of all information processing techniques.

The CIA SAFE System will combine computer and microfilm storage capabilities to support approximately 1350 professional intelligence analysts. These analysts are of the economic, scientific, military, and political persuasions. They lean heavily on their individual or private files and in varying degrees on the services of a central library. Their interests often parallel those of their counterparts in academia, industry, libraries, newspapers, etc. We are not talking about ephemeral information coded on the back of a matchbook cover! We are talking about thousands of pieces of information to be read and processed every day.

Historically, systems built solely by computer personnel who felt they knew what the user wanted have not been successful. We have not made that mistake here. SAFE, to the greatest extent possible, has been designed by the analysts. In addition to a continuous program of analyst interviews and briefings, the basic SAFE concepts were tested in 1974 in a pilot system which was to have lasted for one year. However, it proved so popular that it was retained and is now known as the Interim System.

After this introduction and explanation, it now seems appropriate that this opus be retitled: "A Plan to Build a Fixed Cost, User-Designed and Pilot-System Tested Computer and Microfilm System, Optimizing the Private and Central File Relationship, Creating a Partially Paperless Environment, in Support of the Political, Military, Economic, and Scientific Analysts of the CIA."

Characteristics of the Users

Currently, we estimate that fully operational, SAFE will support around 2000 users. Of these, approximately 16 percent will be management, 17 percent intelligence assistants and clericals, and 67 percent intelligence analysts. Therefore, the majority of our efforts are directed toward satisfying the needs of the intelligence analyst. There is no typical intelligence analyst. Each one is responsible for the analysis, synthesis, and presentation of intelligence information in his particular area of interest. These ares of interest include: politics, science, economics, military, biography, geography, cartography, photo interpretation, and weaponry. In turn, the topics are in many cases geographically oriented. The analyst is involved with current reporting as well as in-depth research, and is more often a specialist than a generalist. The intelligence reports they write must provide accurate knowledge and estimates of the economic, military, political, and scientific capabilities of foreign countries. They must be timely enough to meet the needs of those concerned with crisis situations (current awareness) as well as those interested in long-term trends.

Analysts receive the majority of their information on a continuing basis through the Agency's dissemination system (see Figure 1). This system routes publications, reports, newspapers, books, etc., in addition to a large number of telegraphic dispatches or cables. These items may have been specially ordered by individual analysts, or may correspond to "profile" or reading requirements that the analysts have on file.

In addition to their own files created from information received through the dissemination system, analysts can call upon the services of the Office of Central Reference. These services include a central library containing 100,000 volumes, 1700 different newspapers and journals, millions of documents, an extensive reference collection, and an experienced staff of professional librarians. There are also professional researchers

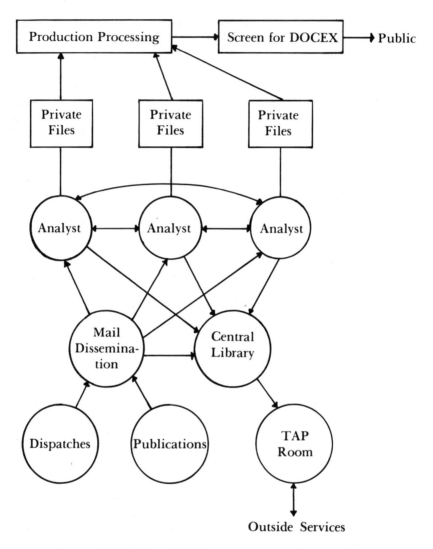

FIGURE 1. CIA DISSEMINATION SYSTEM

divided into branches of special interest (many of which correspond with those of the analysts). These branches maintain a bibliographic data base which indexes a collection of 3 million intelligence documents. A TAP (Terminal Access Point) room provides access to numerous commercial and classified data bases, including the New York Times Information Bank, Lockheed Dialog, SDC Orbit, MEDLINE, and several intelligence community data bases.

Analysts read, review, extract/abstract, comment on, and highlight their information, keeping about 20 percent of what they receive. Retained items are eventually filed according to various methods of indexing, subject headings, thesauri, etc. The nature of a particular file organization is solely dependent on the individual mission of an analyst; in other words, the analyst is not forced to conform to a predefined way of entering data into a file.

When an assignment is received, the analyst searches his files and retrieves relevant information. These data are reviewed and interpreted, conclusions are formed, estimates are formulated, predictions are made, and actions are recommended. All of these elements are formed into an intelligence report. The analyst then coordinates and consults with others, rewrites or makes changes as necessary, and publishes a finished product which is disseminated through established channels.

Unclassified documents are reviewed for public interest. If it is felt that there will be interest, the documents are released. CIA publications available to the public may be obtained in one of three ways: (1) USGPO (United States Government Printing Office), (2) NTIS (National Technical Information Service), or (3) DOCEX (Documents Expediting Project) through the Library of Congress. Well-known examples of documents released this way include the famous oil document that President Carter mentioned in his spring 1977 news conference, and the *China Atlas*. Other examples are the *National Basic Intelligence Factbook*, *Soviet Civil Defense*, *Chinese Coal Industry*, etc.

Steps Toward Paperlessness

Over the years, the volume of items retained by analysts, as well as the Office of Central Reference, has grown to an unmanageable size. Simply stated, the size of the various document collections was and is a major factor in our looking toward paperlessness. Indeed, it is no joke that the floor loads are being exceeded and eventually, if help is not found, the file collections will have to be housed in the basement (terra firma at last), and of course, as the collection gets larger, the probability of finding anything gets smaller. Thus, by necessity, we have had to look at alternatives, i.e., microform and machine-readable data bases.

The advantages of paper reduction, in addition to increasing the storage space, are several. First, by storing documents in machine-readable form instead of paper we can make use of information retrieval and text-search capabilities to retrieve those items relevant to an analyst's particular, immediate need rather than having to get involved in a time-consuming manual search. Second, reducing the amount of paper will, of course, remove much of the burden caused by the large amount of paper-handling presently taking place, thus saving processing time and reducing mistakes. Since a considerable amount of coordination is required among the intelligence producers, a paperless communication capability both before and during the production process should speed the process and improve the product considerably. Table 1 summarizes these attributes of paperlessness and associates them with the various functions of the analysts' information world.

TABLE 1. ADVANTAGES OF PAPERLESS COMMUNICATION
RELATED TO VARIOUS INFORMATION FUNCTIONS

Attributes of Paperlessness	*Mail Dissemination*	*Private Files*	*Central Index Files*	*Central Document Files*	*Production Processing*
Reduce size of storage		X		X	
Improve search capability	X	X		X	
Improve document retrieval and display		X		X	
Decrease paper-handling time/ errors	X				X
Make remotely located files more available			X	X	
Improve communication among analysts					X

Thus, paperlessness has its desirable attributes, but it is not without its problems. One problem is the cost involved in converting to paperlessness. For example, the cost to have the Office of Central Reference convert all documents to machine-readable form would definitely be prohibitive. Another problem is the readability and "caressability" of paper. Analysts, like most of us, have a love affair with their paper dolls and this is not easy to break. And finally, paperlessness alone will not solve the communication problem unless an analyst-to-analyst communication mechanism is established.

The SAFE concepts rest on two preliminary efforts. The first was the development of a machine-assisted dissemination system; the second was development of some models of analysts' private files.

Figure 2 is an overview of the dissemination system before the introduction of machine assistance. Note that electrical dispatches (such as cables and receipts) were converted to paper and then read for dissemination. This seemed like an appropriate spot for us to begin our paperless processing operations because the conversion of these items to paper seemed an unnecessary step. We spent two years perfecting a computer text-search dissemination system, which we dubbed MAD (Machine-Assisted Dissemination), which processed the electrical dispatches as they were received.

The MAD operation worked in the following way (see Figure 3). All of the dispatches were formatted to make the text-search operation as effective as possible. Then an initial computer scan of the text compared each word against words in the "Dissemination Dictionary #1." If the proper words were present in a dispatch, and if they appeared in the proper order and with the proper logic, then the dissemination addresses would be automatically appended. Finally, the dispatches were sorted and the proper number of copies were printed. The first dictionary contained, for example, the names of certain kinds of reports which were always sent to the same customers. Hence, a purely clerical function of addressing these kinds of reports was now done by computer.

Those dispatches which were not disseminated by the first process were again scanned by computer against "Dissemination Dictionary #2." In this case, the computer would again compare every word of text with the dictionary words, and proposed dissemination addresses were placed on the message. However, a human disseminator would look at the proposed dissemination, check it against his set of requirements, and add to or change the proposed dissemination as appropriate. All of this was done on a cathode ray tube (CRT) device. The disseminator would then release the item for printing. The proper number of copies in sorted order would then be printed. At this point the paper delivery system took over. Through these actions we had succeeded in reducing the clerical functions and putting the disseminators in a paperless environment.

As time went on, we added the capability of writing special tape files as well as producing paper output. These tape files would contain all dispatches that met a given set of profile conditions. They were produced wholly from the machine's capability to find words and combinations of words in proper order and with proper logic within the text of the dis-

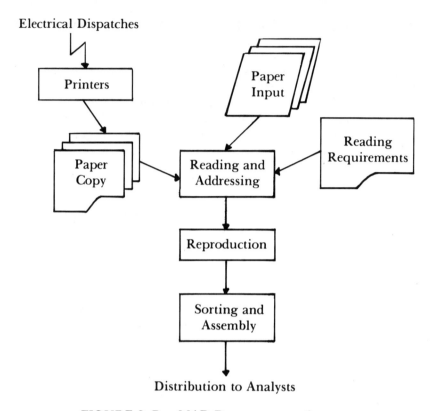

FIGURE 2. PRE-MAD DISSEMINATION SYSTEM

patches. These files were searchable on the Library's Rapid Search Machine (RSM), a stand-alone computer device developed by General Electric that text-searches computer tapes. These tapes were a step toward improving the analysts' search capability.

Analysts depend heavily on their own or private document collections. In some instances these collections have grown very large and the documents have become increasingly hard to find. To improve the storage and searching of these private collections, we introduced the rather simple notion of microfilming the documents and building computer-based indexes to represent them. The indexes were built on-line and were subject to certain limitations on size and complexity, but the actual design of an index record was up to the individual analyst. One analyst indexed documents according to a "who, what, when, where, how" scheme, while another set up a simplified classification schedule. The key to success was

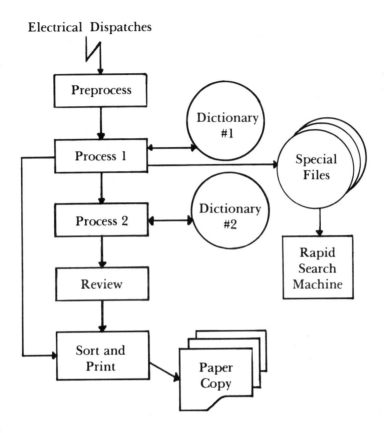

FIGURE 3. MAD System

to make input by the analyst as simple as possible and to let the file be designed by him to meet his individual needs.

From these initial developmental studies we derived a number of significant results:

1. disseminators can make the change from reading paper copy to reading dispatches on-line most readily;
2. the ability to do text searches was a popular innovation;
3. under certain circumstances, analysts will use microfilm in lieu of paper copy; and
4. analysts are enthusiastic about on-line indexes to their private files, even though the actual building of the indexes was considered a chore.

A Pilot System

Armed with this information from our developmental studies and the new emphasis on automation of user files, we began to study the relationship between the analysts' private files and the central library file. The study focused on three questions. How redundant are they? How redundant do they need to be? And the most important question, to what extent could the central library file be used in lieu of or as a complement to the analysts' files? To answer these questions, and because information is only as valuable as it is accessible, we postulated a pilot system that would allow analysts to have as much information at their fingertips as possible.

The pilot system allowed the analysts a continuous spectrum of on-line services, from receipt and disposition of their "mail" (that is, their electrically disseminated dipatches), through the building and searching of their private files and the use of the large central index file, to the use of a large, 4- to 5-week collection of electrical documents. In addition, the analysts had the capability to compose memoranda on-line and to route items from one analyst to another.

There were forty users from four branches representing the major disciplines (political, military, scientific, and economic). We asked them to use the pilot system capabilities as appropriate during the day, and to record basic facts about each use. After nine months of testing, we held a structured interview with each of the users. The most significant findings were:

1. Analysts are not willing to give up the use of paper completely. Paper will still be necessary for cut-and-paste, marginal notes, etc. They are willing, however, to use the processes that store it, search through it, etc.
2. The analysts did, slowly but surely, learn to depend on the pilot system.
3. The best way to introduce office automation is to get an analyst to volunteer to use the capabilities and then let his peers look over his shoulder at the results of his work. A dedicated, convinced user of the system is the best advertisement we have.
4. Analysts would query the central file directly. This previously required a professional researcher to act as an intermediary. The analysts were willing to learn how the big file was organized in order to get the most out of it. However, the occasional user or nonuser of the system indicated that his future preference would be to continue to use the researcher as a go-between.
5. Analysts were very willing to let other analysts have access to their private files.
6. A new category of worker might well appear who would do the "dog work" required of the system; that is, perform data entry, make routine searches, enter compositions into the system, etc.

The analysts' enthusiasm for the pilot system led to a 1974 report that recommended continuing the system as the Interim System and to begin work on an agencywide system—SAFE.

Target 1984

The SAFE System will provide intelligence analysts with a highly reliable, dynamic set of tools. The system, when completed, will be a 24-hour-a-day, 7-days-a-week, dedicated on-line computer and associated microfilm system that provides:

1. faster distribution of incoming intelligence,
2. improved organization of and retrieval from central and personal electrical or hard-copy files,
3. procedures for composing and coordinating information, and
4. indirect access to other intelligence community and commercially available computer systems.

The system will be implemented in a phased approach so that the users will get the assistance they need most at the earliest possible date.

The first phase of SAFE, "Current Awareness," will make electrically received messages or documents (cable traffic) available to the current intelligence analyst as quickly and as completely as possible (within five to fifteen minutes of receipt by the Agency). A SAFE Message Analysis (SMA) module will process and format the incoming messages; then, based on analyst reading requirements contained in profiles, disseminate them. The results of this effort are forwarded to analyst mail files. They are then available for viewing on-line by each analyst at his SAFE terminal. Analysts will be able to process the mail in a variety of ways: file, route, reject, print, and so forth. In addition, all documents that enter SAFE will be retained in a 24-hour text file.

An important adjunct to the mail receipt and disposition will be the capability to "text search" the items within the mail files and those within the 24-hour text file. Analysts will also be provided with a capability to compose articles on-line. This is intended to allow an analyst to capture his thoughts as he reads his "traffic." It is also to be used for forwarding comments to associates, and perhaps for quick text preparation to meet tight deadlines.

The second phase of SAFE, "Private File Management," will provide analysts with an efficient means of creating, searching, and maintaining their own personal files. The analyst will be able to perform detailed filing of material. He may extract data from messages and place them into a file; annotate what he reads and then file it; underscore or otherwise highlight parts of the message significant to him; and/or apply index terms for retrieval purposes. Information can be retrieved from these files by looking for specific index terms or by searching the full text of messages and/or annotations.

Documents not received as electrical transmissions may be indexed, and the resulting indexes which are maintained in SAFE may be searched by computer. The documents may be filed locally—i.e., in a safe or a desk drawer—or in the ADSTAR System. In the ADSTAR System, the documents are microfilmed and held in a central repository. They can be retrieved and displayed on an ADSTAR terminal located in selected regional areas.

SAFE is designed to allow an analyst to input a single search strategy and get references to both hard copy and electrical items. The electrical documents will be displayed on his CRT; the hard copy documents on his regionally located ADSTAR terminal.

In the third phase of SAFE, "Retrospective Search," several retrospective search services are introduced. Access to the multimillion-record central index file (RECON), maintained by the Office of Central Reference, is made available. This index file points to documents that the office is required to retain for use by analysts throughout the intelligence community. Analysts will be able to view the results of searches against this file on their own CRT or on an ADSTAR terminal. Analysts will be able to perform text searches of electrical documents, referenced either by results of RECON searches or by results of searching a "catalog file" which references all items under SAFE control.

An additional source for retrospective search exists in the Office of Central Reference TAP Room where links to data bases external to the Agency (the New York Times Information Bank, for example) are available. These services will be made available to the analyst by having him contact the TAP Room on his SAFE terminal and provide a statement of his needs to TAP Room personnel, who will then run the query against the appropriate data base and alert the analyst when the results are ready.

In the fourth phase of SAFE, "Intelligence Production," the entire process for producing finished intelligence may be accomplished via SAFE. The simple composing capability of the first phase will be expanded to handle all text-editing and word-processing techniques, and to coordinate the entire production process for finished intelligence. A by-product of this phase will be to direct the finished intelligence back into SMA for input to the Agency mail files and the document file. In this fashion, past intelligence becomes available for future analysis.

The target date for total system implementation is 1984. We anticipate that SAFE will rapidly become an indispensable aid to the intelligence analysts. It will reduce the amount of paper; provide the analyst with faster, more complete mail receipt; and give him the most complete and accurate retrieval of information possible. The concepts being incorporated into the design are extendible and will be sufficiently flexible to meet changing patterns of analysis that will certainly occur. With SAFE, the intelligence analyst will have the tools necessary to produce the comprehensive and timely intelligence needed by policy-makers to meet the challenges of today's world.

LEONARD G. LEVY
Combustion Engineering, Inc.
Stamford, Connecticut

A Pilot Implementation of Electronic Mail at Combustion Engineering

During the past century, the Industrial Revolution has brought about remarkable increases in output per worker. Now the same forces of technology that effected the spectacular growth of productivity in the factory are being applied to office and administrative areas. The results of this effort are grouped under the generic heading, "Office of the Future." Included in this broad category are the discrete subjects of facsimile transmission, word processing, teleconferencing, personal computing, private data bases, and electronic mail.

The term *Office of the Future* is a vague one. It has been used in the periodical literature to describe a most varied potpourri of hardware and concepts. Some descriptions sound like a page from a science fiction novel. Others involve significant changes in personnel, job descriptions and management organization.

In most discussions of the Office of the Future, there is mention of direct cost savings in postage and an increase in secretarial productivity (linked to the use of word-processing equipment). It is expected that many companies will pursue the main components of the Office of the Future in order to cut costs. Some companies may be forced to change their office structures because the availability of new career choices for women will make secretarial talent scarcer and more expensive. In addition to the savings in postage and increased secretarial output, Combustion Engineering (C-E) is interested in two important benefits it expects to receive from its venture into the Office of the Future. The first is an increase in executive productivity which will result from the manager's ability to interact with his peers without the need for face-to-face or "phone-to-phone" contact. The second benefit is the speed with which an executive (even when out of the office) can find out what is happening and take appropriate action.

Combustion Engineering is in an ideal position to begin implementing the Office of the Future. It is a large ($2.3 billion annual sales), highly diversified supplier of energy equipment and building materials. C-E has a central computer processing facility in its Windsor, Connecticut, data center, and an international data network, consisting of 80,000 miles of leased telephone lines in North America and more than 20,000 miles in Europe, linking C-E sales and production facilities to the data center.

In addition to the ability to implement the Office of the Future, C-E has a need for its capabilities to unite a widely decentralized and highly diverse management organization. And it has a desire to provide its management with the best tools possible for their activities. The implementation of the Office of the Future at C-E began with a pilot installation of electronic mail. Electronic mail is the backbone of the Office of the Future. It is the thread that will ultimately link all the other parts and was the logical place to begin our implementation. The pilot project was designed and programmed in 1977 and was operational from January 1 to June 30, 1978.

While the term *electronic mail* is not quite as vague as the phrase "Office of the Future," it too has different definitions in different contexts. Some people use the term when referring to facsimile transmission (especially the new high-speed "fax"). In other companies, the term is used to denote a linkup of word processors or minicomputers in a store-and-forward or message-switch network. The meaning of the term "electronic mail" at C-E is very similar to what is meant by the computer message systems (CMS) mentioned in current literature. The concept can be defined more clearly by describing what electronic mail accomplishes and how it works.

Objectives of Electronic Mail

The purpose of electronic mail is to improve the efficiency and effectiveness of written communication by utilizing the power of the computer and the speed of data transmission. The objective is to make it faster, cheaper and easier to transmit information from person to person by applying the latest developments in data processing technology. It is expected that electronic mail will:

1. increase the speed of communication by making messages available to the recipient, regardless of location, instantly upon completion (or dispatch) by the author;

2. reduce the cost of communication by utilizing the existing data network to process messages at a cost substantially lower than that of first-class mail; and

3. improve the effectiveness of communication by providing a simple, easy-to-use system for the creation, transmission, retrieval and follow-up of messages.

Description of C-E's Pilot Project

To begin the movement toward the Office of the Future at Combustion Engineering, we designed and installed a prototype system for the "automatic transmission of mail" (ATOM). The ATOM System was the hub of a pilot project, the purpose of which was to provide information concerning the costs, benefits, desirability and usefulness of electronic mail at C-E, and was available to a selected group of approximately fifty users.

The ATOM System consists of a series of computer programs resident on the Amdahl 470 at the data center. We often referred to the Amdahl as the central post office where we all had post office boxes. During the pilot operation, we examined ways in which electronic mail could be implemented throughout C-E on a production basis that would maximize benefits and reduce costs.

The duration of the pilot project was six months, with monthly reviews scheduled. Participants in the pilot study were expected to evaluate the system which they used, and to suggest changes and improvements that should be made before participation in the system was opened to other operating areas.

The approach taken in implementing the ATOM System at C-E was (1) to build around the extensive international data network which was already in place, (2) to utilize the data management and retrieval capabilities of the INQUIRE software package, (3) to explore the use of the word-processing capabilities of minicomputers, and (4) to use the Network Operating System (NOS) of the Control Data Corporation (CDC) Cyber computer for on-line data entry. The pilot system was installed using IBM's Time-Sharing Option (TSO). This made access to mail contained in the system possible from any existing TSO terminal. The pilot system was also used to test a variety of new terminals which ranged from stationary typewriter-quality devices to lightweight portable models with thermal printers.

In summary, one could say that the ATOM System provided each participant with a secure mailbox housing all mail sent to or from that participant. By using a computer terminal, the participant was able, from any location in the world, to create, scan, read print, pend, forward (with notations), or archive mail sent to him or her by others.

Creation of new documents was possible in two ways. Documents could be created on-line as part of the user's dialogue with the ATOM System, or off-line on a word-processing minicomputer to be transmitted to the system as a high-speed batch (Remote Job Entry) submission. Documents could also be created on-line to the Cyber computer and sent over the IBM-CDC link. All the mail sent to the system was prepared with the assistance of some type of word-processing text editor. For those items entered directly into the system, the text editor of IBM's TSO was used. For those created off-line on a word processor, its text editor was used; and for those created on-line to NOS, the University of Calgary's text editor was used. Each of these offered significant assistance in the creation of a document. This assistance was particularly important when making changes or corrections to the document.

Mail could be retrieved from the system by either a manager or a secretary. An important consideration in the system design was to make it convenient for an unassisted executive in a remote location to operate the system without difficulty or any special "data processing" training. This was accomplished by creating a user dialogue that prompted for all necessary inputs and used simple English statements. In this "unassisted" mode of operation, the executive would connect his portable terminal to the system and begin the dialogue. He would first see a count of what was in his mailbox. He could request more information about the documents in his mailbox (author, subject, etc.), or he could choose to read his mail. He might start with the rush documents, then read the short ones, and request that the long documents be sent to his nearest high-speed printer. He may use his terminal to forward messages to other people, or he may enter short messages directly from the terminal. If the manager chooses to enter correspondence into the system by dictating to his secretary, the message would be typed into a word-processing system (where it would be stored on a magnetic recording medium) and a draft printed out. After the draft was reviewed, corrections to the recorded document could easily be made. The finished letter would be transmitted to the Corporate Data Center for processing by the ATOM System's "postmaster." The postmaster function is performed by a batch program executed each time a group of letters is received from a word-processing machine, or each time a letter is entered and "mailed" from a portable terminal.

In addition to the transmission of mail from person to person, or from a person to a predefined group of people, the ATOM System has a "suspense file" or "follow-up" capability in which a document marked as pending is held in the system until the specified date on which it is to reappear in the owner's mailbox.

Features of the ATOM System

The capabilities offered to the participant in the ATOM System pilot project were designed to parallel closely the way we work (or would like to work) at our desks.

Immediately upon logging onto the system, the user receives a summarized count of what is in his "in-basket" awaiting his review. Once this display is completed, the participant can enter any of the twenty-one commands in the system repertoire. These commands are grouped into five functions (see Table 1). Following is a detailed description of the way in which the system operates.

TABLE 1. ON-LINE FACILITIES OF THE ATOM SYSTEM

Function	Command	Operand
Retrieval	COUNT (CO)*	
	INDEX (I)	IN (I)
	VIEW (V)	OUT (O)
	PRINT (P)	RUSH (R)
		NEW (N)
		UNSEEN (U)
		PENDING (P)
		ALL (A)
		or message numbers
Composition and	CREATE (C)	
Editing	EDIT (E)	File name
	MODIFY (M)	Message number
	FORWARD (F)	Message number
	VIEWHELD (VH)	File names
Distribution	HOLD (H)	File name
	SEND (S)	File name
Disposition	PEND (P)	Message numbers
	DELETE (D)	Message numbers
	DELFILES (DF)	File names
Information and	BOXID (B)	Characters
Assistance	WHOIS (W)	Characters
	HELP (HE)	Command name
	FILES (FI)	
	PASSWORD (PW)	OLD, NEW
	PAGE (P)	Screen lines
	QUIT (Q)	

*The short form of the command is in parentheses.
Notes: A comma, but no space, must come between the command and the operand. VIEW, PRINT, PEND and DELETE commands will work with a range of operands (### to ###) in place of a string of message numbers.

When a user signs onto the system, he is asked to supply an appropriate user identification code (Mailbox ID) and a unique password. If the user responds properly, he receives a display acknowledging that he is using the Electronic Mail System, and counts of the various types of messages (i.e., incoming, outgoing, new, etc.) in his "in-basket." After displaying these counts, the system subsequently prompts the user for a command. The list of commands that he may choose from can be categorized as: composition and editing commands, distribution commands, retrieval commands, disposition commands and information commands. Each of these can be abbreviated by using the first (or if necessary to resolve ambiguity, the first two) characters of the command name.

Composition and Editing Commands

The CREATE command is used to enter a new message into the system. Each message is composed of two parts: the heading and the text. When this command is given, the system prompts the user for heading information, which includes the mailbox identifiers of all intended recipients. The copies addressed to the recipients can be distinguished as originals, carbon copies or blind carbon copies. Additionally, the system will prompt the user for a subject, a date and a pending date. The user is also asked to indicate whether the message is rush, confidential or registered. Upon completion of the heading information, the user is prompted to enter the text of his message.

If a mistake is made during the composition of a message, or if changes need to be made to a message that has been held prior to distribution, the user would utilize the EDIT command. This command makes available all of the text-editing capabilities of IBM's TSO. However, it was found that most users needed only a small subset of these editing facilities. With the edit functions, users may insert, delete and modify lines of text, or replace one set of characters with another prior to making the message available for distribution.

If, however, a message has already been distributed, and the sender wishes to change its contents and redistribute it as a new letter, he or she may employ the MODIFY command. This command retrieves the original text from the user's outgoing "mailbox" so that either the heading or the text portion of the letter can be altered and redistributed.

Distribution Commands

In the event that a user wishes to save a message so that he or she may continue to work on it at a later time, the HOLD command is used. By supplying a "file name" with the command, the heading and text of the message are retained under this name and can be recalled for subsequent editing and distribution.

When the user wishes to distribute a message to all of the identified addressees, he or she simply enters the SEND command. The use of the command itself will send the current message; but if one or more file names are supplied, the named message files which have been saved with the HOLD command will be sent instead.

Often a recipient wishes to comment on a message and then redistribute it to different addressees. To accomplish this, the FORWARD command is used. This command retrieves the message from the user's "in-basket," prompts for a new addressee list and then for the comments. When the comments are followed by the text delimiter (*), the message and the comments are distributed to all intended recipients.

Retrieval Commands

When a user signs onto the ATOM System, a count of his messages is automatically displayed. However, the user may enter the COUNT command at any time. This command, with the appropriate subcommand, will display a count of new, unseen, confidential, pending, rush, incoming or outgoing mail. If the user simply types the word COUNT, the system will display a count of all messages in his or her mailbox, as well as the individual counts of each type of message listed above.

Generally, a user will want to see a summary of his or her mail without having to view the entire contents of each individual message. Thus, an INDEX command is provided which will display a list of the message numbers, senders, subjects, lengths and types of messages that have been received. If the user wants to be even more selective, the summaries can also be presented on the basis of whether they are incoming, new, unseen, rush, pending, or outgoing (e.g., the command INDEX,NEW will display summaries of all messages received since the last session).

At some point, the user will obviously want to read his mail. To do so, the VIEW command is used. The command by itself will present to the terminal all messages in the user's "in-basket." However, here too the user may want to be more selective. Entering one or more of the message numbers displayed in an index summary, or any of the message types mentioned in connection with the COUNT or INDEX command, will result in a display of the text of all messages specified.

Most managers have preferred to use a CRT teletypewriter device. Such users may wish to have a "hard copy" of certain messages. Consequently, through use of the PRINT command, all messages marked as incoming can be automatically routed to an appropriate line printer associated with a user's mailbox identifier. In many instances, however, the user may wish only to print messages of particular types. This can be accomplished by supplying the appropriate type name along with the

PRINT command (e.g., PRINT, NEW will route to an appropriate printer all messages not yet indexed).

Disposition Commands

Whenever a user wishes to have a memo "surface" in his or her mailbox on some future date, the user can employ the PEND command. Several messages can be pended at once, but this command must be used in conjunction with a pending date. Messages can also be given a pending date when they are created and forwarded. This capability can be used to establish a "tickler" or reminder file.

To remove the reference of a message from a mailbox, the DELETE command is used. This command, accompanied by a message number, logically disconnects a user from a specified message. The message will not actually disappear from the system until after all recipients have deleted it. Users are allowed to specify one or more message numbers (up to ten) following any invocation of the DELETE command.

Information Commands

Because messages are distributed on the basis of a user's mailbox identifier, it is important for the sender to be able to determine infrequently used identifiers. By supplying the intended recipient's name or some part of the name with the BOXID command, the system will display the names of one or more individuals, depending on the uniqueness of a matching character string, their locations and their mailbox identifiers. Conversely, a user may know the mailbox identifier but simply wish to verify the name, address or organizational entity of an individual within C-E. For this facility, the user enters the WHOIS command and supplies the mailbox identifier in question. The system responds with a display showing the mailbox identifier, the name associated with the identifier, the location and the internal C-E group/division/department code.

For beginning users, or users having infrequent exposure to the system, a HELP command is provided. Used by itself, this command lists all of the ATOM System commands along with their respective abbreviations. However, by supplying a command name with the HELP command, the user obtains a brief description and instructions for its use.

A major feature which was intentionally omitted from the ATOM System would have allowed for the sophisticated retrieval of documents (for example, by subject, author or phrases in context). There are two reasons why we have omitted this capability:

1. To be consistent with common business practice, it was decided to keep the "in-basket" and "file cabinet" separate. Most of us read our mail,

and then decide whether or not to keep it and where to file it. It is a good practice to keep the "in-basket" empty and we encourage that.

2. For purposes of training and implementation, it seemed easier to split the system in two parts; the first part is electronic mail and the second part is another component of the Office of the Future, commonly called the personal data base. This feature, which we have named "Archive," will be added to the production system as a second stage in the implementation. When installed, this feature will allow a system participant to select specific documents (either inbound or outbound), assign subject or file codes to them, and have them routed to the "Archive File Management System." The Archive will be an INQUIRE data base and will allow for the retrieval of documents based on any selection criteria (from, to, etc.), including words or combinations of words in text. We presently have "correspondence control systems" of this type operational.

The Objectives of the Pilot Project

The major goal of the pilot project was the selection of the best approach to use in implementing electronic mail at C-E. To arrive at this determination, many individual subjects had to be researched, including noncost advantages and benefits reported by participants, acceptability and adaptability of this new form of communication to users, acceptability of the system's behavior to users, and pilot costs and savings versus those of conventional office operations. The aggregate experience and supporting information obtained through the use of the pilot system will be the means through which the desirability of extending the application companywide will be determined. There are many individual subjects which were researched as part of the overall project. Some of these are:

1. *Hardware evaluation:* The pilot project was used to test various input and retrieval devices to ascertain their acceptability to the user population.
2. *Test of software:* The pilot project allowed us to test the "human engineering" of the ATOM System and the dialogue which takes place between the user and the computer.
3. *Determination of costs:* While an estimation of costs based on hypothetical usage of the system is possible, the pilot allowed actual costs to be recorded based on the use of the system in a working environment.
4. *Evaluation of the benefits:* The pilot operation was used to measure the tangible benefits and estimate the value of the intangible benefits derived from use of the system.

5. *Development of usage statistics:* As part of the research which was performed during the pilot project, the system gathered some basic statistics on usage, such as (a) the length, in lines, of the minimum, maximum and typical message; (b) the maximum and typical number of addressees for a message; (c) the use made of "group codes" and standard distribution lists; (d) the number of messages sent per day (maximum, minimum and typical), and classified as rush, confidential or registered; and (e) the number of sessions per day per user (maximum and typical), and the time and duration of these sessions.

6. *Analysis of user experience:* As another part of the research project, each participant was requested to comment on the benefits realized from the use of electronic mail, and to suggest changes that should be made to the system to improve its effectiveness. Each participant was requested to complete a monthly questionnaire.

An analysis of this questionnaire helped define how the ATOM System was used in actual practice and how the system may be improved:

1. Do managers participate directly, or do their secretaries do both input to and retrieval from the system?
2. Is the system used to reply to messages, and how often are they forwarded for reply or information?
3. Is the system used after hours to extend the workday?
4. Is the system used from off-site locations, and are portable terminals worthwhile?
5. Are "group codes" useful in addressing messages, and are standard distribution lists helpful?
6. What suggestions, complaints or comments can be collected from the participants?
7. Has the use of the system resulted in changes in work habits and what benefits, if any, resulted?

The extent of the information we were able to obtain from the evaluation of the pilot project explains why we took the approach of designing and installing a prototype instead of relying on market research studies and statistical analyses. We believed it vitally important to observe the human interface with electronic mail in a "nonlaboratory" environment.

Tangible Benefits

A primary objective of the pilot implementation was to identify and evaluate the benefits to be derived from the use of electronic mail. A partial list of anticipated benefits includes the following items:

1. elimination of postage and interoffice mail costs;
2. elimination of telecopier and TWX usage;
3. reduction in use of photocopying machines since there is no need to mail a copy to a recipient who is on the system;
4. significant increase in the productivity of the input typist through the word-processing machines used for input to the ATOM System;
5. elimination of the need to perform key-entry to correspondence control (Archive) systems since the key-entry of documents to the mail system will serve both functions (note: the feed between the ATOM System and the Archive System will allow for increased and improved use of file retrieval systems); and
6. reduction in the need for file storage space due to the archiving feature of the system which eliminates the need for subject files (or other cross-reference collections). If the full text of a document is retained in the Archive, only current working files need to be kept in the office.

Intangible Benefits

Some of the intangible benefits to be derived from use of the electronic mail system are as follows:

1. Information is available sooner, allowing management to speed up the decision process. The system also makes it easier and more convenient for people to share knowledge. The result is twofold: better decisions made more quickly.
2. The system is available most of the day anywhere in the world and is designed to be readily usable by people who are not data processing personnel. This allows management and key staff personnel to read or compose messages without regard to place or time, thus extending the productive day for system participants.

MURRAY TUROFF
Director
Computerized Conferencing and Communications Center
New Jersey Institute of Technology
Newark, New Jersey

STARR ROXANNE HILTZ
Chairperson
Department of Sociology and Anthropology
Upsala College
East Orange, New Jersey

Electronic Information Exchange and Its Impact on Libraries

It has become common parlance that we are entering the "Information Age." We would like to take the reader with us on an exploratory voyage to the edge of some current information-age computer technology that may transform the library. A precondition for joining this expedition is an understanding of the "new world" which we hope to discover and build. It is a societal state in which the library has become one of the anchors of what we call "The Network Nation"—an era in which the amalgamation of computers and communications will reduce the time and cost needed to span distances between people and information, and among people communicating, to practically zero.

We are today awash in a sea of information. The library, the journals, the publishers, and the professional societies are segments of the ecological system that populates this ocean. These organisms serve the function of information exchange. One can view the library as a beacon of light to the user; however, if the user no longer sails the waters for which they provide guidance, then libraries lose their function and justification. True, just as for the right whale, one has a certain sentiment for the library; but as humankind has destroyed the right whale so it can allow the extinction of libraries if they no longer serve to light the way. There is nothing sacred about any library, any journal and publisher, or any professional society. If other, more useful mechanisms arise to provide information exchange functions, these entities will disappear unless they adapt to the new ecological environment. Somehow, the barnacles of tradition have to be scraped away.

Following is a description of an alternative technology to provide information exchange. It is not a library or a journal, yet it provides some of the functions of both. Perhaps someday it will become the heart of a new concept of the term *library*.

A specific representation of this technology is the Electronic Information Exchange System (EIES) now operating from the New Jersey Institute of Technology (NJIT) with support from the National Science Foundation. We will concentrate on a few of the current applications and facilities which may be relevant to the role libraries and librarians can play in the future.

Some Capabilities of Existing CCS

The term *computerized conferencing system* (CCS) will be used here to refer to systems structured to create a shared communication space within a computer to be used for the formation, collection, processing and dissemination of information and opinions. What is it like to participate in a CCS? Imagine that you are seated before a computer terminal, similar to an electric typewriter with either a long scroll of typed output or a TV-like screen for display. The terminal is connected to an ordinary telephone. You dial the local number of your packet-switched telephone network service which provides a low-cost link to the computer-host of the conferencing system. You type in a few code words to identify your conferencing system and yourself.

A conferencing system such as EIES will inform you of all of the communications since you last accessed the system that have been directed to you or to the group conference of which you are a part. Then it will lead you through the sending and receiving of text or graphic communication by asking a series of questions and responding to your answers.

There are four main communications capabilities or structures provided within EIES (see Table 1). In addition, there are a multitude of advanced features available.

TABLE 1. EIES COMMUNICATIONS FEATURES

Feature	*Replaces*
Messages	Letters
	Telephone calls
	Face-to-face conversations
	Visits
Conferences	Face-to-face conferences or meetings
Notebooks	Sending of drafts or preprints
	Necessity for coauthors to be in the same place
Bulletins	Newsletters
	Eventually, journals and abstract services

Technological Features for an Electronic Journal:
Collection, Submission and Public Access

"The Living Library," a concept attributed to Gaston Berger, suggests that if a subject is little understood or seen as difficult, it is better to spend time discussing it with several experts than to spend it on library research. We propose that the concept of a "living library" is what computerized conferencing is all about. A computerized conferencing system makes it very easy for people to find one another by topic of interest and to exchange their reflections on subjects that are difficult or not well defined. This is not a replacement for the book or journal article, but an improvement of our ability to deal with formulative and transitory information. Libraries have yet to deal with this area in any effective manner, with the exception of collections of working drafts maintained by some company libraries in a research-oriented operation.

During the past three years, EIES has built up a file of conferences on a diverse array of topics. We at NJIT have also observed a range of human behavior patterns reflecting the groups conducting the conferences. Some of these observations indicate future roles for libraries and librarians, if one agrees that libraries should move in the direction of handling formulative and transitory information.

In particular, we noted that certain individuals had developed the habit of copying into their notebooks items from different conferences. This occurred when some topic of interest to them represented a lateral information cut across the various topics defining the conferences they were in. Later, they might utilize this "collection" as the basis for a paper or a completely new conference with other individuals having similar interests.

The pattern of the EIES operation is to utilize observations of this sort to aid and facilitate the users' information behavior through improvements in the design of the system. Therefore, as a result of our observations, we have recently incorporated a lateral information capability called "collections." A collection on EIES works as follows:

1. The user forms an outline on any topic of interest. The outline has a title for each item and there is a 9-level hierarchical numbering scheme using the standard period notation to separate levels, such as 1.2.3. This outline may be modified by the addition of new sections or subsections or by the reordering of items. The user defines a title and abstract for this outline and may have as many different outlines as desired. The user may also designate others he or she wishes to have read and/or write privileges for the outline. The outline represents a rather flexible set of labels for the user's electronic file cabinet.

2. Any time the user encounters some text item that would fit within this outline, a single command may be used to file it at the appropriate location.
3. In line with the philosophy of promoting communications on EIES, the act of collecting an item automatically creates a one-line notice to the author of the item, notifying him or her that the text item was collected, by whom, and under what collection. The author is free to view the abstract of that collection but must get permission from the "collector" to see the actual collection contents.
4. Since the collection really holds only a pointer to an actual item, the author of the particular item is free to edit or delete it at any time. Therefore, the author can pull an item out of a collector's file if he or she wishes.

Note that a collection could be used merely to allow a person to structure his or her own personal notebook, to organize a paper or a book, or to allow a group to collect everything on a particular topic of common interest. Another key point is that the collection potential is based upon what a person can read rather than just on what he or she has written.

One could well imagine an electronic environment where certain individuals become noted for their ability to collect informative compilations of knowledge and where collections are traded or brokered. We feel that the collection concept represents the transition of EIES from a versatile communications and text-processing system to a more pleasing merger of communication and information systems. The collection also allows a person to perform the same sort of function on the transitory and formulative information composing this system's data base that a research librarian would perform on the library's book and paper collection. However, librarians will take on new roles in this type of environment. These roles could span the range from observer, such as the anthropological participant observer, to group facilitator, who guides and organizes discussions. This latter role, of course, implies an entirely new set of talents that must be incorporated into the educational process of future librarians.

Another analogy that has been applied to EIES is that of a blooming and buzzing garden, in which certain individuals play the role of bees, flitting from conference to conference, bringing about the cross-fertilization necessary to trigger new growth in the discussions. Their other function is the high energy or low entropy extraction and production of the honey or collection for the rest of us to feed on, as we now do on good books or papers. The model of the future librarian may well be that of the "busy buzzing bee."

The collection also makes it possible for an author to "publish" his or her own works electronically and include constant updates in the text. Royalties might be computed by charging a nominal fee per page retrieved by readers, with the computer doing the bookkeeping. Unlike more traditional publishing, readers might directly question the author or comment on the work; these exchanges could be made available to subsequent readers as supplements.

A simpler process than collections is "submissions." Any author can execute a "submit" command identifying the locations of the abstract and pages of his or her paper. The text item that the submission command creates may serve as a message to individuals or be placed in a conference or notebook. Anyone printing out that text item as part of their normal communication process will be presented with the abstract for the paper. The receiver may then execute a "read" command referring to that text item and the whole paper will be printed. This submissions capability in essence opens a window or creates a beacon into the author's notebook that others may look through or be guided to.

The final component necessary for the electronic journal is access or dissemination beyond the limited membership of EIES; that is, to the public. This is provided for by "public slots" which can be accessed by up to 1000 individuals, each with a subaccount.

The Electronic Journal

When we first began design of EIES, we laid out a very specific plan for an "electronic journal." Three years of operation and hundreds of thousands of text pages later, we realize how wrong we were. Our initial thoughts were very much along the lines of mimicking a formal journal and imposing this structure on all "bulletins" or journals on the system. What has evolved, however, is a multitude of alternate subfunctions from which user groups can piece together the type of "journal" operation that satisfies their needs, desires and norms. The scientific user groups can create their own personal "animal" that swims and dives in the manner and style they wish.

The collection capability and the submit and read commands provide the building blocks for the emergence of electronic journals on EIES. There are currently four prototypes in existence or in the development stages.

The simplest is *Chimo,* a newsletter with items about the members and groups on EIES and new system features. It uses the read feature for its "supplements": full-length papers which have been keyed into EIES by and are made available to its members.

There is also a public conference called Paper Fair which can be considered a totally unrefereed journal. Any member of the system can put a paper into Paper Fair, and any member can read the papers there and enter their reactions or comments into the Paper Fair conference.

A subsystem of EIES called Legitech has been operational since January 1978. Its design is unlike that of traditional journals, but, as will be discussed later in this paper, it provides a similar function.

Finally, under development is the first electronic journal which is similar to existing print-based journals. Its initial issue should be "published" by 1980. It will be a journal for the research specialty known as "mental workload," the study of person/machine interfaces in the operation of complex systems, such as the controls in the pilot's cockpit or in a nuclear plant. This particular specialty area does not now have a print-based journal.

One Example of an Electronic Journal:
The Classic Model, with Variations

The electronic journal on mental workload is to be advertised, refereed, edited—just as are traditional journals. The plans are to advertise in wide-circulation print journals, such as *Science*. Any interested person can subscribe to membership in the journal. Subscribers will receive instructions and access code to dial into EIES on a public-membership slot; markers will be kept on each of the approximately 1000 members expected to be able to share access to a slot.

Anyone signing on under a journal subscriber identification code will not see the regular EIES interface, but will be welcomed to the journal "Mental Workload" (or whatever title is chosen). The subscriber will be asked if he or she wants to read abstracts, search authors or titles, print articles, or comment on articles or the journal system. An editor will preserve the anonymity tradition of journal publishing. When an article is submitted on-line (with the submit command), the editor will assign reviewers, who will have access to the paper without knowing the author's name. Likewise, the reviewers will send their comments to the editor, who will remove the identity of the reviewers before sending the comments to the author.

When an article is in final form and accepted, it will be "published," rather than held for issues at specific times. Another difference from the traditional journal is that all reader comments will be collected and made available to other readers, along with any responses from the author. Such comments on articles can be signed or unsigned.

This is not difficult to do technologically, and will result in a much shorter cycle from completion of research to dissemination of findings, as well as lower costs, since each reader prints only those articles of interest. The interesting problem is the motivational one. How do you motivate people to take the risk of expending effort to write for and review an electronic journal which has no established prestige-granting rating in the scientific community? For besides serving as official archives of research findings, journals also serve to bestow prestige.

As with new print journals, part of the answer is to try to obtain initial reviewers and authors with established reputations. As of summer 1979, all the software for the electronic journal was in place and working. However, none of the invited authors had actually submitted an article. The technology is here; the norms and reward structures needed to make scientists ready to use the technology have not evolved. As Roistacher points out, another "crucial social aspect of a virtual journal is not merely that scholars submit articles but that they read and cite articles in virtual journals at least as frequently as conventionally published work."[1] Even with a potential 1000 "subscribers," relatively few scholars would have access to the journal. The secondary readership of library copies is not likely to occur, unless libraries subscribe and have terminals available for their patrons to access on-line journals.

Legitech: A New Kind of Electronic Information Network

Legitech is the name of a network of approximately forty state science legislation advisors and many federal representatives who are using EIES as an information exchange. It is included in this paper as an example of the "usual" EIES interface and features tailored to users' particular needs to create an information-sharing and access resource.

When the average user of EIES signs on, he or she receives the following "menu" of choices:

ACCESS TO:
MESSAGES	(1)
CONFERENCES	(2)
NOTEBOOKS	(3)
BULLETINS	(4)
DIRECTORY	(5)
EXPLANATIONS	(6)
REVIEWS	(7)
COMPOSITION	(8)
MONITORING	(9)

However, the state science advisors have some very unique kinds of information which they create and share. These are called "inquiries," "responses," "leads," and "technology briefs." Thus, they have customized their own interface on EIES. When a Legitech member signs on, he or she receives the following messages to read and choose among:

WELCOME TO LEGITECH.
PLEASE WAIT WHILE YOUR PENDING ITEMS ARE FOUND.

WAITING:
    2 INQUIRIES

ACCESS TO:
    INQUIRIES   (1)
    RESPONSES   (2)
    LEADS   (3)
    BRIEFS   (4)
    YOUR SELECTIONS (8)
    EIES   (9)

LEGITECH CREATED BY P+T, JIM WILLIAMS, AND HARRY STEVENS

A typical set of interactions is shown in Figure 1. As illustrated, a request for information on a topic can result in suggested "leads," such as people or books, or "responses," which are more complete replies. Eventually, each "inquiry" entered will build up its own associated list of leads and responses. Thus, whenever a state advisor has a question, he or she can check EIES to see if there are already any stored answers or leads, and if not, enter it as a new inquiry. One can imagine that a similar structure could be created for interlibrary loan requests, or for "referential consulting networks" for questions which "stump" the local librarian.

When all of the responses have been received, someone often takes the responsibility to edit them into a more polished, integrated "brief" on the topic. These are made available not only on-line, but also by mail. The titles of finished briefs are published in a number of newsletters and made available in hard copy for a small fee. This off-line, secondary distribution thus provides the "mass circulation" that is characteristic of more traditional journals.

FIGURE 1. SAMPLE ITEMS FROM LEGITECH

WELCOME TO LEGITECH.
PLEASE WAIT WHILE YOUR PENDING ITEMS ARE FOUND.

WAITING:
    2 LEADS
    4 RESPONSES
    12 INQUIRIES. . .
    ACCEPT WAITING ITEMS (Y/N)? y

N74 NP34 PHYLLIS KAHN (PHYLLIS, 707) 1/30/79 1:49 AM L:8
KEYS:/INQUIRY #34/INFORMATION SERVICES/
TOPIC:
    INFORMATION SERVICES
QUESTION:
    How does your state budget funds for information services and what sort of justification is required for equipment upgrades? Has there been any person or committee paying attention to this aspect of appropriations?

FIGURE 1.—*Continued*

SELECT ABOVE INQUIRY TO RECEIVE BACKGROUND, RESPONSES, AND LEADS (Y/N)? y

N75 NP47 VERNER R. EKSTROM (OKLEG, 715) 2/8/79 3:10 PM L:17
KEYS:/RESPONSE #47/RESPONSE TO INQUIRY #34/INFORMATION SERVICES/
RESPONSE:
> The Data Processing Planning and Management Act of 1971 (Title 74, Sec. 118) provides that several state agencies including all of higher education may maintain their own data processing installations but others may not. For those who have their own they are budgeted out of their appropriations. Others pay for their services from the Division of Data Processing Planning through a revolving fund established by the act. DDPP services over 30 state agencies. A bill has been introduced to expand the scope of the agencies and to provide funding for the development of common systems such as payroll, personnel and inventory systems and to fund the development of systems in agencies not having the capability of doing their own. It is also planned to gain greater control over the development of all systems through the appropriations and budget process and review of state agency data processing programs by the Legislative Council. There is much I could say to elaborate on our program. Please message me further if you would like. Chimo-Verne.

N75 NP53 JOHN BAILEY (726) 2/8/79 9:47 PM L:7
KEYS:/RESPONSE #53/RESPONSE TO INQUIRY #34/INFORMATION SERVICES/
RESPONSE:
> Maine has a couple of executive orders on this. The state got burned several times in a row in hardware acquisitions, so the government ordered all state agencies (except the universities) to use the state's Central Computer Services. There is, in addition to the usual contract review, a special committee that must approve all computer-related acquisitions.

N74 NP 36 JENNIFER BRANDT (JENNIE, 747) 1/31/79 5:21 PM L:11
KEYS:/INQUIRY #36/STATE BILL STATUS SYSTEMS/
TOPIC:
> STATE BILL STATUS SYSTEMS

QUESTION:
> Are there any state legislatures which have dial-up access to their bill status computer systems? The White House is interested in the possibility of accessing these systems. Is this feasible?

SELECT ABOVE INQUIRY TO RECEIVE BACKGROUND, RESPONSES, AND LEADS (Y/N)? y

BACKGROUND:
> The White House information center needs to provide information in response to White House staff inquiries concerning state legislative issues. In the policy analysis and review of pending federal proposals, it would be useful to review pending state legislation.

N76 NP17 GARY NALSON (GARY G., 706) 2/6/79 4:19 PM L:12
KEYS:/LEAD #17/TYPE = PERSON/LEAD TO INQUIRY #36/STATE BILL STATUS SYSTEMS/
RESPONSE:
> George Reischeck
> NYS Secretary of the Senate Staff
> New York State Capitol, Albany, NY
> George maintains the computer bill tracking system that is used by both houses of NYLEG. They have remote terminals to access system.

FIGURE 1.—*CONTINUED*

N75 NP37 G. WILLIAM HARBRECHT (MTLEG, 717) 2/1/79 6:19 PM L:8
KEYS:/RESPONSE #37/RESPONSE TO INQUIRY #36/STATE BILL
STATUS SYSTEMS/
RESPONSE:
Montana has a computer bill status system. To call in, dial (406) 449-3064 and
ask for Val. She will determine the status of the bill for you. If you want to
connect your computer terminal directly into the system, it will be necessary for
you to contact Diana Dowling, Legislative Council, State Capitol, Helena,
Montana 59601.

N75 NP40 STEVE FISHER (NBLEG, 728) 2/5/79 6:21 PM L:3
KEYS:/RESPONSE #40/RESPONSE TO INQUIRY #36/STATE BILL STATUS
SYSTEMS/
RESPONSE:
Nebraska has no computer bill status system. However, the status of any bill can
be found by dialing (402) 471-2271

N75 NP45 ROGER SWENSON (ORLEG, 716) 2/6/79 7:50 PM L:9
KEYS:/RESPONSE #45/RESPONSE TO INQUIRY #36/STATE BILL STATUS
SYSTEMS/
RESPONSE:
Oregon has a bill status system—call (503) 378-8551. If you wish to tie directly
into the computer system, contact Earl Vogt, Oregon Legislative Information
System, State Capitol, S-408, Salem, Oregon 97310, or message me.

N75 NP55 VERNER R. EKSTROM (OKLEG, 715) 2/11/79 11:22 AM L:26
KEYS:/RESPONSE #55/RESPONSE TO INQUIRY #36/STATE BILL STATUS
SYSTEMS/
RESPONSE:
Oklahoma is still experimenting with a computer bill status system but our
efforts have been stymied by a combination of lack of interest and support from
our House, poor response and reliability of our computer system, lack of
adequate support from our computer systems and programming staff, and lack
of enthusiasm for our proposals from the Senate staff. In 1976 and again in 1977
we installed and ran the Florida system for the Senate but it was ill-suited to our
particular needs and would have required extensive modification for eventual
use. In 1978 we used ATMS II to store a document on the status of each bill, a
document indexing all bills, a document showing the bills in each committee,
and a document showing the bills introduced by each legislator. Before being
fully usable this approach would require special software—interfaced with
ATMS—to permit multiple updating with one transaction. It would also
require a considerable improvement in our computer terminal response time to
support such a transaction and is using software developed essentially in
Missouri although they are modifying it substantially. Unfortunately, this
system is stand-alone and will do little to support the House, Legislative
Reference Library, other state agencies and certainly not the general public
including other state legislatures. Incidentally, you should be aware the NCSL
has some interest in state computer efforts relating to bill status.

Almost Instant Literature Review

When journals and other information sources go electronic, the flood
of new publications will undoubtedly make it even harder for people to
keep their heads above the oncoming waves of information without a

knowledge-worker's life preserver—the peer review of the importance and quality of new sources. Current book reviews in most scientific fields tend to be a year or two behind the publication date, and many books get only a very short review because of a lack of space. New journals tend not to be reviewed at all, let alone constantly updated or assessed, in locations where possible consumers can gain access to the reviews.

There have been several examples on EIES of "electronic book reviews" which were composed and published shortly after initial distribution of a book. The most interesting form this has taken is the joint or group book review, in which several people critique a new book or journal from different points of view, and the author or editor responds. For example, the new journal *Social Networks* was reviewed in *Chimo* approximately a week after it came out, and responses from the journal editor followed the next week.

Such multiple, interactive and quick reviews are potentially invaluable to readers outside a specialty who want to know what possible relevance a publication has for them. Because current reviews are largely done by an author's peer from the same specialty, this is a unique kind of information resource, other than hearing about a book by "word of mouth."

Human Factors and the Automation of Existing Traditions

Often, the initial ideas which people have for use of electronic information exchange technology are to automate exactly the communications conventions and concepts that characterize the traditional media. Thus, for example, we have "electronic mail" systems which refer to "letters," "mailboxes" and even a "postmaster." In actuality, when one mails a letter it cannot be retrieved for modification or even deleted before delivery; after all, once a letter is dropped into a mailbox, there is no way to get it back. Extending this practice to electronic mail serves no useful function.

Likewise, there is no reason an electronic journal needs to have any limitation on the amount of material published, or any fixed publication schedule for new items. Roistacher suggests that the assigning of referee scores can serve the function of assessing quality without preventing publication of articles:

> The virtual journal's essential addition to the evaluation process would be that each referee would give an article a numerical score ranging, for instance, from 0 to 100. The referee score would not only allow the virtual journal to publish all papers submitted, but would also allow readers to treat papers as if they were published in a series of journals of differing prestige. Referee scores would be published with the journal's table of contents and

could be used as retrieval items in bibliographic information systems....Low scoring articles would tend to be withdrawn until a satisfactory score is obtained.[2]

However, before disregarding all conventions made unnecessary by the new technology, one would do well to ask if there is any definite gain for the users in making such an alteration in their habits. There may indeed be some useful functions served by the prevailing practices. For example, the traditional journal or newspaper appears on a regular publication schedule. And, sure enough, our first operational electronic journal, *Chimo*, does too; it is "published" every Monday.

There was a discussion of whether it was necessary or useful for an electronic journal to be a "periodical" in this sense. Certainly there is no technological need, since one does not have to set up a press run or activate a distribution system to disseminate a new issue; discrete items could be disseminated immediately upon acceptance. However, the habits and motivations of the humans in this communication system seem to support the carry-over of this convention. It appears that both the authors and the editorial board need predictable deadlines; this provides a motivation for them to schedule a definite time within a week to finish their work—that time, of course, is usually right before the deadline. So, while publication weekly rather than continuously might seem to slow the production and dissemination of new items, ironically, this convention actually effects human motivational factors which operate to speed them up. In addition, at least some readers like the predictability of a new issue every Monday morning, waiting on-line. They have stated that it has become something of a ritual, the way reading the Sunday paper is for others. Our generalization is that the design of new systems must take into account the motivations and habits of the people who create and exchange information, not just the technological possibilities.

NEW ROLES FOR LIBRARIES AND LIBRARIANS

Both professionals and the general public need and are seeking better ways to deal with wisdom, lore and raw data. There are many opportunities for the library to develop important new functions and services such as facilitating access to models and becoming key nodes in a network of computer-based resources.

The "personal computer" is now available for less than $1000 and is spawning an avid hobby market. There is little doubt that computer and information technology will flow into the home within the next decade in forms far beyond that suited to this market. It is very likely that the first major consumer item derived from a general-purpose microcomputer system will be an intelligent typewriter or home word-processing system. With almost no added cost for hardware, such a system will have the capability to serve equally well as a computer terminal, a personal electronic file and notebook system, and an electronic home library. Such a system will have a replaceable memory unit very much like today's "floppy disk" (a storage device), which will hold about 50,000 words and cost about $10. Such a system currently costs about $6000 but is likely to drop to less than $1000 by the mid-1980s. This means that during the 1980s a growing population of individuals and organizations will be able to access directly a wide range of digitally based information and communication services.

The library today is a rather prominent member of the societal fleet of institutions. However, it is beginning to exhibit all the problems of the supertanker, representing a pinnacle of specialized, functional accomplishment and a singularity of purpose that may limit significantly the channels it can navigate and the forms of information it can deliver. Its inertia and size may very well make its turning radius far too large to maneuver in the storms of technological change so rapidly forming on the horizon.

The library is still synonymous with printed forms of information that have a high degree of permanence. However, societal needs for information are beginning to require an ability to handle transitory and raw information.

The Microprocessor as Distiller

In "The Rime of the Ancient Mariner," Coleridge speaks of "Water, water, everywhere, nor any drop to drink." Sometimes the would-be users of data bases and models that are stored on remote computers feel the same way. They are thirsty for the information contained in the potentially accessible data base, but they do not know how to get through the unpotable protocols of an unfamiliar system.

A capability that can be incorporated into a computerized conferencing system is a microprocessor with its own computer-controlled dialer. Programmed to participate as a full-fledged member, it has the same powers of interaction as any human member, and can perform such tasks as linking a user to any data base or model in any computer in a network. The microprocessor linked to EIES is currently called "Hal," but maybe we should rename it "Ahab."

Potentially the most important uses for the library of such a microprocessor are to access data bases such as NTIS, Chemical Abstracts or an interlibrary loan catalog. The microprocessor has the advantage that the entire protocol for accessing the information, extracting the desired items, and sending the answer to the user can be programmed into it. Thus, the user does not have to remember N different protocols for N different systems, but can be prompted by a series of questions.

This is increasingly important with the proliferation of on-line data bases of potential interest to the library patron. ASIS recently published a directory which lists more than 300 different computer-readable data bases.[3] As Williams pointed out, most on-line systems are now used by intermediaries because of the time needed to gain familiarity with the multiple command languages.[4] The microprocessor, however, can steer the user through such barriers and enable him or her to obtain the desired information without taking up the time of the trained specialist.

When tied to an interlibrary loan request system, the microprocessor might be able to search for an item and automatically send a message to the computer in the library where the book is cataloged to determine whether it is available.[5] If a desired item is located and is available, the system can then be used to send a message requesting that the item be sent.

Referential Consulting Networks

Given the availability in libraries of computer terminals for public access and use, and for on-line searches of computer-based journals and abstract files, a CCS might be used by librarians themselves to form what Manfred Kochen called a "referential consulting network."[6] Kochen argued that since information is now located in many places other than the traditional books and journals under the librarian's care, it is time for the reference librarian to become a general community knowledge resource, an "information-please" professional ready to locate any needed information. For those inquiries that cannot be answered using the resources stored in the local library, a network of reference librarians and "on-call" experts willing to share their knowledge resources might be developed. Every reference librarian is, for some types of questions, an expert consultant. With a system similar to Legitech, the reference librarian unable to find something could enter the item as an inquiry. The answers supplied by others could then be appended to the original request. We have then a new kind of information system, in which the users are also the creators of the information, and of the indexing or key-wording used for its storage and retrieval.

Models as an Information Resource

One of the most potentially valuable resources laying buried in the depths of computers are models that can be used for the analysis of data or for prediction and simulation. Unfortunately, the "lore" on how to run these models has generally made them inaccessible to those who are not in close proximity to the designers. It is as if the model were an elegant ship enclosed in a glass bottle, and nobody but the builder knows how it was done. An operational example of such a model is HUB, designed by the Institute for the Future. To run a modeling program, the user of HUB simply sends a message to the program; part or all of the program can be run and the results entered into a conference transcript to be shared with others.[7]

The advantage of locating access to a model within a conferencing system is that if any difficulties are encountered in running or interpreting the model, a message can be sent to the designers or documenters detailing the difficulty and asking for instructions or explanations. In addition, one person in a conference system familiar with a particular model or data base is the only one who needs to know the details of access. He or she can set up the programming specifications for the interface. From that point on, any other potential users need only fill out a form provided by the microprocessor or "hub" which asks all the questions needed to access and run.

Riding Out the Copyright Storm

Having used a conferencing system to navigate successfully through the narrow and tricky channels of access to remote data bases and models, the library may find itself tossed about in a storm of controversy over copyrights and data rights, and threatened on all sides by legal barrier reefs.

Since a user in a computer conferencing system can copy the results of a data base search or a run of a model, both of which are shared with others, it is possible for there to be copyright/data right violations. Problems even more severe are introduced when conferencing systems have international membership, thus opening the way for an information flow in violation of the tariff regulations or data protection laws of the sending or receiving nation.[8]

For example, the "mental workload" journal initially had approximately one-third of its editorial board located in Great Britain. It was supposed to have international contributors and readers as well as editors. However, the British Post Office ruled that it would be illegal for British scientists to participate in EIES, because that would violate its monopoly agreement on the transatlantic transmission of messages. So much for the new technology; it is prohibited by laws formulated before it existed, and by vested interests in outdated communications technologies.

The merging of communication and information systems, commonly thought to be very divergent, creates new systems that span the gulf between them. On EIES to date we have had not only the exchange of professional information in the form of discussions on topics, but also such activities as job advertising, proposal writing, on-line consulting, drafting of papers, setting of standards, arranging for professional meetings, and so on. There are a number of individuals now performing their consulting tasks through the system. At least two consultants are earning their livelihood via the system. We feel that ultimately the key to the success of these systems is that the writings of an individual or a group be viewed as the property of the individual or group. The EIES environment makes it very easy to conceive of user charges based on material printed which incorporate royalties for the responsible author or group. Such a system would provide the incentive for authors and groups to develop material relevant to the needs of information seekers. In such an environment, the librarian becomes the person who can add value to information by organizing it and facilitating people's awareness of its existence or relevance. In principle, "librarians" can also receive royalties for such services in addition to those received by the authors. If organized libraries do not act on these innovations, then it is very likely that commercial services will emerge for people who wish to function in this type of environment. In other words, if the libraries do not begin to experiment with this new area of information collection and dissemination, they may lose the opportunity to do so.

These communication/information systems could also create a marketplace for information. It is extremely difficult now, with the current system of publication services dominated by organizations, to establish the worth of any item of information or of a particular author in terms of technical or professional information. The unit of information never gets finer than a collection of papers in a book or journal. We conceive of a future where the unit of information is an individual idea or concept and a bid or barter system' can be superimposed on the information exchange process. In fact, one can conceive of a futures market for information which would represent the ultimate stimulus to authors whose writings make up the commodity base.

We have suggested a few ways in which systems like EIES might be used in libraries in the future. The points we would like to stress in conclusion are as follows:

1. Computer technology is now fairly reliable and cheap. A small library network could subscribe to a system such as EIES, or a larger network could have its own dedicated minicomputer-based system.

2. Advanced features and an imbedded programming language in EIES, plus microprocessors, can be used to tailor the interface and capabilities of such systems to the requirements and functions of particular users, such as libraries.
3. There is need for experimentation with such systems to discover what kinds of interface, features, training, documentation and pricing are best suited to specific purposes of libraries.

With a modest investment in field trials and experiments now, library professionals could acquire the skills and knowledge to navigate the computer networks of the 1980s with ease and confidence. The alternative is to wait until a combination of technology, economics and the rising flood of information force the abandonment of current print-based practices, leaving libraries to "sink or swim."

ACKNOWLEDGMENT

This paper is drawn from research supported by the National Science Foundation (DSI-77-21008 and MCS-78-00519). The opinions expressed herein are solely those of the authors and do not necessarily represent those of the National Science Foundation.

REFERENCES

1. Roistacher, Richard C. "The Virtual Journal," *Computer Networks* 2:23, 1978.

2. Ibid., p. 20.

3. Williams, Martha E., and Rouse, Sandra H., eds., comps. *Computer-Readable Bibliographic Data Bases: A Directory and Data Sourcebook.* Washington, D.C., American Society for Information Science, 1976.

4. Williams, Martha E. "Networks for On-Line Data Base Access," *Journal of the American Society for Information Science* 28:247-53, Sept. 1977.

5. Rouse, Sandra H., and Rouse, William B. "Assessing the Impact of Computer Technology on the Performance of Interlibrary Loan Networks," *Journal of the American Society for Information Science* 28:79-88, March 1977.

6. Kochen, Manfred. "Referential Consulting Networks." *In* Conrad H. Rawski, ed. *Toward a Theory of Librarianship.* Metuchen, N.J., Scarecrow Press, 1973, pp. 187-220.

7. Spangler, Kathleen, et al. "Interactive Monitoring of Computer-Based Group Communication." *In* Richard E. Merwin, ed. *AFIPS Conference Proceedings: 1979 National Computer Conference.* Montvale, N.J., AFIPS, 1979, vol. 48, pp. 411-14.

8. Williams, op. cit.

ADDITIONAL REFERENCES

Bamford, Harold E., Jr. "A Concept for Applying Computer Technology to the Publication of Scientific Journals," *Journal of the Washington Academy of Sciences* 62:306-14, Dec. 1972.

Hiltz, Starr Roxanne, and Turoff, Murray. *The Network Nation: Human Communication via Computer.* Reading, Mass., Addison-Wesley, 1978.

"La Bibliotheque Vivante" (letter received by Georges Gueron, communicated to Robert Theobald, and passed to the authors over EIES), Jan. 1, 1979.

Turoff, Murray. "The EIES Experience: Electronic Information Exchange System," *Bulletin of the American Society for Information Science* 4:9-10, June 1978.

_____, and Hiltz, Starr Roxanne. *Development and Field Testing of an Electronic Information Exchange System: Final Report on the EIES Development Project* (Research Report No. 9). Newark, New Jersey Institute of Technology, Computerized Conferencing and Communications Center, 1978.

WILLIAM J. KUBITZ
Associate Professor
Department of Computer Science
University of Illinois
Urbana-Champaign

Computer Technology:
A Forecast for the Future

In order to understand the impact of computer technology in the 1980s one must first understand the force underlying its ever-widening proliferation: electronic integrated circuit technology. Integrated circuit technology's impact on society will rank in importance with the invention of the steam engine and other such technological innovations—or perhaps surpass them. This technology is presently in its infancy. Most of us are aware of some of the early progeny: calculators and electronic watches and games. Some may be aware that it is now possible to buy a small home computer for about $700. This is just the beginning of what will become a wide variety of products which will affect every person. The reason? Low cost. The semiconductor process continues to enable ever-greater complexity at ever-decreasing cost. The future will bring lower-cost storage, processing and communications.

The processing of electronic signals can be performed in two basic ways: analog and digital. Although impressive gains have been made in both technologies from an electronics point of view, the greater visible impact will be from digital electronics and the discussion here will be confined primarily to advances in that area. Indeed, digital electronic circuits need not be "computers" in the commonly used sense, but I will further restrict this discussion for the most part to digital computer and digital storage technology.

In this discussion, I will concentrate on developments that will have a significant impact on libraries and library users. The impact on users will be in terms of the improved methods of using libraries they will have at their disposal because of other, nonlibrary related developments. The impact of digital technology on libraries will affect both their internal operation and the services they can provide.

From the user's point of view, a library is a place to obtain information in printed form that he cannot afford, or does not wish to buy because the use would only be short-term, or both. From a computer technologist's point of view, a library is a data bank or memory—a storehouse of information. It is primarily a particular kind of memory, commonly called read-only memory or ROM because users do not normally put information in—they just take it out. One does not "write" into the memory. Technologically, this simplifies the storage problem and lowers the storage cost, as shall be shown. The commonly used computer memory must have the capability of being both written and read and is called R/W memory. Libraries have another interesting property from a data bank point of view: the goal of making access to information as simple and inexpensive as possible. Thus, data security, which is so desirable in most large data banks, is not wanted at all. Of course, the physical form of the information in libraries must be protected, but not the information itself.

The basic needs of a library are for extremely large amounts of storage space, and some specialized processing, especially for searching the data bank. The processing and storage requirements, excluding those associated with the collection, are similar to those of other businesses. There is also a need for low-cost processing to handle the day-to-day business transactions. The users need low-cost terminals and a convenient means for browsing. To show how all of these things may come about, five areas will be discussed: microcomputers, large computers, terminals and home electronics, data communications, and memory and storage.

All of the above areas will have an impact on the future of libraries, as well as society in general, and the largest impact may well be from the combination of them rather than from their individual contributions. For society, the greatest impact will result from the single-chip computer and low-cost memory. For libraries, the greatest single impact may come from the development of the optical disk. It provides the first really low-cost mass storage. Before discussing the above items individually, a general discussion of electronic technology will be given in order to provide some perspective on the developments in this field.

Electronic Technology

The first electronic computer, ENIAC, was constructed using vacuum tubes. Electronics has since become almost entirely solid-state through a succession of transitional eras leading to the present one, in which many circuits are classed as large-scale integrated (LSI) circuits. These eras can be characterized as follows:

1. 1950-60: discrete (single devices);
2. 1960-71: integrated circuit (small-scale to large-scale integration); and
3. 1972-present: microprocessor (large-scale to very large-scale integration).[1]

Table 1, which compares ENIAC to a modern microprocessor, illustrates the incredible changes that have taken place in the last thirty years.

TABLE 1. COMPARISON OF ENIAC TO
MODERN MICROPROCESSOR

Item of Comparison	Microprocessor as Opposed to ENIAC
Size	300,000 times smaller
Power	56,000 times less
Memory (RAM)	8 times more
Speed	20 times faster
Number of active elements (tubes or transistors)	Approximately the same
Number of passive elements (resistors and capacitors)	80,000 fewer
Add time	Approximately the same
Failure rate	10,000 times better
Weight	Less than 1 lb. vs. 30 tons

Source: Hogan, C. Lester. "WESCON Keynote Address," *Progress: The Fairchild Journal of Semiconductors* 6:3-5, Sept./Oct. 1978.

During 1965-78, the number of devices per chip doubled each year. This "law" has become known as Moore's Law, named after Gordon Moore of the Intel Corp. who first made the observation. It appears that this behavior is continuing, although there are projections that the doubling may occur only every other year after 1980.[2] To provide perspective, the number of components per chip for several years is given below:

1. 1965: 30 components/chip
2. 1975: 30,000 components/chip
3. 1978: 135,000 components/chip
4. 1980: 1,000,000 components/chip[3]

These chips are typically about 1/4-inch square. The individual elements on them are defined by a photographic process. The minimum element size is dependent on the wavelength of the light used, which is currently an ultraviolet ray of approximately 250×10^{-9} meters. Presently, the smallest dimensions on the chips are about 3-4 micrometers (10^{-6}

meters). By the early 1980s this will be reduced to less than 1 micrometer, and by the late 1980s it will be further reduced to 0.05-0.005 micrometer. By comparison, a human hair is about 80-100 micrometers in diameter. In the past twenty years the number of minimum elements that can be put on a chip has gone from 10^3 to 10^7. At the same time, the number of elements needed to implement one bit (the smallest amount) of digital storage has decreased from 10^3 to 10^2 elements.[4] The reduction in this element size over the years is shown in Figure 1.

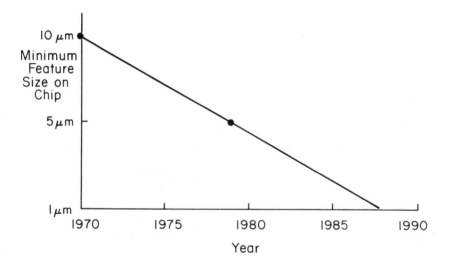

FIGURE 1. MINIMUM FEATURE SIZE VS. YEAR

At present there are no physical limitations to this continuing reduction in the size of the minimum element—called the minimum feature size. There are many technological problems which must be solved but physical limits will come into play only when atomic dimensions are approached. Increasing the size of the chips themselves is limited by our inability to produce perfect, defect-free crystals of silicon, the material from which the circuits are commonly started. Growing these crystals in space may prevent defects and this will be attempted as part of the space shuttle program. The major difficulty at present is knowing what to make and making it at a reasonable cost. An extensive effort is underway now to automate the design process so that these very complex chips can be designed at a more reasonable cost. Recently, the number of man-hours per month required for definition and design has been doubling every year.[5]

Because of this extremely high density of elements per chip, it has been possible to put a very large amount of memory (currently sixty-five kilobits) on a single chip. It has also been possible to put most of a 16-bit computer on a single chip. Although the design costs are high, they are prorated over an incredible number of chips, making the cost per chip very low. For example, 100,000 bits of memory cost $1.26 per bit in 1954 but had fallen to less than $0.01 per bit by 1978.[6] The situation is one of getting more and more for less and less. Figure 2 shows a typical semiconductor learning curve. This curve illustrates how the relative cost of a device falls rapidly as the total number of devices produced increases. The largest impact of this phenomenon has been in the area of computer technology and associated devices, although a broad spectrum of electronics has been affected. The two major results are low-cost processing and low-cost storage. These will have a profound effect on our society in the future.

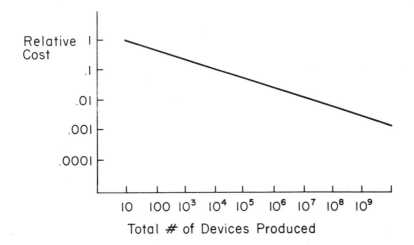

FIGURE 2. SEMICONDUCTOR LEARNING CURVE

Computer performance per unit cost has been increasing at 25-30 percent per year. The revenues of computer manufacturers and computer service firms have been doubling every five years and are projected to be $64 billion by 1981. It is projected that 8.3 percent of the GNP will be spent on computing by 1985, which does *not* include the use of microprocessors in automobiles and consumer electronics items.[7] Thus, this figure does not include the home computer which will be almost as common as the home television by the late 1980s.

Microcomputers

The term *microcomputer* was coined to describe any computer which uses as its processing element a microprocessor. The microprocessor is the single-chip "computer" about which so much has been written. However, it is important to realize that it takes more than the microprocessor chip itself to construct a useful, working computer. Nonetheless, the term microcomputer is often used rather loosely in reference to the processor chip itself. The processor chip performs all of the powerful functions usually associated with computers but provides no interface that a human can interact with and usually has only a small amount of memory. These "single-chip computers" will be referred to here as *processors* to preserve the distinction between the processor itself and a full-fledged computer.

The first microprocessor appeared on the market in 1972. Since that time the number of different microprocessors available has followed an exponential growth, as shown in Table 2. In the semiconductor industry the design cost of a single complex chip is extremely high, but if that cost is spread over millions of chips the price of a single chip can be extremely low. For example, in 1978 16 million of the simplest types of microprocessors were sold to toy and game manufacturers. This brought the price of these devices down to the one-dollar level. Texas Instruments alone sold over 9 million of these, thus producing around $9 million in revenue. The most expensive units at present sell for about fifteen dollars.[8] These are the larger, more powerful microprocessors.

TABLE 2. GROWTH OF TYPES
OF MICROPROCESSORS

Year	Number of Types of Microprocessors (approximate)
1972	1
1974	10
1975	30
1976	70
1977	100
1978	130

Source: Verhofstadt, Peter W. "VLSI and Micro-computers." In *Computer Technology: Status, Limits, Alternatives (Digest of Papers, COMPCON Spring '78)*. New York, Institute of Electrical and Electronics Engineers, 1978, p. 10, Figure 1.

The computing power of a microprocessor depends on, among other things, its speed of operation (to perform an addition of two numbers, for example) and what is known as its word length or precision. The word length is measured in bits (*binary* digi*ts*) and is an indication of how large a number can be processed and stored in the machine. For example, most large computers use a word length of about thirty-two bits. Eight bits is often used to represent one alphabetic character, so thirty-two bits could represent four alphabetic characters. The early microprocessors could only operate on four bits—quite adequate for games and simple control functions but not sufficient for "real" computing. These early microprocessors were quickly followed by a succession of ever more powerful ones:

1. 1972: 4 bits
2. 1974: 8 bits
3. 1978: 16 bits
4. 1981: 32 bits
5. 1985: 64 bits[9]

As shown above and in Figure 3, it is projected that by 1981 a 32-bit microprocessor chip will be available. In word length this is the equivalent of large machines commonly used in business today. In overall processing capability, it will enable the construction of a computer with a single-chip processor equivalent to the best of what are called minicomputers. (Minicomputers are currently 16-bit machines which do not use single-chip processors and are thus faster, roughly speaking.) It is estimated that the design of a 32-bit processor will require fifty man-years of effort. A 64-bit chip, as projected for 1985, would have a word length equivalent to that of a present-day "large-number cruncher," such as those produced by Control Data Corp. Presently, designers are investigating how to put such a large "mainframe" computer on a chip. It is projected that by 1990 it will be possible to put as many as 250,000 logic gates on a chip.[10] That is equivalent to a large IBM computer and makes possible a single-chip processor capable of executing 1 million instructions (operations) per second.

The Z 8000 microprocessor, recently announced by the Zilog Corp., illustrates what is currently available. It is a 16-bit processor, the equivalent of current minicomputers in word length. It operates at 4 million steps per second, making it ten times faster than previous microprocessors. The chip is 238 by 256 mils (approximately ¼-inch on a side) and contains 17,500 transistors.[11]

The implication for society is that by the mid-1980s processors with the capabilities of computers currently used in small businesses will be readily available on a personal basis. It is important to realize that the more

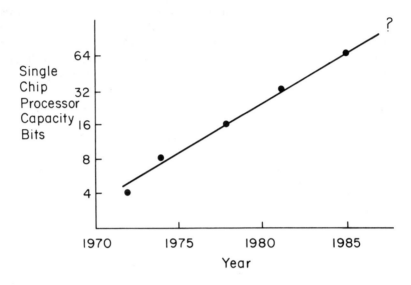

FIGURE 3. PROCESSOR CHIP CAPACITY VS. YEAR

powerful processors will not be significantly more expensive than the small ones. The cost is determined almost completely by the volume produced, not by the complexity of the device. Thus, it may be cost-effective to use a more powerful processor even if its capabilities are not totally exploited. A brief summary of data gathered by *Business Week* follows which illustrates the volume of microprocessors shipped in recent years as well as the projection to 1980:

1. 1976: 2.3 million
2. 1978: 27 million
3. 1979: 57 million (estimated)
4. 1980: 100 million (estimated)[12]

Because of this extremely high volume, the cost of computing has been falling at 30 percent annually.

In 1975 there were eight companies in the microprocessor business and total microprocessor sales represented 3 percent of total semiconductor sales. In 1978 there were twenty companies with $376 million in sales, representing 5 percent. In 1983 it is estimated that sales will be $1.5 billion and represent 11 percent of total semiconductor sales. One-third of last year's microprocessor chip production went into games. One-half of last year's games sales were electronic. It is projected that the sales of microcomputers will go from $135 million in 1978 to $670 million in 1982. Small business system sales are projected to be $1.5 billion by 1987.

Thus, in the 1980s we will see powerful small computers readily available for use in any endeavor one wishes to undertake. Every business and most homes will have at least one such computer. The heart of the system will most likely be a 32-bit single-chip processor. The processor will be used in conjunction with a color cathode ray tube display (TV), a keyboard, and a large amount of low-cost storage. It is projected that the television set, the TV games and the home computer will probably become indistinguishable in the 1980s and that by 1987, one-half of the U.S. households will have so-called smart terminals.[13] However, smart terminals will be indistinguishable from small computers. It is also probable that voice output will be available, as well as some restricted form of voice input. This will be discussed later in more detail.

The major factor in the decreasing cost of computing is the falling cost of the electronics. To use a computer, however, it must be programmed. The cost of software (or programs, as opposed to hardware or electronics) has been increasing. In 1973 software represented 5 percent of the microprocessor system cost; in 1978 this increased to 80 percent and people are worried about having to spend "$150,000 on software to use a $10 microcomputer."[14] This paradox arises for a number of reasons. As the microprocessors themselves become more complex, users attempt increasingly complex tasks requiring exceedingly complex software. It is estimated that the average professional programmer produces only ten good lines of code per day when working on complex software. Software is a relatively new discipline and there is still a great need for good "methodologies." In recognition of this need, a discipline of "software engineering" has sprung up. It is hoped that some control can be gained over design and management of software.

Unfortunately, improvements in software reliability may not be visible because the complexity of the software is increasing so fast. There have been several developments which make the future look more promising. In answer to the need for better programming languages, an improved language called PASCAL was developed; it has proved very popular in recent years and has almost become a de facto standard in the mini- and microcomputer world. Another development is "solid-state software" or firmware, in which the software is put into the hardware in the form of read-only memory. This does not, of course, make the software any better but it does provide some advantages in terms of speed. In addition, it provides some protection against theft of a manufacturer's software, which is developed at great expense. Perhaps the biggest advantage is that ROMs are now large enough to store large software programs; hence, the interface to the user is greatly improved, making computers much easier to use. Also, ROMs are now large enough to store an interpreter for a language such as BASIC. Another improvement in user interface is a shift away from procedural languages to the introduction of query systems. These allow a user to give instructions to the machine and obtain information from it in a question-and-answer mode. With the development of speech input and output it is even possible that this man/machine communication can be a spoken dialogue.

Large Computers

The changes in large computers in the 1980s will be less dramatic than those in other areas. The biggest change will be toward lower-cost processing due to the increasing complexity and decreasing cost of semiconductor electronics. The smaller large computers will have been replaced by what were once called microcomputers. Most computer users will have their own machine for their own purposes and time-sharing systems as we know them will be a thing of the past. One projection of developments for large, general-purpose computers is summarized as follows:

1. 1985: equivalent of IBM System 32 for $1000; equivalent of IBM System 370/125 for $5000; compilers implemented as dedicated processors within the system
2. 1986: equivalent of IBM 370/135 for less than $20,000
3. 1990: speech recognition for data entry, data processing and word processing; structured programming languages dominate computer languages; application and system software supplied as plug-in modules; manufacturers derive almost all income from software; and operating systems totally in hardware[15]

In the future, large computers will be relegated to two primary uses: large numerical computations (number-crunching) and management of central data banks. It is projected that raw number-crunching power will grow from 50 million instructions per second (MIPS) to 500 MIPS in the late 1980s.[16] For this discussion, data bank management is the more important use. Extremely large data banks will be available in the 1980s. Because of the relatively high cost and large amounts of data stored, these will be centralized resources upon which users can draw, much like conventional libraries in function. In fact, libraries will begin to take on the form of data banks, storing their contents in machine-readable form.

These central systems require a large computer for data management. It is likely that these large processors will not be general-purpose computers but, rather, specialized machines designed to perform very high-speed searching, sorting and data transfer operations. Such "service centers" will offer both software and data to users over communication links. The users will, for the most part, do their processing locally on their own machines; a service center would be contacted only when some software or data were not locally available, and on those rare occasions when local processing capabilities were not adequate to handle the problems at hand. The vast majority of the use would be in the nature of library use: checking out information and programs. It is even possible that something akin to the Library of Congress might be desirable, i.e., a national data resource center. Presently, data banks already exist for:

1. corporate and business management (personnel, vendors, accounting, inventory);
2. financial and banking matters (security position, customer accounts, investment analysis);
3. government information (legislative actions, constituent opinion, balloting);
4. legal information (laws, precedents); and
5. airline reservation systems (crews, passenger reservations).[17]

In the future, it is possible that many other data banks will exist for newspapers, periodicals and journals; musicians and composers; writing letters, memoranda, documents, texts, pamphlets and books; and preparing and maintaining retail catalogs, telephone directories and event calendars.

The data need not all be physically located in one place—it is only necessary that the various parts of the data bank be linked by high-speed data communication links. With large amounts of low-cost storage available locally, calls to the central data bank can be minimized. Since the cost of the local processing will be very low, and the cost of communications relatively high, minimizing the number of calls to the data bank will be important.

Terminals and Home Electronics

In recent years, low-cost electronics has had a significant impact in the home. We have seen a revolution in terms of the calculator, watch and game industries. Less visible but equally important changes have taken place in appliances, such as ranges, sewing machines, dishwashers, microwave ovens and washing machines. The auto industry is also poised to take the electronics plunge in the 1980s. The major revolution in home electronics is just beginning: the low-cost computer and the changes it will bring.

As discussed, low-cost, powerful single-chip processors will exist in the early 1980s. To make a powerful home computing system, one needs an output display. That already exists in the form of the color TV in almost every home. One also needs input—a keyboard—and large amounts of low-cost storage. Inexpensive keyboards are readily available now. Of course, voice output (and perhaps input) may also be possible. Low-cost memory will be copiously available in the 1980s. For the home computer to access data from a central data bank, a data quality communications link must exist. As will be discussed later, this will be provided by the "telephone" company or by cable television systems, or both. It is projected that the market for intelligent terminals (i.e., computer terminals which contain a computer) will grow from $300,000 in 1978 to $750,000 in 1982.[18] That doesn't even include home computers—just computer terminals used primarily in business. The following developments for terminals are projected for the 1980s: color displays and printers, and touch input on display; speech output and input, and flat panel displays; and expanded character sets (mathematical symbols, for example).[19]

Color displays, speech output and expanded character sets are certainly possible in home terminals. In addition, it has been predicted that a book-size display will be available in the 1980s.[20] Such a display will allow all written material to be stored in digitally encoded form. One would simply play the book through the home computer center and read it off the display. One need not go to the library to browse, of course, since that will be done by interrogating the library computer system or by perusing the latest acquisitions on TV. A more detailed description of such systems, and storage of books, will be given in a later section.

By the late 1980s television manufacturers will probably include a computer as part of the television set. It is rumored that in 1979 home computers will be announced by Texas Instruments and by Atari (an electronic game manufacturer). By 1981 home computers will be an established consumer item ranging in price from $500 on up.

Several other developments must be mentioned here. First, automated checkout or point-of-sale systems are well established in the retail sales business. This same concept can be applied to libraries to automate discharges. It simply requires a universal book code (UBC) system similar to the universal product code system used in grocery stores. Of course, it is possible that one need never actually go to the library in the future. Users would use their universal charge card, an idea already well into the serious discussion stages by the banking industry. This card would be used for everything: check cashing, bill paying, grocery purchases, travel, buying clothes, and checking out library books.

Second, relatively inexpensive language translation is now possible. Both Craig Corp. and Lexicon Corp. now market language translators for about $200.[21] These can translate words and simple sentences from one language to another. The languages of translation can be changed by replacing a plug-in cartridge (memory chip). At present, these operate only in a text input/output mode, but voice output should be possible in two years.

Finally, voice output is now possible at reasonable cost. Texas Instruments marketed a toy called "Speak and Spell" for Christmas in 1978 which had a 200-word vocabulary. The toy pronounces a word and the child must spell it correctly. Again, plug-in modules can be used to change the vocabulary.

Thus, terminals with rudimentary speech output in several languages are possible by the mid-1980s. Speech input is more difficult and will probably be available in the late 1980s and then only in primitive form.

Data Communications

The present communications situation in the United States is extremely confusing because the government is heavily involved in regulation of this industry and is unable to decide what to do. As a result, it is difficult to predict what might happen since political rather than technological reasons may control its destiny. There are two types of communications which impact the computer business: the television broadcasting industry and information transmission companies. It is important to realize the fundamental difference here. Broadcasting involves one source sending the same information to everyone. Information transmission companies (voice and/or data) allow a single source to send information to a single destination, although a broadcasting type of operation is possible.

The former is the less complex and involves the broadcasting by television networks and stations of digital information which can be received on television sets (which will soon be part of home computers). Two developments require mention here: Teletext or Viewdata and cable television. The idea behind Teletext or Viewdata is to transmit textual information simultaneously with ordinary programming. A special decoder in a television set allows this textual information to be displayed on the screen. Many pages of data can be transmitted and the user can select the page to be viewed. The format is usually twenty lines of text with forty characters per line. Such a system has operated in Britain and France on a trial basis for some time and is now being tried in the United States. Cable TV can do this and more since more information can be transmitted over the cable. In either case, such information as weather, travel advisories and stock market reports have been carried, and it is just as possible to list all of the latest acquisitions of the local library. Since home computers will be able to read and store this data in the late 1980s, it would be possible, for example, to transmit the local paper to everyone during the night so that it would be available for reading in the morning.

The other important area of communications is the voice and data transmission business. Briefly, the situation is as follows. The United States has an excellent telephone system which was set up to transmit voice. In 1956 the telephone companies agreed not to get into the computing business. (As hard as it is to imagine now, the fear was that the fledgling computer industry would not survive.) As a result, the telephone system never started "thinking digital" and made no move to serve the needs of computers "talking" to computers, i.e., data transmission. Computers require transmission 10,000 times faster than that for voice. As a result, independent companies were allowed to begin operation to serve the rapidly growing need for data transmission. This meant that the telephone company was missing out on a potentially more lucrative market than voice communications. To compound the matter, the world's largest computer company, IBM, entered the data communications business while the world's largest communications company, AT&T, was left with their agreement not to offer any computing services. In the meantime, AT&T has belatedly decided to become involved in data communications in a big way. They will probably offer terminals as well as data transmission services (processing). They can ill afford to wait for the government to make up its mind. This simple explanation doesn't do justice to the complexity of the issue. It is clear to most people that this vigorous industry probably no longer requires extensive government regulation or protection.

An all-digital "telephone" system would allow digital transmission into and out of every home. This is a very expensive proposition because much of the present system would have to be changed. A digital system would allow voice, facsimile, television and data transmission with almost equal ease. The announced contenders in the satellite data transmission sweepstakes, and the services they intend to offer, are summarized in Table 3.

The Advanced Communications System (ACS) is AT&T's new, all-encompassing data service which will compete directly with SBS and XTEN. Because of another agreement, the telephone companies do not own satellites. They use the services of the Communication Satellite Corp. AT&T expects to have 137,000 ACS business customers by 1983. SBS is aiming at large corporate customers and expects to provide 200,000 two-way voice circuits by 1985.[22] XTEN will also serve business. AT&T is not happy about the offering of voice services by others. The following kinds of services have been discussed:

TABLE 3. SUMMARY OF COMPANIES PLANNING
SERVICES FOR SATELLITE DATA TRANSMISSION

Company	Planned Service
American Satellite Corp. (uses Western Union & RCA satellites)	Data
AT&T (ACS service)	Voice/data/facsimile
Communication Satellite Corp. and Comsat General (a subsidiary; provide service to AT&T and GTE)	Voice/data
Intelsat (international)	Voice/data
RCA American Communications Inc. (satellite service)	Voice/data/cable TV
Satellite Business Systems (SBS) 1980 (IBM, Comsat, Aetna Insurance)	Voice/data/TV
Telesat Canada	Voice/data/TV
Western Union (Westar)	Voice/data/TV
Xerox (XTEN system)	All data services

Source: Hindin, Harvey J. "Transmitting Data by Satellite Calls for Special Signal Handling," *Electronics* 52:91-98, March 29, 1979.

1. direct TV broadcasting;
2. video conferencing;
3. video phone;
4. high-speed computer links;
5. high-speed facsimile transmission of documents and pictures;
6. vehicular communications between individual ships, aircraft, etc.;
7. tele-mail: post office to post office by facsimile;
8. tele-medicine: consultation and transfer of records;
9. tele-reference: a central reference service;
10. tele-shopping: selecting merchandise via TV with automatic billing; and
11. tele-education: TV classes.

The plans to transmit electronic mail have also drawn the postal service into the fray. It is projected that by 1985 low-cost facsimile transmission will be available at a transmission rate of two seconds per page.

For the most part, these systems simply provide an information transmission service and do not offer any information processing. AT&T has not been clear on this point, however, and may offer some processing services. As a result of these developments, it is quite likely that in the 1980s we will see the establishment of a two-way data transmission link in every home, either by cable television, the phone company, or both. To be really useful, this link needs to be designed for high-speed transmission. That opens up the possibility of electronic mail, newspapers and the other things mentioned above. For this to happen, much of the land-based system must be capable of handling higher-speed transmission. This transition has already begun with the increasing use of optical transmission of data over glass fibers. The eventual extension of high-speed links into the home will make it possible to browse in the library at home and, once a selection is made, have it transmitted to the home computer system where it would be stored to be read whenever desired. Because communication costs are apt to be high, it is not yet clear whether it will be cost-effective to transmit a book such as *Hawaii* to one's home, or whether it would be better to pick it up (on disk) at the library. Another problem is the large amount of *writable* storage that would be needed at home. The discussion in the next section illustrates that low-cost disk storage will make the storage of documents in machine-readable form a reality.

Memory and Storage

Computer memory can be classified in a number of different ways. We have already made the distinction between R/W memory, which can be read and written at will, and ROM or read-only memory, which can only be read after it is initially written. R/W memory can be further classified as random access memory (RAM) or as serial access memory (SAM). Random access memories are built up from a large number of very dense semiconductor memory chips and have the additional feature of access time that is quite short. The access time is the time that elapses between the request for data and the data's availability. On the other hand, in serial access memory, the data is stored in sequence and to get to the desired information one must usually pass by a good deal of data that is not needed. Thus, the access time for SAM is longer. SAM is usually provided by magnetic disk and magnetic tape. Because of the way in which RAM and SAM are implemented, RAM is more expensive than SAM but SAM has a much higher capacity than RAM. These are well-known tradeoffs and are illustrated in Figures 4 and 5. Figure 4 shows how various types of memory vary in cost as a function of the access time. The costs shown are for the early 1980s. The current costs are up to a factor of ten higher than those shown. Figure 5 shows how the capacity of different types of memory varies with access time.

Both figures demonstrate what has become known as the "access gap," the region between approximately 1 microsecond (millionth of a second) and 1 millisecond (thousandth of a second). In this region there has traditionally been no appropriate technology with which to implement

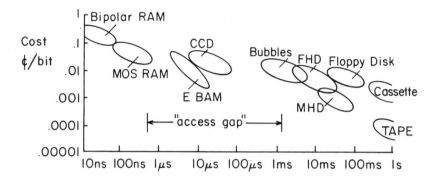

FIGURE 4. MEMORY COST VS. ACCESS TIME

Source: Hindin, Harvey J. "Communications," *Electronics* 51:178-87, Oct. 26, 1978.

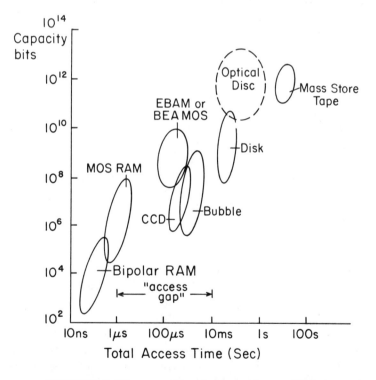

FIGURE 5. MEMORY CAPACITY VS. ACCESS TIME

Source: Lennemann, Eckart. "Tape Libraries with Automatic Reel Transport." *In* Walter E. Proebster, ed. *Digital Memory and Storage.* West Germany, Friedrich Vieweg & Sohn, Verlagesellschaft, 1978, pp. 65-78.

memories. In the last five years, however, several contenders have appeared and these are shown in the figures. Basically, the following memory technologies are shown:

1. semiconductor memory: bipolar and MOS (metal oxide semiconductor) RAM;
2. gap fillers: electron beam accessed memory (EBAM; also called BEAMOS for beam accessed MOS), and charge coupled device (CCD);
3. magnetic disk: fixed head disk (FHD), moving head disk (MHD), and floppy disk (flexible disk);
4. magnetic tape: cassette (about ¼ inch), standard computer tape (½ inch), and mass tape; and
5. optical disk: video and optical digital disk.

There is insufficient space here to discuss all of these in detail, so emphasis will be placed on the first and last. Before that, however, a few brief, general comments are in order. It is desirable to have a computer's processor operate as fast as possible in order to accomplish as much as possible. The processor must obtain its data and instructions directly from its memory, so the memory must also be fast. Thus, semiconductor memory is used directly by the processor. To do useful processing, a lot of semiconductor memory is needed, making the inexpensive, large-capacity, fast semiconductor RAM very important. The "gap fillers" are relatively new and by no means established. Brief mention will be made of their status. Magnetic disk and magnetic tape technologies are old and well established, and will also only be mentioned briefly. Optical disk technology has finally arrived and has profound implications for society, and libraries in particular. Because of this, some emphasis will be given to this subject.

RAM

Random access memory is fast read/write memory which is used in large quantities by computers. Currently, it is always semiconductor memory of which there are two types—bipolar and MOS. These will not be discussed here, save for the observation that the most dramatic changes in density (bits per unit of chip area) and cost have been for the MOS type. It is the decreasing cost and increasing density of semiconductor RAM chips which, along with the development of powerful microprocessors, is making the computer for everyman a reality.

In the last decade the speed and reliability of semiconductor RAM has increased by an order of magnitude. At the same time, the size, power and cost have all dropped by a factor varying from 100 to 1000.[23] In 1978 the cost per bit was 0.08 cent. In 1983 it is projected to be 0.02 cent. Thus, one can purchase four times as much for the same price. This dramatic change in cost per bit over the years is shown in Figure 6. The cost is projected into the 1980s.

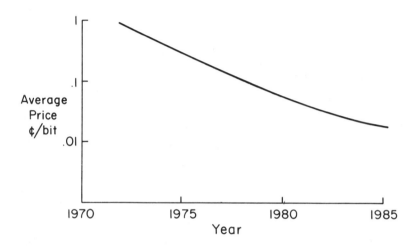

FIGURE 6. Semiconductor RAM Price Projection

Roughly speaking, memory chip costs drop by 50 percent every three years. The major reason for this dramatic cost change is the rapidly increasing capacity of a single chip of semiconductor RAM. Figure 7 shows the change in capacity with time. Again, roughly speaking, memory chips quadruple in capacity every two years. Most of this increased capacity has been achieved through higher density on the chips, not by using larger chips. The chip capacity is projected to be 1 million bits by 1985, or 1000 times more than in 1971. However, it is projected that the chip will be only twice as large in area.[24] The projection for the number of devices (transistors) per chip is given in Table 4. The projections for the mid-1980s are made on the assumption that the memory will be based on the charge coupled device (CCD) technology. At the present time one company is developing a chip with 1,000,000 transistors.[25] It is not a memory, but rather a solid-state imager which could be used in television cameras.

While cost has been decreasing and capacity increasing, two other important changes have also taken place: access time and power consumption have both decreased. There are very few analogous events in history. The result is that by 1987 one will be able to obtain twenty-seven times as much memory per dollar as in 1978.[26] If a new technology (based on Josephson junctions) being pursued by IBM proves feasible, the speed of both logic and memory could increase by a factor of 100-1000 by the mid- to late 1990s.[27]

TABLE 4. PROJECTION OF NUMBER
OF DEVICES PER CHIP

Year	Capacity (kbits)*	Number of Transistors per Chip	Access Time (ns)†
1977	65	100,000	100
1981	256	300,000	50
1985	2,000-4,000	400,000	?

*thousand bits
†billionths of a second

Source: Moore, Gordon. "VLSI: Some Fundamental Challenges," *IEEE Spectrum* 16:30-37, April 1979; and Allan, Roger. "VLSI: Scoping Its Future," *IEEE Spectrum* 16:30-37, April 1979.

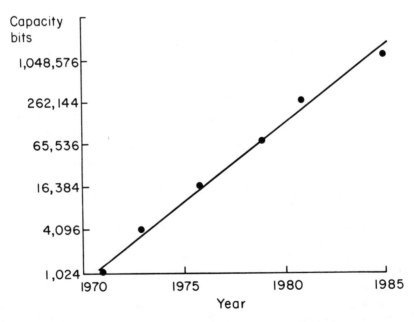

FIGURE 7. MEMORY CHIP CAPACITY VS. YEAR

Bubbles

Magnetic bubble devices have been in development for ten years and are now an accepted form of serial access-type memory. The present capacity is around 10^6 bits on a single chip. The projected access time and capacity for these devices are summarized in Table 5. It is possible that bubble devices will begin to replace magnetic disks by 1985, but that is uncertain.[28] At present, bubble devices are priced at about 0.1 cent per bit but should drop by a factor of five or so in the 1980s.

Charge Coupled Devices

Charge coupled devices have been in development for about eight years and have not yet had any major impact on computer memory usage. CCDs have been successfully designed and built, but RAM technology has kept pace in capacity and price so there has been no market for these devices. However, it will be difficult for RAMs to become much larger and, thus, CCDs will become important. In principle, CCDs have a higher density. A projection for access time and capacity of CCDs is given in Table 6. At present, CCD prices are around 0.1 cent per bit.

EBAM/BEAMOS

EBAM devices also fall in the access gap. They have large capacity and fast access. An EBAM system with a capacity of 10^9 (one billion) bits and an access time of 80 microseconds has been announced for 1980.[29] Each storage unit in the system can store 128 million bits, or 128×10^6 bits. Plans are under way to develop a device which can store four times that much, or 512×10^6 bits, and it is felt that by the mid-1980s a single device can be developed with a capacity of 10^{10} bits and an access time of 20 microseconds.[30] This is not an easy technology to use and it remains to be seen whether it can compete on a cost basis with memories such as the optical disks.

Disk and Tape

Magnetic disk technology is already highly developed and little can be expected in terms of major increases in capacity. Costs are projected to drop, as shown in Figure 4. The same is true for ordinary magnetic tape. There is one development in the use of tape that should be mentioned, the "mass tape stores." These are automated tape systems in which many tapes are arranged in pigeon holes; a mechanism automatically retrieves and mounts the tape so that it can be used. The tapes in these systems are wound on drums much like old-time phonograph records. Examples of such systems are the IBM 3850 with 378×10^{10} bits, and the CDC 38500 with 512×10^9 bits.[31] Tape cassette systems have also been developed which can store 400×10^6 bits.

TABLE 5. PROJECTION OF ACCESS
TIME AND CAPACITY OF BUBBLE
MEMORY DEVICES

Year	Capacity (kbits)	Access Time (ms)
1977	100	3
1980	256	1.5
1985	1000	1

Source: Capece, Raymond P. "Memories," *Electronics* 51:126-32, Oct. 26, 1978; Toombs, Dean. "An Update: CCD and Bubble Memories," *IEEE Spectrum* 15:22-30, April 1978; and _____. "CCD and Bubble Memories: System Implications," *IEEE Spectrum* 15:37, May 1978.

TABLE 6. PROJECTION OF ACCESS
TIME AND CAPACITY FOR CHARGE
COUPLED DEVICES

Year	Capacity (kbits)	Access Time (ms)
1977	65	100
1979	256	100
1982	1000	100
1987	4000	100-400

Source: Capece, Raymond P. "Memories," *Electronics* 51:126-32, Oct. 26, 1978; Toombs, Dean. "An Update: CCD and Bubble Memories," *IEEE Spectrum* 15:22-39, April 1978; and _____. "CCD and Bubble Memories: System Implications," *IEEE Spectrum* 15:36-39, May 1978.

Optical Disks

The optical disk has the potential to bring about revolutionary changes in consumer electronics, computers, education and libraries. It is the highest-density and lowest-cost form of storage yet developed. There are two basic approaches to recording on these disks: an analog method which yields a color television picture, and a digital method which yields data as digital bits. These disks are about the size of ordinary long-playing phonograph records. The analog type is often called an optical video disk since it provides a video or television signal compatible with color television. At present, the video disks are prerecorded whereas the digital disks can be written. Once written, however, the disks are read-only since the writing is permanent. Both types will be discussed here because either, or a combination of the two, would be very useful for document storage.

Video Disks

There have actually been two approaches attempted for producing the analog-type video disks—an optical method, and a nonoptical, mechanical approach.[32] In the mechanical approach, the disk works very much like a phonograph record in that a stylus traverses a very narrow groove (1.4 micrometers). This "pickup" detects the signal by means of a capacitance variation. The disk rotates at 450, 900 or 1800rpm depending on the system, and contains from thirty minutes to an hour of color television programming per side. A price of $10-20 per disk is projected. This stylus-type player is being developed by RCA and the Japan Victor Co.

The other approach is optical and seems to be the better one. RCA is apparently developing an optical version also,[33] as is the Philips Corp. of the Netherlands and various subsidiaries. This disk, too, is the size of a long-playing phonograph record, but the readout is by means of a tiny, solid-state laser diode. There is no physical contact with the disk, so it is easy to implement both random access to any picture and stop-motion. In addition, the lack of physical contact means that there is no wear. There is one TV picture per revolution of the disk and up to one hour of programming per side. In total, a single disk contains about 54,000 color television pictures. Unlike the RCA system, this one has actually been test marketed in the United States under the name Magnavision by the Magnavox Co., a subsidiary of Philips. The system was developed jointly by Philips and MCA, a corporation which distributes motion pictures, among other things. Players and disks were sold in Atlanta in fall 1978. The players cost $695 and were made by Universal Pioneer Corp. of Japan. The disks are manufactured by Philips/MCA Discovision which through MCA has access to movies from Universal Studios, Paramount and Walt Disney. The disks sell for $15.95 (for such recent films as *Animal House* and *Saturday Night Fever*), $9.95 (for older films, such as Marx Brothers' and TV movies), down to $5.95 for the lowest-cost ones. At present, the disks are rigid like phonograph records but they may be made in flexible form in the future and sold rolled up in a tube.

Pioneer Electronics Corp., a U.S. subsidiary of Universal Pioneer, is marketing an industrial version player also. This unit has slow motion, fast motion, stop action, playback and remote control. It also contains a built-in microcomputer to make the system interactive and can be interfaced to external digital electronic systems. Its price is $2500. The Army, Navy, Air Force, MIT and Utah State University have already placed orders. General Motors has ordered 7000 players to be used by dealers in North America. The "programs" will contain descriptions of new autos and training programs for mechanics and sales personnel. It would also be possible to use disks for parts inventories much as microfiche is used now. The digital version may be better suited for that, however.

Optical Digital Disk

Again, both RCA and Philips have been the major developers of the optical digital disk. In this case the RCA approach is similar to Philips's. The disks can be written once, and this can be done by the user. By employing a laser diode to burn away a thin metallic film which has previously been evaporated on the plastic disk, holes are created. The holes, about 1 micrometer in size, signify a bit which is a one, and no hole indicates a bit which is a zero. The capacity of these disks is 10^{10}-10^{11} bits each. The data can be read from them at rates of 50-200 million bits per second. Philips has built a working prototype and expects systems to be available in two to three years.[34] The characteristics of the Philips DRAW (Direct Read After Write) System are as follows:

1. 30 cm. disk (12"),
2. 10^{10} bits,
3. writes at 10 million bits per second,
4. average access time is 250 ms. at present, and
5. disk turns at 150rpm (2.5 revolutions per second).[35]

To appreciate how significant this development is, consider the capacity of one unit of high-density magnetic storage in constrast to that of the optical disk (capacity is indicated in millions of bits):

1. tape: 728
2. disk: 560
3. optical disk: 10,000

Of course, the optical disk cannot be erased and reused as can the others, although simple duplication, with changes, onto a new disk is possible. The digital disk has about one-sixth the bit density of the optical video disk since error control and formatting are not needed on the latter.

The projected cost for the disk is $10, or 10^{-7} cents per bit! Presently, the bit density is a factor of ten higher than the best magnetic recording. Current research is aimed at achieving 10^{11} bits with a data rate of 50 million bits per second and an access time of less than 100 ms. Based on what has been achieved to date, an optical disk system can be built which can store 2×10^{14} bits in six square meters of floor space (10^{11} bits per disk is assumed). Then 10^{15} bits could be stored in a 30-meter-square room (10^{10} bits is enough to store 500,000 typewritten pages). Assuming that an average book contains 500 pages, each disk (in current use) can hold 1000 books. The University of Illinois Library contains 5,622,938 "volumes." Again assuming an average volume of 500 pages, 5623 present-day disks are required. Only 563 would be needed for the 10^{11} bit disks, since each of these would hold 10,000 books. This means that only a 2-meter square area of floorspace is required to store the entire library. On the other hand, if one wished to plan for future expansion and used the 30-meter-square area that holds 10^{15} bits, there would be room for another 94,370,000 volumes to be stored before a library addition would be needed! Of course, the volumes would have to be recorded. Once in a readable form, the entire library could be copied onto new disks in a few months, working 8-hour days.

The impact that optical disks could have is obvious from the above figures. They can be used for books, journals and all manner of educational materials, from fix-it instructions to academic texts. They could also be used for computer programs, quadraphonic records, games and movies with 4-channel sound from the "movie-of-the-month club." They are an almost ideal archival storage medium. At present, the shelf life is at least ten years and probably much more. This is in contrast to magnetic-type memory which must be rewritten every three to four years. The morning newspaper could come on a disk. Subscribers to magazines could get a copy of *every* magazine published each month. Academicians could receive *all* journals and simply read those they wished to. Library patrons could check out disks, or perhaps they would simply have one made containing the books they wanted. At $10 per 10,000 books, that's only 0.1 cent per book plus the recording charge. It is assumed, of course, that publishers will supply books in disk form—perhaps an updated disk each year. Of course, they probably won't send a disk but will simply transmit new books, as they are published, to libraries for recording. One book can be "read" in 0.2 seconds and sent to a home recorder. Thus, one could simply browse through the card catalog using the home computer system and, having selected the desired volume, have the book sent over a high-speed link to the home recorder. After storing it, one could curl up next to the fire with the flat panel display and read, referring occasionally to the full-color pictures from the book displayed on the computer's color television screen.

Summary

The ever-increasing complexity and lower cost of integrated circuit and computer technology will radically change our lives in the next twenty years. The availability of low-cost computing and storage will make computers available and economical for everyone, whether in business, industry or the home. What we now call "microcomputers" will become as powerful as present-day large computers, but will sell for under $1000. Large central data banks will be formed as repositories of information. High-speed digital communications links will be readily available by way of satellite transmission in space and optical fibers on the ground. Digital communications will be brought into the home via the telephone system or cable TV or both. This will allow the user to call the central data banks using the home computer system. The home computer system will have color TV, voice output, limited voice input, possibly a facsimile printer, and an associated flat panel character (book) display. Libraries will evolve toward becoming just one of many data banks. Optical disk storage will provide a solution to the document storage problem. Users will be able to browse through the library or shop from the home computer center. Books can be selected, transmitted to the user and stored locally, and then read using the book display. Banking and financial transactions will also be handled this way. Almost every device in the home that does anything will be electronically controlled. Newspapers and bulk mail will come over the computer system. Magazines will arrive on disk or be transmitted and recorded on the home disk under control of the computer system.

REFERENCES

1. Hogan, C. Lester. "WESCON Keynote Address," *Progress: The Fairchild Journal of Semiconductors* 6:3-5, Sept./Oct. 1978.

2. Ibid.

3. Ibid.; and Triebwasser, Sol. "Impact of Semiconductor Microelectronics." In *Computer Technology: Status, Limits, Alternatives (Digest of Papers, COMPCON Spring '78)*. New York, Institute of Electrical and Electronics Engineers, 1978, pp. 176-77.

4. Keyes, Robert W. "Physical Limits on Computer Devices." In *Computer Technology...*, op. cit., pp. 294-96.

5. Ibid.

6. Caswell, Hollis L., et al. "Basic Technology," *Computer* 11:10-19, Sept. 1978.

7. Triebwasser, op. cit.

8. Verhofstadt, Peter W. "VLSI and Microcomputers." In *Computer Technology...*, op. cit., pp. 10-12.

9. Moore, Gordon. "VLSI: Some Fundamental Challenges," *IEEE Spectrum* 16:30-37, April 1979; and Allan, Roger. "VLSI: Scoping Its Future," *IEEE Spectrum* 16:30-37, April 1979.

10. Triebwasser, op. cit.; and Gossen, Richard N. "100,000+ Gates on a Chip—Mastering the Minutia. l. 64-kbit RAM—Prelude to VLSI," *IEEE Spectrum* 16:42-44, March 1979; and Heilmeier, George H. "100,000+ Gates on a Chip:

Mastering the Minutia. 2. Needed—Miracle Slice for VLSI Fabrication," *IEEE Spectrum* 16:45-47, March 1979.

11. Shima, Masatoshi. "Two Versions of 16-bit Chip Span Microprocessor, Minicomputer Needs," *Electronics* 51:81-88, Dec. 21, 1978.

12. "The Microprocessor: A Revolution for Growth," *Business Week* 26:42B-42X, March 19, 1979.

13. Ibid.

14. Ibid.

15. Yencharis, Len. "Technology Survey Predicts Big Jump for Computer Hardware and Software," *Electronic Design* 27:40, 51, March 29, 1979.

16. Turn, Rein. "Computers in the 1980s—and Beyond." In *Computer Technology...*, op. cit., pp. 297-300.

17. Apfelbaum, Henry, et al. "Computer System Organization: Problems of the 1980's," *Computer* 11:20-28, Sept. 1978.

18. Shima, op. cit.

19. Caswell, et al., op. cit.

20. Gossen, op. cit.

21. Caswell, Hollis L., et al. "Now, an Electronic Translator," *Business Week* 25:42D-42E, Dec. 25, 1978.

22. Hindin, Harvey J. "Communications," *Electronics* 51:178-87, Oct. 26, 1978.

23. Spencer, Ralph F., Jr. "VLSI and Minicomputers." In *Computer Technology...*, op. cit., pp. 13-25.

24. Gossen, op. cit.

25. Moore, op. cit.

26. Caswell, et al., "Basic Technology," op. cit.

27. Turn, op. cit.

28. Yencharis, op. cit.

29. Mhatre, Girish. "Electron Beam Accessed Memory Expected by 1980," *Electronic Engineering Times*, p. 37, Nov. 13, 1978.

30. Smith, D.O. "Electron Beam Accessed Memory," In *Computer Technology...*, op. cit., pp. 167-69.

31. Lennemann, Eckart. "Tape Libraries with Automatic Reel Transport." *In* Walter E. Proebster, ed. *Digital Memory and Storage.* West Germany, Friedrich Vieweg & Sohn, Verlagesellschaft, 1978, pp. 65-76.

32. "Stylus Glides Over Grooveless Videodisk," *Electronics* 51:67-68, Oct. 26, 1978; "Videodisks for 1979: A Trio Rushes the Market," *Optical Spectra* 13:14, March 1979; "RCA Finally Commits to Marketing its Laserless Player of Videodisks," *Laser Focus* 15:20, 22, March 1979; and " 'Industrial' Laser Player of Videodisks will be Offered in Summer by MCA," *Laser Focus* 15:22, 24, March 1979.

33. Kenville, Richard F. "Optical Video Disc for Digital Mass Memory Applications." In *Computer Technology...*, op. cit., pp. 170-72.

34. "RCA Finally Commits..," op. cit.; " 'Industrial' Laser Player...," op. cit.; Kenville, op. cit.; Kennedy, George C., et al. "Optical Disk Replaces 25 Mag. Tapes," *IEEE Spectrum* 16:33-38, Feb. 1979; "Optical Disks Point to Future Data Systems," *Optical Spectra* 12:26-29, Dec. 1978; and Belmon, H.C. "Diode Laser Recorder Gives 10^{10} User Bits per 12" Disk," Apelboorn, The Netherlands, Philips Data Systems, Nov. 1978. (Press release.)

35. Kennedy, op. cit.; "Optical Disks Point...," op. cit.; and Belmon, op. cit.

F. WILFRID LANCASTER
Professor
Graduate School of Library Science
University of Illinois
at Urbana-Champaign

LAURA S. DRASGOW and ELLEN B. MARKS
Research Associates
Graduate School of Library Science
University of Illinois
at Urbana-Champaign

The Role of the Library in an Electronic Society

In 1978 the Library Research Center of the University of Illinois Graduate School of Library Science was awarded a grant by the National Science Foundation to investigate the impact of a paperless society on the research library of the future. The basic premise underlying our ongoing research is that many types of publications can be distributed more effectively in electronic form and that, in fact, future economic factors will dictate that they be distributed electronically. Within the long history of human communication, the print-on-paper era will prove to be a short one: a period of little more than 500 years. Clearly, we are evolving out of this paper-based era into one that is electronic. We are presently in a transitional phase in the natural evolution from paper to electronic communication. This transitional phase appears to have three major characteristics: (1) the computer is presently used to print on paper, (2) printed data bases exist side by side with their machine-readable counterparts, and (3) new data bases are emerging only in electronic form. By and large, machine-readable data bases have not yet replaced print-on-paper data bases, but this will undoubtedly occur quite soon.

Full transition will occur when the communication structure is adequate to allow electronic distribution to a large part of the audience that needs to be reached (it has been estimated that there will be around 100 million terminals in the United States by 1995), and when the on-line market is large enough to support the costs of data base construction. It is clear that the market *is* there. We will soon reach the time when the electronic revenues exceed the revenues derivable from the print market.

Problems of the Present System

To understand the reasons for this evolution we need only look at the problems that exist in the ways and means now used to distribute information.[1] The three most basic problems at present are: (1) the enormous growth of the information produced, (2) the escalating costs, and (3) the general inefficiency of current processes of production and distribution.

Obviously, as knowledge itself grows, the literature of science, social science and the humanities must also grow to keep up with new research and thinking. The real problem in information distribution is one of packaging. How can we "package" and distribute the results of scientific research, for example, in the most effective and efficient way possible? The growth problem in publication is multidimensional: there is continual rapid growth in the *number* of packages available, in the *size* of the packages available, and in the *diversity of forms* in which information is distributed.

The most obvious example of the increase in the number of packages is, of course, the science journal. In the 1660s there were two journals providing information to the scientific community. Now the best available estimate indicates there are 50,000 science journals worldwide, and that this number is increasing at a rate of about 4 percent a year compound growth.

The size of the individual packages is increasing as well. The *Physical Review*, for example, published less than 2 million words in 1937. By 1968 that same journal was publishing 22 million words a year. *Biochimica et Biophysica Acta* is now doubling in size in 4.6 years.[2] The body of literature published by the American Institute of Physics doubles every eight years.[3]

Growth is even more dramatic in the secondary literature, which obviously must grow to keep pace with the primary literature. It took *Chemical Abstracts* thirty-two years to publish its first million abstracts. However, the latest million abstracts, the fifth million, took only 3.3 years to be published. *Chemical Abstracts* is currently publishing at the rate of approximately 400,000 abstracts per year (i.e., a million abstracts in 2.5 years). It is apparent that soon *Chemical Abstracts* may be faced with the task of publishing 1 million abstracts a year. When this occurs, very few institutions will be able to afford a version printed on paper. *Chemical Abstracts*, of course, is not the only secondary publication struggling to make a vast body of literature available.

Publishing costs are skyrocketing. Inflation in the publishing industry is grossly out of step with inflation in the economy as a whole. In a period in which the general rate of inflation (as measured by the Consumer Price Index) was 40 percent, some secondary publications increased 850 percent in price.[4] The cost of the *Bibliography of Agriculture* has gone from $10 in 1963 to $245 in 1978-79. In the same period, *Biological Abstracts* rose from $225 to $1300 and *Psychological Abstracts* from $24 to $315 (a 1475 percent increase in fifteen years)!

These figures illustrate some very cold facts. Unless the average salary paid to a psychologist, biologist or agricultural scientist has increased upwards of 850 percent in the last ten to fifteen years, or unless the budget of a library has increased tenfold in this 15-year span, these publications become increasingly less accessible in printed form. In the extreme example, a subscription to *Chemical Abstracts* in 1940 cost $12 a year ($6 a year for American Chemical Society members); now in 1979 it costs $4200. The meaning of these figures is clear. These publications began as services to meet the needs of, and be used by, individual subscribers. They were once quite accessible to the individual chemist, psychologist, agriculturist, and so on. But secondary publications have priced themselves out of the individual market and even beyond the resources of many smaller institutions. Not only are they now an "institutional phenomenon," but they tend to be accessible only in the larger and wealthier institutions. This decline in the accessibility of printed secondary literature can only continue. Information will become increasingly less accessible as long as we continue to print, publish and distribute in the same way we have been for the last 300 years.

And it is not just the secondary literature that is doomed to inaccessibility; the same beast preys on the primary literature. The problem is explicit if we look at average subscription costs for libraries. The average subscription price in the United States for a journal in chemistry and physics was approximately $24.48 in 1967-69; the average subscription price for a journal in chemistry and physics in 1978 was $108.22. In education, journal costs rose from $6.34 to $19.49 in the same period, and in business the rise was from $7.54 to $21.09.

Even these average price increases are grossly out of line with the general rate of inflation in the economy. And if we look at extremes (e.g., *Inorganica Chimica Acta* cost $24 a year in 1970 but now costs approximately $640) the outlook appears more bleak still. Clearly, there is no future in this economic picture, no future in an enterprise whose costs are increasing so much faster than those elsewhere in the economy. But growth and costs are not the only problems. As the literature grows, it becomes increasingly scattered and, consequently, it becomes increasingly hard to find, increasingly hard to keep abreast of, increasingly hard to identify through an indexing or abstracting service in a particular subject field, increasingly difficult to collect in a library specializing in the field... and so on.

The growth in science itself leads to more people having more things to say and therefore writing more. Delays in the distribution of information increase because large numbers of authors are competing for publication space that is limited and costly. Often this limitation is artificial, created by publishers to keep their escalating costs somewhat within bounds. So, a substantial number of papers submitted are rejected, not on grounds of quality, but because the publisher simply cannot afford to print them. Thus, a deserving author may have his article rejected by one or more journals before it is finally accepted and published. This results in considerable delays in publication and distribution, a situation which appears inevitable in our present dissemination system.

What all this portends is that the primary literature of science is headed in the same direction as the secondary literature—becoming more and more a purely institutional phenomenon, with the number of individual subscribers declining relative to the institutional subscribers year by year. In fact, many of the more expensive science journals have not a single individual subscriber.

The fact is that the science journal, in its present form, is an inefficient dissemination mechanism. As Herschman has pointed out, the science journal tries to serve three distinct purposes:

1. *social function:* It is an effective way for authors to earn academic "brownie" points.
2. *archival function:* Libraries collect issues, bind them and preserve them, thus providing a good archival record of the history of science.
3. *dissemination function:* It is an inefficient way of packaging and distributing information.[5]

The science journal seems to serve the author better than it serves the reader because much of what a subscriber pays for is often irrelevant to his interest, the distribution mechanism is costly and wasteful, and the printed journal lags far behind the "cutting edge" of science research.

The journal is inefficient because much of its contents are irrelevant to any one user or reader and because much of what the reader pays for he or she already knows about! Typically, a published paper reports results of research completed eighteen months to two years prior to publication, and that research was probably begun three to four years prior to publication. Most probably the author whose work is described in a current journal has moved on to another, new research project. In no way can the science journal be considered a reflection of what is happening in science today. At best, it is reporting on what happened in science in the immediate past. The science journal is more archival than current, and of course the secondary services that index and abstract these journals are even more archival.

Looking further into the economic picture, we see that libraries are in a very bad economic situation because they represent labor-intensive activities heavily dependent on other labor-intensive activities (publishing) for their resources and raw materials. Neither libraries nor publishers, up to the present, have benefited significantly from automation in the way that certain other industries (e.g., the rubber and plastics industries) have. Data from Purdue University on sixty-two major U.S. research libraries show that these libraries' budgets increased 133 percent during 1966-75, but the money they had available for materials purchases only increased by 89.7 percent, the difference being largely accounted for by the increase in personnel costs. These libraries actually purchased only 35 percent more materials in 1975 than in 1966; the difference between the 35 percent and the 89.7 percent due to the sharp increase in the cost of materials.[6]

There is no future in this economic situation either, in which budgets are doubling approximately every seven years, but purchasing power in terms of new materials is increasing by only 35 percent. The future lies, quite clearly, in increasing automation; and not only increasing automation of certain selected processes. We have that already. It doesn't simply mean automation of circulation procedures in the library. It means automation *throughout the entire communications cycle* by which the results of research in science, social science and the humanities are distributed. In the next decade, manual processing costs are expected to increase by a minimum of 6 percent per year, whereas communications costs are expected to decline at an annual rate of 11 percent, computer logic costs at approximately 25 percent per year and, most dramatically, computer memory costs at 40 percent per year. Even if it were not economically feasible to distribute information electronically at present (in fact, one can show that it is already economically attractive to replace print-on-paper with electronic distribution[7]), it is clear that the future lies with electronic distribution.

Advantages of Electronic Distribution

The advantages of electronic distribution of information are obvious and some have already been achieved through machine-readable data bases and on-line access. These advantages are:

1. *increasing accessibility:* It is probably true that just as information is getting less accessible and more costly in printed paper copy, it is getting more accessible and less expensive in on-line, machine-readable form.
2. *decreasing cost:* The cost of access to information in electronic form is rapidly decreasing.

3. *transformed economic picture:* New alternatives arise with electronic information distribution. Before on-line access became a reality, a large capital investment was required to make a data base accessible. To make *Chemical Abstracts* available in printed form requires a capital investment of $4200, excluding costs of storage and handling. Clearly, if only forty-two searches a year are performed in *Chemical Abstracts* the cost *in data base access alone* is $100 per search. But with electronic distribution the economic picture is completely changed. Printed materials need no longer sit on library shelves to be accessible. We can access them *when we want them, on demand.* In other words, information distribution is changing to an on-demand, pay-as-you-go situation. A client can access when he or she needs to and pay for only as much as he or she uses. This completely transforms the economic picture of information distribution and operation of information services.

4. *emergence of new forms:* Electronic forms not dreamed of ten years ago have been developed. One such form is the "electrobook," a hand-held microprocessor closely resembling a pocket calculator.

5. *more rapid dissemination:* Information is more quickly disseminated when the print phase is skipped entirely.

6. *more effective access:* We can afford many more access points and use more complex search patterns and strategies than with print-on-paper formats.

7. *new capabilities:* Electronic publishing can incorporate analog models, three-dimensional representations, and other "razzle-dazzle" features impossible in printed forms. Electronic publishing can be dynamic whereas print on paper is static.

The Role of the Library

The purpose of our present National Science Foundation study is to investigate, at least in a preliminary way, what may be the effects on libraries and librarians of the predicted transition from a print-on-paper to a paperless society. The investigation is being conducted by means of: (1) a detailed review of the relevant literature, (2) a Delphi study in which forecasts relating to the future of publishing are being collected, and (3) the development of a scenario to depict what libraries and librarians may be doing in 2001.

The Delphi study, in two rounds, is being conducted with representative samples of librarians, publishers and "technologists." The questionnaire (see Appendix I for a specimen page) seeks the informed opinion of this group on the probability that selected events relating to electronic publishing will be technologically and economically feasible, and will actually have occurred by certain dates. Also, opinions on the desirability of the events were solicited. The first round of the study has been completed and the results tabulated. In the second round, the group forecasts for each event (see Figure 1) were sent back to each participant, with an indication of his or her position relative to the group as a whole. In addition, comments of participants in the first round (see Appendix II) were sent out to all participants. We hope, of course, that the results of the second round will produce a greater consensus of opinion than those of the first. The results of the Delphi study, the scenario, and our interpretation of both will form the backbone of our report to the National Science Foundation.

The scenario was developed and refined as follows:

1. Group or individual interviews were conducted with senior staff members of the University of Illinois Library at Urbana-Champaign. The interviews were largely unstructured and were designed to determine what changes would be likely to occur in the functions/responsibilities of these librarians if certain predicted changes in the publication/distribution of information come to pass. Discussions were stimulated by such questions as, "If *x* were to occur, what effect would this have on your own professional activities?"

2. A first draft of a scenario was developed as a result of these interviews.

3. The first draft was circulated, for review and criticism, to the deans and directors of all accredited library schools, to one-half of the directors of the member libraries of the Association of Research Libraries (the other half was invited to participate in the Delphi study), and to selected librarians in industry. On the basis of feedback from this group, a second draft was prepared.

4. The second draft scenario was distributed to all participants at the 1979 Clinic on Library Applications of Data Processing, and was also published in the journal *Collection Management*, with a request for input from the profession at large.[8]

Presented here is the second-draft scenario. It is set in the year 2001 and looks back at the developments of the preceding twenty-five years.

The Scenario

Looking back from the vantage point of this, the first year of the twenty-first century, it is clear that the library profession has not escaped the upheaval that has beset all segments of society in the past twenty-five years. Indeed, it has undergone changes that, in their own way, are as

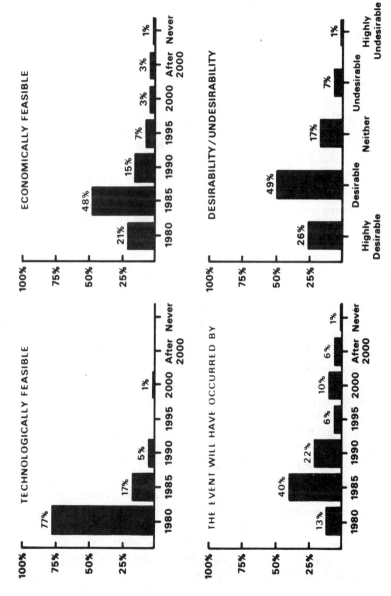

FOR THE FIRST TIME THE PUBLISHER OF AN EXISTING REFERENCE BOOK DISCONTINUES ITS PUBLICATION AS PRINT ON PAPER AND REPLACES IT WITH A MACHINE-READABLE FILE OF COMPARABLE SCOPE

FIGURE 1.

dramatic as those encountered in education, in medicine, in banking, in transportation, and in many other branches of commerce and industry. It would have been impossible for the profession to resist this change, even had it wanted to, in the face of the rapid developments that have affected the publishing industry and transformed the entire process by which information products are created, distributed and paid for.

It is in special libraries, particularly those in industry, that the change has been most pronounced, but academic libraries also look much different than they did in the 1970s, and even public libraries have not escaped the process of change.

While developments affecting the information professions have been numerous and diverse in the last three decades, two major trends can be recognized as predominating. The first is simply the rapid decline of the *artifact*—particularly the printed book—as the primary device for storage and transmittal of recorded knowledge, and the replacement of these artifacts with *data,* derived from many sources and presented in many different formats, virtually all of these data now being accessible electronically.[9]

The second trend, a natural concomitant of the first, has been increasing diversification in the profession. This diversification can be thought of in terms of the "deinstitutionalization" or, perhaps more accurately, the "reinstitutionalization" of many information professionals. It seems undeniable to claim that, while the library as a collection of artifacts has declined substantially in importance in the past twenty years, the information specialist has grown considerably in stature, in recognition and in rate of compensation. This development has occurred primarily as a result of the deinstitutionalization/reinstitutionalization process. Although firms of "information consultants" and even "freelance librarians" existed much earlier, it was the 1980s before it became widely recognized and accepted that information specialists no longer needed to function within the four walls of a library—that computer terminals, in effect, gave these professionals access to vast electronic "libraries," whether they chose to work within a formal institutional environment, a private office, or from their homes. In the 1980s, then, we witnessed a veritable boom in employment opportunities for qualified information specialists outside the traditional library setting: as members of health care teams; in legal practices; as resource personnel at various levels of national, state and local government; as members of research and development teams in academia and in industry, and so on. At the same time, the rapidly increasing demand for information services led to the formation, throughout North America and Western Europe, of many new companies of information consultants. In the years since 1980 the composition of the information profession has gradually changed to the present point at which the number of individuals providing information service who are not library-affiliated exceeds the number who are so affiliated.

To understand the differences between librarians and other information specialists today and those of, say, 1975, it is necessary to look at the changes that have taken place in the publishing industry, in the way in which information products are distributed and used, and in libraries themselves within the last quarter of the twentieth century.

The Publishing Industry Since 1975

The roots of what has become known as the "electronic age" in publishing can be traced back to the early 1960s when computers were first used to drive photocomposition devices. This led to a period of transition in which computers were essentially used as devices to print indexing and abstracting publications, magazines and journals, certain types of reference books, catalog cards, and so on.

The so-called secondary publications, especially those in the sciences, were at the forefront of this development. It was not long before the machine-readable data bases generated through this publishing operation were used in computerized literature searching activities, both retrospective searching on demand and selective dissemination of information (SDI). In the 1960s such services were largely performed by using computers in an off-line, batch-processing mode. Search strategies for many different information needs were put into machine-readable form and matched against data bases in a complete batch, the results being printed out and delivered to the requesters. So-called scientific information dissemination centers emerged in this period. Through licensing agreements with data base producers, such centers were able to offer SDI and retrospective search services from many different data bases, and the volume of use generated by these centers kept cost per search or per user interest profile down to acceptable levels. SDI service, in particular, was an economical application of computers even in the 1960s, though retrospective searching was still quite expensive. In fact, a retrospective search over five years of some data bases could cost as much as a whole year of SDI service from the same data bases.

It was not until the 1970s that a significant switch from off-line to on-line access occurred. The on-line retailers of information, such an integral part of information provision today, emerged in the 1970s, although in those days there were only three or four major centers of this kind. The move to on-line processing greatly increased the accessibility of data bases and substantially decreased the cost of searching them. Cost reduction was dramatic in this period. In the early 1960s a realistic cost for the conduct of a single retrospective search by computer (if the full costs of data base preparation were distributed over the various services provided) was several hundred dollars. Through on-line access the cost for the same search in 1978 had dropped to perhaps $10.

It was in the 1970s too that telecommunications networks, to support data processing activities, emerged. The early networks were those of the Tymshare Corporation and the Telenet Corporation. Before the end of the 1970s these networks, which were based on analog communication (voice-grade telephone lines), had spread to Canada, Central America and Western Europe. It was not until the 1980s that the worldwide satellite networks, based on digital transmission, emerged. In the 1970s it was an extremely expensive proposition to search a data base located on a computer in, for instance, Los Angeles, from Rio de Janeiro or Sydney, for this required a voice-grade telephone connection for the duration of the search. Now, of course, the cost of the link between Sydney and Los Angeles is only marginally greater than the cost of the digital link between New York and Los Angeles.

The period 1960-80 can be regarded as one of transition from print-on-paper to electronic publication. This transitional period had three major characteristics:

1. computers were used to print on paper and the resulting product was distributed, in a completely conventional manner, through the mail;
2. printed data bases and their machine-readable equivalents existed side by side but, by and large, the former had not been replaced by the latter (before the end of the 1970s, however, a handful of secondary data bases had completely converted from printed to electronic form); and
3. new data bases emerged in machine-readable form only, without ever existing in paper form. (The majority of these were actually *data banks*—files of numerical, statistical, physical, chemical and commercial data—which essentially could be regarded as types of "reference books" that emerged in the electronic era. Some, however, were data bases of bibliographic references such as the Information Bank of the New York Times and ABI/INFORM, a data base of business information.)

Up until the end of the 1970s, on-line access was very largely restricted to secondary data bases. Reference retrieval had greatly outstripped document delivery, which was still based almost entirely on paper and microform copy distributed through the mail. While some journals were photocomposed in the 1970s, thus leading to the creation of machine-readable files of complete text, very little use was made of these primary data bases in machine-readable form and none could be accessed on-line. A notable exception to this general pattern was the field of law, for the full text of substantial bodies of legal material was accessible on-line as early as the late 1960s.

Before the end of the 1970s, however, new forms of publications began to emerge. In 1978, for example, the first periodical commenced publication in cassette form. This was a popular "magazine" of instructional and recreational materials designed to be used with an early version of a home computer. In the same year the first self-contained electronic "book" appeared. The forefather of our present electrobooks, this was a bilingual dictionary, in the form of a hand-held minicomputer, with interchangeable modules covering various pairs of languages. In 1978, however, an electrobook cost considerably more than an equivalent book in print-on-paper form. The first one, in fact, cost over $200, which, at the present time, has the equivalent purchasing power of about $1500!

In the 1970s there were no real on-line journals apart from one or two experimental and rather informal journals existing within computer conferencing and other types of networks.

Electronic publication of primary literature lagged some years behind electronic publication of secondary literature and followed the same general pattern of development. The text of several primary journals, all in the sciences, became accessible through on-line service centers early in the 1980s. By the end of this decade, a majority of the North American journals of a research nature in the sciences and social sciences could be accessed on-line. A substantial level of on-line access to humanities journals and to journals produced outside of North America did not occur until the 1990s.

The 1980s was a decade of remarkable progress in publishing; it was also a period of great turmoil for the publishing industry and for the library profession at large. Secondary publications began to disappear in printed form as terminals became commonplace and storage and access costs continued to decline. New "reference books" emerged, both in the form of electrobooks and data banks accessible on-line. Many existing reference books were converted from print-on-paper to electronic form in the 1980s, including data handbooks, dictionaries, directories, bibliographies and concordances—a development that continued throughout the 1990s.

By the late 1980s, some printed journals began to disappear, to be replaced by on-line access to text and by journals issued on tape cassettes, videodisks and other electronic forms. This transformation, substantially achieved for the sciences and social sciences by 1995, was forced on the publishing industry by several factors:

1. *costs of print-on-paper publication that continued to escalate at rates far beyond general inflation in the economy:* All but the largest circulation

journals in the sciences had begun to price themselves beyond the resources of the individual subscriber by 1980. By 1985 they had substantially priced themselves out of the individual subscriber market entirely and many had priced themselves beyond the resources of the smaller institutions.

2. *competition from newer journals that began their existence in electronic form:* These journals, which were becoming economically viable by the mid-1980s, were beginning to reveal signs of social acceptance, and were offering modes of presenting information (e.g., electronic analogs of equipment and dynamic displays of research data) that were completely impractical in the print-on-paper journals. Only in the handling of high-quality photographic material could the print-on-paper journals offer substantial advantages over the electronic journals, a situation that had altered radically by 1990.

3. *the emergence, by 1985, of a pay-as-you-go, on-demand society:* The market for information products had begun to change dramatically. The market for many types of printed products was declining rapidly but, to compensate, a vast market was emerging—one of individuals and institutions willing to pay for on-line access to the electronic equivalents of these publications when the need arose. Publishers of data bases in dual (printed and machine-readable) form were deriving less than 20 percent of their income from on-line access royalties in 1978. Some of these publishers had reached the 50 percent level by 1985. By the end of the 1980s the market for secondary publications in printed form had dwindled to an insignificant level in the developed world and only the developing countries, still lagging technologically despite great progress, were expressing need for printed formats. By this time, however, the great cost of the printed versions was making this mode of distribution completely unprofitable and on-line access was subsidizing the printed forms. The same phenomenon, delayed by some years, was beginning to be felt by primary publishers before the end of the 1980s. By 1995, of course, print on paper had virtually disappeared for all secondary publications, for much of the primary literature of the sciences and social sciences, and for many types of reference works.

4. *developments in other segments of society which created demand for access to literature though on-line facilities or in other electronic forms:* In the 1970s there occurred many developments that were to become essential components of present electronic communication systems. Computer conferencing, the paperless office and electronic transmission of mail were all in their infancy in the 1970s. By the late 1980s, these various separate developments had been brought together into integrated systems. When scientists, attorneys, physicians and other profes-

sionals began to receive much of their mail at terminals, and also to communicate with colleagues through the same networks, demand for access to literature in the electronic mode increased considerably.

It was in the 1980s that on-line access to the text of technical reports, patents, standards and specifications first occurred.

The Publication Situation Today

In 2001, of course, publication in print-on-paper forms is the exception rather than the rule. While a few high-circulation journals have been able to retain their printed form, most of the research literature (whether in the sciences, social sciences or humanities) exists only in electronic versions. Some journals are issued on electronic media for use with domestic television receivers or home computers; these journals can also be accessed through the network of on-line service centers. There is little doubt that the explosive growth of the home computer market has made a significant contribution to the social acceptance of electronic publication. Most journals, together with files of technical reports, patents, standards and specifications, can only be accessed on-line. Patents, standards and specifications can still be obtained in paper or microform, but most of the use is now on-line. Technical reports are available in microform but rarely in paper form; again most of the use is through on-line access. All secondary data bases (including the national bibliographies of all the developed countries) exist only in machine-readable form, accessible through on-line terminals.

For popular magazines, fiction, other works of imagination, and recreational materials in general, print on paper has been replaced much less extensively. While attempts have been made to publish such literature in electronic form, no significant market has yet developed. The great cost of publication on paper, however, including the escalating costs of distribution through "conventional" mail service, has caused a very drastic reduction in the number of magazines available and new titles of fiction and other recreational works are now published in numbers that are only a fraction of those released annually some twenty years ago. It is just not economically feasible to sustain a print-on-paper publication unless an extremely large market can be reasonably assured; thus, the present situation of few new titles but massive print runs on each. The recent emergence of completely portable electronic readers may stimulate the market for popular reading in electronic form. The market for fiction and other imaginative works in audio form is also growing.

The substantial move toward electronic media in education has virtually eliminated the "textbook," even at the elementary level, and the on-demand news services offered through television and through several of the on-line networks have decimated the ranks of printed newspapers. A few regional papers remain but increasing production costs and declining sales put the future of these in grave doubt.

"Reference books" are rapidly disappearing in print-on-paper form. The last English language encyclopedia to be published in paper form appeared some eight years ago and it is very unlikely that we will see another such publication. Many "pocket" reference books, such as monolingual and bilingual dictionaries and handbooks of engineering and scientific data, have been replaced by electrobooks. More extensive data bases—full-scale dictionaries, encyclopedias, directories, concordances, biographical dictionaries and similar tools—are available on-line. The contents of most of the electrobooks can also be accessed on-line.

Electronic reference tools offer many advantages over the print-on-paper tools. Many are updated on a continuous basis, which is especially valuable for directory-type information. The search capabilities are also very much greater because many more access points can be provided economically. To quote but one example, biographical files can be searched not only on names or parts of names but on biographical details of the subjects covered, such as profession, education, dates of birth and death, place of birth, titles of works written, and so on. It is a simple matter to identify, for example, the names of novelists born in Stoke on Trent, or born in September 1933.

Electronic publishing has produced reference works that would not have been economically viable in print-on-paper form. A good example can be seen in the concordances that now cover complete groups of poets. It has also allowed the publication of reference tools with capabilities far beyond those possible with print on paper. In particular, electronic analog models of equipment and other devices are now commonplace in encyclopedia-type data bases.

A potential obstacle to the transition from print-on-paper to electronic publication, stressed by many early skeptics, actually proved to work in favor of the electronic medium rather than against it. Communications networks, especially those providing "on-demand" services to the home, proved to be extremely effective channels for the advertising of many types of products and services. Loss of advertising revenue to the publishers of printed journals, as advertisers switched to electronic media, was an additional incentive to these publishers to convert to an electronic mode of distribution.

Influence on Information-Seeking Behavior

Computer-based information systems were well received in the 1960s and 1970s by many scientists and social scientists and by the legal and medical professions. They were also well accepted by the majority of librarians. In the 1970s most on-line searches were mediated searches conducted by librarians or other information specialists on behalf of the ultimate users. By 1985, however, the wider accessibility of terminals, together with the greatly increased demand for on-line searches, which was beginning to exceed the capacities of libraries and information centers, had produced a change in this pattern of use—more and more scientists, social scientists and other professionals were using on-line systems directly. At least, they were conducting their own searches in those data bases they had most need for and had become most familiar with. They still tended, as they do today, to go to the information specialists for searches in less familiar areas or in less familiar data bases. Unmediated on-line searches, of course, became increasingly feasible with the emergence of more user-oriented searching software, especially those software packages permitting interrogation of data bases in sentence form.

Data banks and electrobooks, when these began to replace printed reference books, were well received. Even in the humanities the reception was more cordial than might have been expected. One reason was simply the realization that computer facilities made possible the production of reference aids (e.g., rather comprehensive concordances and detailed indexes to older historical and literary materials) that would not have been economically viable in print-on-paper versions. Also, the great power of the computer in linguistic studies and in textual analysis had become widely recognized. Scholars in the humanities recognized the benefits that could be derived from computer processing facilities and, in general, were quite receptive to new bibliographic and other tools as they became accessible on-line.

On-line journals were received cautiously. The first successful electronic journals were those introduced to serve communities that were considered most likely to be receptive to this medium. These communities included computer programmers and other segments of the computer industry, information science, medical electronics and electronics in general. Electronic journals also emerged rapidly in highly specialized fields, especially interdisciplinary research areas, where the community to be reached was too small to support a journal in printed form. Many of these electronic journals arose out of specialized conferences set up within computer conferencing networks. The majority of these journals, from the beginning, imposed editorial and refereeing standards roughly comparable to those of reputable journals in the print medium. After an initial "teething" period they were well accepted, becoming cited in other journals (both electronic and paper) and, somewhat later, indexed by the major services. As acceptance occurred, and it was recognized that a paper published in a machine data base having a high standard of peer review carried as much "weight" (for purposes of promotion, tenure and salary review) as one accepted by a "conventional" journal, it became increasingly easy to attract high-quality contributions. The speed with which contributions could be reviewed and published, and the new reporting capabilities afforded by the electronic medium, were major factors leading to a switch of allegiance from paper to electronics on the part of many authors.

The first electronic journals were introduced by new publishing entities. The traditional publishing industry was (predictably) antagonistic to the newer competitors and was itself reluctant to change. Conversion of existing journals to electronic formats was forced on the industry, however, as the electronic journals gained in strength and acceptance. Not only were the conventional journals losing authors to their electronic competitors, they were also losing subscribers through their own escalating costs. The most expensive of the science journals were the first to convert but a more widespread and rapid conversion began toward the end of the 1980s.

Paradoxically, although the research community was quite willing to accept new journals and new tools in electronic form, it was highly resistant to the disappearance of the familiar printed journals. It was only in the past decade that the inevitability of this conversion process was accepted. A major reason for the change in attitude has simply been the emergence of a new generation of scientists and professionals in other fields, a generation that has grown up with on-line systems, especially as a result of the widespread use of such systems in education.

The completely integrated approach to information handling that we now know, while it had its origin in the 1970s, has really only reached full implementation in the last ten years. In science, commerce and most other fields, professionals now receive much of their mail electronically. SDI services direct to their attention citations or abstracts of new publications (articles, reports, patents). Such notifications form one category of message that is awaiting the user when he or she logs onto a network, the other major category being notifications of mail. The text of the majority of sources referred to by the SDI services can be directly accessed on-line. Although some individuals still insist on making hard-copy prints, personal electronic files have virtually replaced paper document files. Almost all commercial and professional correspondence is now handled through on-line processing and the majority of offices are now paperless. Computer conferencing is widely accepted and more and more individuals find it convenient to work from their homes, only visiting their parent offices at irregular intervals.

A major use of on-line systems is simply to provide an electronic "work-space" which can be used as an informal notebook and for the composition of reports. The versatility and simplicity of current text-editing systems has made on-line composition of reports virtually universal. Communication among authors, editors and referees is handled entirely in an on-line mode. Publications are more "dynamic" now than they were in the past. The speed with which research results can be reported has led to the wide recognition and acceptance of the "transience" of publications. It has become very common for investigators to publish the results of a research project as a series of progress reports, each one essentially replacing its predecessor. This trend has been facilitated by the changes in reporting itself brought about by the electronic medium, which places much greater emphasis on tabular, diagrammatic and other concise representations than on narrative text. The typical electronic journal most closely resembles the "brief communication" or "letters" journal of the print-on-paper environment.

Terminals in offices and homes are used to search for information as well as to receive information, compose reports, build and index files, and communicate with other individuals. Searches extend from personal files to files of parent institutions and out into the universe of available resources in machine-readable form. On-line directories and referral centers identify sources (personal as well as data base sources) having the greatest likelihood of satisfying particular information needs.

The majority of individuals in all fields now conduct their own searches, at least in those data bases that are most familiar to them. The low cost of on-line access to many data bases, coupled with the emergence of an international standard query language and the capability for natural language interrogation in sentence form in most networks, makes direct, unmediated searching the mode of access preferred by the majority. For the less familiar data bases, on the other hand, there is a strong tendency to delegate the search to an information specialist. Directories of these, indexed by subject or data base expertise, can be accessed on-line through several of the existing networks. Communication between information specialist and customer is generally on-line, the results of the searcher's efforts being transmitted directly to the customer's terminal. The work of these information specialists, both those with library affiliations and those without, is discussed in the next two sections of this report.

The Role of the Research Library

The decades from 1980 to the present have been decades of remarkable change in libraries. The period of transition from a largely paper-based society to a largely paperless one was also one of considerable trauma in the profession. The rapid emergence of more and more machine-readable data bases (both primary and secondary) in the 1980s coincided with a period of wholesale conversion from card catalogs to on-line catalogs, especially in academic libraries. Gradually it became recognized that the catalog of a library could no longer be restricted to coverage of items physically present within the walls of the institution. Since an increasing number of sources were not purchased outright, but were accessed on-line as the need arose, it no longer made sense to retain this artificial distinction. By the middle of the 1980s, several of the on-line catalogs were including entries for data bases frequently accessed on behalf of users. The justification was simply that if a data base was readily accessible to users, it was quite immaterial whether it was physically present in the library (as paper, microform, disk, tape, electrobook or some other electronic form) or accessible through on-line connection.

The inclusion of entries for data bases not actually "owned" paved the way for the development of our present multisource catalogs. These catalogs, now virtually universal in academic, special and all but the smallest of public libraries, include entries for all materials held by the network or networks that a particular library belongs to. In addition, they include entries for all externally accessible data bases, primary and secondary, that any member library chooses to include. While entries for "physically owned" items still exceed entries for externally accessible sources, especially in those networks incorporating large academic libraries (which still have substantial quantities of older printed materials), the ratio is gradually changing as more and more sources become accessible only through on-line connection.

The emphasis in cataloging has changed in the electronic medium. The concept of a "main entry" has disappeared, since an entry can be accessed by many different approaches, including complete or partial names of authors (personal or corporate), editors and publishers, complete or partial titles, or any combination of these. Descriptive cataloging of North American materials is now entirely centralized, through cooperation between the Library of Congress and the publishing industry, and descriptive entries become available for network use at the same time that a data base becomes accessible to on-line users or at the time that a printed, tape, disk, microform, electrobook, or other publication is released for sale.

Subject cataloging has increased in importance since electronic catalogs make it economically feasible to provide multiple access points. While library networks maintain cataloging staff to augment the limited subject access approaches provided by the Library of Congress, and to catalog materials added by network members that have not been covered by the Library of Congress, catalog departments have disappeared in all but the larger academic and public libraries. Even in the very large libraries these departments have rapidly dwindled in size in the past twenty years. The

principal functions performed by these staffs are cataloging of local interest materials, cataloging of printed materials from foreign sources, and
augmentation of subject access points for materials of special interest.

On-line catalogs, of course, include entries for materials in all forms:
printed, microform, tape, disk, electrobook, on-line data bases and other
electronic forms.

The dwindling of cataloging in individual libraries is part of the
larger dwindling away of technical services in general. Since libraries are
now acquiring much less material of their own, the acquisition activity is
of much smaller volume than it was twenty years ago, and binding in
academic libraries is now mostly restricted to older materials of historical
interest.

While libraries have declined as institutions, and library technical
services in particular have dwindled, remaining library activities are
highly service-oriented. A better understanding of the present situation in
libraries can be gained from a brief review of developments since 1980.

Academic and special libraries were generally highly receptive to
on-line services providing access to secondary data bases when these were
introduced in the 1970s, but it was not until the 1980s that the on-line
services began to impact seriously the sales of their printed equivalents,
and libraries began widespread cancellation of printed subscriptions in
favor of on-line access on demand. This, of course, was a major contributor
to the market shift from printed to machine-readable forms.

Library attitudes toward other data bases and electronic forms were
mixed. Electrobooks were ignored at first, or looked at with considerable
suspicion. When it became evident that these forms were "here to stay" and
that they are in fact a legitimate and useful form of publication, libraries
began to acquire them along with other forms.

Because libraries in the 1980s were already using on-line secondary
data bases extensively, they were not slow to make use of other on-line data
bases as they became available, including the data banks that began to
replace conventional printed reference books; data bases of patents, laws,
standards and specifications; data bases of technical reports; new electronic
journals; and the on-line versions of these journals still available in paper
form. Again, it was the widespread shift from printed journal subscriptions to on-line access to equivalent data bases that led to the subsequent
demise of the printed versions of many titles. By the beginning of the 1990s,
the wide accessibility of text on-line had caused a very considerable reduction in interlibrary loan traffic. Now interlibrary lending is largely restricted to the older books and journals.

Libraries were slower in adopting journals released in the form of tape
cassettes, videodisk and other electronic forms largely because of the capi-

tal investment required in providing an adequate number of minicomputers to make these accessible to library users. Those libraries that did make substantial investments in equipment of this kind came to regret their haste as an increasing number of the journals released in these forms became accessible on-line through the various on-line retailers.

Beginning in the early 1980s, academic and many special libraries have followed a familiar pattern of development:

1. *an increasing portion of the budget allocated to purchase of on-line access to information sources when needed, at the expense of outright purchase:* This move to on-demand, pay-as-you-go operation in libraries has had important cost-effectiveness advantages. It is no longer necessary to "second-guess" demand; libraries now avoid investing substantial sums in materials that are rarely if ever used. This is in direct contrast to the situation some twenty years ago when it was estimated at the University of Pittsburgh, for example, that about 40 percent of the materials acquired by its library received no use.

2. *drastic curtailment of physical growth:* As many fewer materials are acquired, special libraries and smaller academic libraries with active weeding programs have tended to shrink considerably.

3. *staff reduction accompanied by reductions in the size of the library:* Technical services have been practically eliminated but public service staffs have also dwindled as many of the more specialized information services have passed out of the hands of the library.

4. *departmental libraries in academic institutions begin to disappear:* As printed materials have declined in value, and become important mostly in various types of historical research, materials held in departmental libraries are being consolidated with the other collections of older materials.

5. *a partial dichotomy between those librarians that handle electronic information sources and those dealing with print and microform materials:* Most of the information service function has passed to the former although the latter group also perform reference activities on a lesser scale, especially in the humanities and in support of historical research.

6. *members of the professional staff of academic (as well as public and school) libraries tend to be generalists rather than specialists:* In contrast, the staff of industrial and governmental libraries, as well as information professionals not affiliated with libraries, tend to be subject specialists. The latter are likely to have master's degrees in a subject field, as well as a master's degree in information science, while the former are much less likely to have an advanced degree except in librarianship or information science.

It is the special libraries, especially those serving government agencies and industry, that differ most from those of 1980. These libraries now maintain only very small collections of print and microform materials, almost all of their activities being concerned with information service from data bases in electronic form. Librarians in industry have increased considerably in importance since they are likely to have control over indexing and retrieval operations involving the company's electronic mail and its own machine-readable files of technical reports, as well as providing information services from external sources.

The librarian of today has become essentially an information consultant. In the 1970s librarians were intermediaries between those needing information and the electronic files. In the 1980s, with the rapidly increasing availability of on-line terminals, many professionals began to conduct their own searches. They found themselves successful, however, only in those data bases that they used regularly. The explosion in the number and diversity of electronic data bases led to increased reliance on librarians as guides to what is available in machine-readable form and as exploiters of data bases and data banks unfamiliar to the scientist or other professional having need for information. When an individual needs information that cannot readily be found in his own files or other sources he is familiar with, he will frequently consult with an information specialist. This professional recommends appropriate information sources for the requester's own use or conducts a search on the requester's behalf.

In the academic environment, subject-oriented information specialists perform this function. In some academic organizations these specialists are members of the staff of the academic library, even though they may be permanently assigned to a particular academic department. In other insitutions, however, these specialists are completely divorced from the library as an institution. In these cases, the staff of the library itself is composed of information generalists rather than specialists and it is more oriented toward serving the needs of the undergraduate curriculum (both student and faculty needs) and of the administrative staff than it is to serving the needs of advanced teaching and research programs. Information professionals in academic institutions are primarily information consultants to faculty, staff and students. The same function is performed by information staff in industry and in government agencies. The information professional plays an important role in "interdisciplinary linking" by searching data bases in areas that are unfamiliar to users. Another important activity is to keep up to date with new data bases and to inform potential users of the existence of these tools.

The larger public libraries now provide similar services to those members of the community that have no access to academic or special libraries. In addition, they provide adequate terminal facilities to allow requesters to access data bases from the library itself, if they choose to do so. Besides providing books and other materials for recreation and study purposes, many public libraries have raised the level of their information service activities in the last decade. The ability of a public library to provide general question-answering service of a high quality has been considerably enhanced by the wide range of reliable and constantly updated electronic sources accessible to them and by the fact that most such libraries belong to reference service networks in which cooperating libraries maintain an on-line data base of answers and sources for "difficult" questions. A number of such networks are now linked so that a vast "growing encyclopedia" is accessible to even the smallest of institutions.

Many of the large and medium-sized public libraries have taken on important community information services, including the compilation and maintenance of community resource directories that can be accessed through domestic television receivers, as well as other terminal devices, and the organization and control of municipal or county records of all types. Some public libraries are also active in the provision of information service to small businesses in the community, although much of this type of service is now handled by information consulting companies, especially in the larger cities.

School libraries have been widely expanded into learning resource centers, providing access to a wide range of computer-aided instruction facilities and other learning materials in all formats. As in other types of libraries, the professional on the staff of a school library is an information consultant to the teaching staff and to students, and plays an important role in instructing students in the use of information resources. School libraries also provide extensive recreational materials in printed, audio and electronic forms.

Closely related to their role as information consultants is the function that professional librarians now perform in "user education." Beginning in the 1980s, librarians in academic and special libraries have been extremely active in instructing members of their user communities in how to exploit on-line resources effectively. The scope of the instruction encompasses search strategy, use of query languages, use of on-line resource directories, and general surveys of resources available. The instruction may be conducted on a one-to-one basis or through more formal workshops for groups. In the academic world it is now common for information professionals (on the staff of the academic library or school of information science) to present courses on information services and their exploitation within the various academic departments: physics resources for physicists, economics resources for economists, and so on.

The wide move to electronic communication has served to narrow the gap between the "information rich" and the "information poor" countries rather than widening it, as many were predicting a decade or so ago. Just as many developing countries moved rapidly from the age of the oxcart to that of jet aircraft, virtually skipping all the intermediate steps that occurred in the developed world, so many have moved smoothly into electronic information networks without having gone through a stage of well-developed traditional libraries. Satellite communication has served to make information sources more internationally accessible than ever before. The North American networks can communicate, and exchange information, with Euronet, Afronet and similar enterprises in other parts of the world, and international information programs organized by various agencies of the United Nations provide for free interchange of information between the developed and the developing worlds.

Information Professionals Outside the Library

As mentioned earlier, the most spectacular growth in the information profession has been the rapid increase in numbers of information professionals who are not affiliated with any library. This has led to some diversity in terminology. The term *librarian* has clung to those professionals who are clearly affiliated with a library, while those without such affiliation are more likely to be referred to as "information officers," "information consultants," or simply, "information specialists."

In the 1980s there was a short-lived boom in completely freelance information specialists, many working from their homes, but almost all of these have now been absorbed into information consulting companies or into "private practices" closely resembling the group practices that are also common in the health care and legal fields.[10]

While a few freelance librarians could be found in the 1970s (mostly in the large cities) the growth of private information practices has been phenomenal in the last fifteen years. It came about, of course, with the realization that a good reference librarian in the electronic age does not need to operate from a library. Indeed, the needs are not for extensive physical facilities but for a detailed knowledge of electronic information resources together with the terminals and expertise needed to exploit these resources effectively.

These professionals perform in much the same way as their counterparts in academic and special libraries. Although not so much concerned with education and training, they act as information consultants, helping to put those with information needs in touch with data bases or individuals likely to be able to satisfy these needs. Alternatively, they provide a complete service, searching available sources and delivering information, text or source references directly to requesters. These specialists also assist customers in developing suitable interest profiles for use with on-line SDI services.

Their customers are drawn mostly from small businesses and other institutions that lack their own information professionals. As well as providing information services, these information specialists will also consult with these organizations on their internal information problems, including the organization of internal files and the indexing of electronic mail.

Many such information specialists who restrict their activities to particular subject areas—medicine, engineering, economics, and so on—are generally well qualified in those areas, and command high rates of compensation. That information specialists tend now to have a higher level of subject expertise than their predecessors is due largely to the fact that their customers frequently expect them to deliver a precise answer to a research problem rather than merely point them to possible sources that might contain the answer to their question. As mentioned earlier, the information world is much less artifact-oriented and much more data-oriented than it was twenty years ago.

Another type of information specialist is the one who is a member of a research and development team in industry or academia and the one who, as a member of a health care facility, works directly with physicians in providing information as needed in patient care. These professionals, whose importance has now become widely recognized, are integral components of the teams they support, assuming complete responsiblity for providing all information, from whatever source, needed to facilitate the work of the group.

Professional Education

With so many changes taking place in information delivery, it is hardly surprising that education for the profession has also undergone a process of alteration in the last twenty years. All of the major library schools have become schools of information science. Education for professionals in public libraries and in school libraries has changed less than other aspects; it is a separate track in some schools, while others concentrate exclusively on the preparation of students for those branches of the profession. Most professionals working outside of libraries as well as those in academic and special libraries have master's degree in a subject area as well as one in information science.

The information science curriculum differs considerably from the library science curriculum of twenty years ago. Again, the deinstitutionalization process is very evident. "What goes on in a library" is no longer the principal focus of study. In leading schools the curriculum is much broader in scope: communication processes (formal and informal) in general, publication and dissemination processes, interpersonal communication, design and management of information services, factors affecting the effectiveness and cost-effectiveness of information services, indexing, vocabulary control, data base management, information resources and how to exploit these resources effectively ("search strategy" in the broadest sense of the term), and the evaluation of information services. The librarian of today needs to be thoroughly familiar with a wide range of communication activities, including electronic mail systems, computer conferencing, communications networks of all types, and word-processing and text-editing systems and equipment.

As previously mentioned, many schools of information science also offer "service" courses for other academic departments, an activity that has become a major function of several of the leading schools.

There is now great diversification in the employment opportunities open to graduates of schools of information science. They can find employment in special, academic, public or school libraries; in the headquarters of library networks; as information specialists in industry, law or health care; in publishing companies (both primary publishers and the publishers of indexing/abstracting services); in the on-line service centers, in information analysis centers, or as information specialists in group practices or the larger consulting companies.

The developments of the past twenty-five years have not, of course, been free of problems. The conversion to electronics created great economic stress in the publishing industry, particularly for publishers of periodicals who were faced not only with capital investment in new equipment but with a completely different income environment— payment on a "use" basis rather than a "front end" subscription income. This led to the demise of some publishers, the amalgamation of others, and many formal cooperative arrangements, especially the use of cooperative editorial processing centers.

The copyright laws were shown to be woefully inadequate in coping with the conversion from print-on-paper to electronic publishing, and it is only since 1995 that the copyright and royalty situtations have been settled to the apparent satisfaction of all parties concerned.

A specter raised repeatedly in the 1980s turned out to be less of a danger than predicted. The rapid spread of fee-based information consultants threatened to cause a wide rift between "information rich" and "information poor." It was feared that an "information elite," composed of those members of the community who could afford information services, would emerge. This situation did, in fact, exist for a number of years while the "fee versus free" controversy raged throughout the profession. This has largely settled itself as costs have declined and as public libraries and academic libraries came to recognize that information service from electronic sources is as legitimate a service to provide to their communities as the provision of printed materials. It is true, as it has always been, that the wealthier organizations and individuals can afford to purchase a higher level of subject expertise or a more rapid response in information services, but virtually no citizen of the United States is deprived of access to needed information through inability to pay for it. Fortunately, the electronic networks developed in the past twenty years have not created an information elite but have improved access to information for all segments of society.

ACKNOWLEDGMENT

This paper is drawn from research supported by the National Science Foundation, Division of Information Science and Technology (DSI-78-04768).

REFERENCES

1. Lancaster, Frederick W. *Toward Paperless Information Systems.* New York, Academic Press, 1978; and _____ "Whither Libraries?, or Wither Libraries," *College & Research Libraries* 39:345-57, Sept. 1978.

2. Sandoval, A.M., et al. "The Vehicles of the Results of Latin American Research: A Bibliometric Approach" (Paper presented at the 38th World Congress of the International Federation for Documentation, Mexico City, Sept. 27-Oct. 1, 1976).

3. Metzner, A.W.K. "Integrating Primary and Secondary Journals: A Model for the Immediate Future," *IEEE Transactions on Professional Communication* PC-16:84-91, 175-76, Sept. 1973.

4. Between 1963 and 1973, a period in which the Consumer Price Index rose about 40 percent, the subscription price of *Psychological Abstracts* and *Bibliography of Agriculture* rose 850 percent.

5. Herschman, Arthur. "The Primary Journal: Past, Present and Future," *Journal of Chemical Documentation* 10:37-42, Feb. 1970.

6. Drake, Miriam A. *Academic Research Libraries: A Study of Growth.* West Lafayette, Ind., Libraries and Audio-Visual Center, Purdue University, 1977.

7. *See, for example,* Roistacher, Richard C. "The Virtual Journal," *Computer Networks* 2:18-24, 1978; Folk, Hugh. "The Impact of Computers on Book and Journal Publication." *In* J.L. Divilbiss, ed. *Proceedings of the 1976 Clinic on Library Applications of Data Processing: The Economics of Library Automation.* Urbana, University of Illinois Graduate School of Library Science, 1977, pp. 72-82;

and Senders, John W. "An On-Line Scientific Journal," *The Information Scientist* 11:3-9, March 1977.

8. Lancaster, Frederick W., et al. "The Changing Face of the Library: A Look at Libraries and Librarians in the Year 2001," *Collection Management* 3:55-77, 1979.

9. We are indebted to Allen Veaner for first characterizing this trend in this particular way.

10. We are indebted to Estelle Brodman for this idea.

APPENDIX I

Specimen Page of Questionnaire

INDEXING AND ABSTRACTING SERVICES

4. 90% of all indexing and abstracting services are published *only* in electronic form.

    (a) The event could be *technologically feasible* by:

    1980   1985   1990   1995   2000   after 2000   never

    (b) The event could be *economically feasible* by:

    1980   1985   1990   1995   2000   after 2000   never

    (c) The event will have occurred by:

    1980   1985   1990   1995   2000   after 2000   never

    (d) This event is:

    very   desirable   neither desirable   undesirable   very
    desirable   nor undesirable   undesirable

    (e) Comments or justifications:

PERIODICAL LITERATURE

5. The first periodical to begin its life in electronic form will appear. It will not exist in print-on-paper form and it will never have existed earlier in print-on-paper form.

    (a) The event could be *technologically feasible by:*

    1980   1985   1990   1995   2000   after 2000   never

    (b) The event could be *economically feasible* by:

    1980   1985   1990   1995   2000   after 2000   never

    (c) The event will have occurred by:

    1980   1985   1990   1995   2000   after 2000   never

    (d) This event is:

    very   desirable   neither desirable   undesirable   very
    desirable   nor undesirable   undesirable

    (e) Comments or justifications:

SCIENCE AND TECHNOLOGY PERIODICALS

6. For the first time a periodical in science or technology begins to be available in machine-readable form as well as in paper-copy form.

    (a) The event could be *technologically feasible* by:

    1980   1985   1990   1995   2000   after 2000   never

    (b) The event could be *economically feasible* by:

    1980   1985   1990   1995   2000   after 2000   never

(c) The event will have occurred by:

1980   1985   1990   1995   2000   after 2000   never

(d) This event is:

very   desirable   neither desirable   undesirable   very
desirable   nor undesirable   undesirable

(e) Comments or justifications:

APPENDIX II

Comments or Justifications for Question 5

1. Periodicals may start on-line but hard-copy derivatives may follow.
2. More inclined to the belief that ongoing periodicals will take the plunge first.
3. See EIES at NJIT. +NEWS is a formal periodical. Difficult to browse at 30 char./sec.
4. Is being done now—if enough publishers did it, it could become feasible soon—but resistance is high! Lots of people will have terminals—will want it!
5. By your own definition (and mine) this type of publication would not be a periodical. May happen but needs new definition and role.
6. Very limited distribution; 100 to 500.
7. I believe *conversion* from paper to electronic form will be more significant than the indications.
8. CBS Evening News satisfies your definition now. Several in-house periodicals now exist entirely on-line (e.g., ?NEWS on DIALOG, similar feature on ARPANET). Bowker-Ramo Stock Quotation Service is on-line now and profitable.
9. Postage, paper, printing and labor costs will *force* things to go this direction.
10. Public libraries must have good terminals.
11. Message network related; could be home-computer related.
12. *The convenience of paper form is yet to be challenged.*
13. Some computer-related journal (ACM) might, since its users have access to needed technology.

CONTRIBUTORS

LAURA S. DRASGOW is an editor at Research Publications, Inc. in Woodbridge, Connecticut. She received an AB in history and an MS in library science, both from the University of Illinois at Urbana-Champaign. She has worked on a project of the university's Library Research Center to investigate the impact of paperless communication systems on libraries in the future. Her interest in this area continues.

MICHAEL GORMAN is Director of Technical Services and Professor of Library Administration at the University of Illinois at Urbana-Champaign. Past positions include Head of Bibliographic Standards Office of the British Library, Head of Cataloguing for the British National Bibliography, and Bibliographic Consultant for the British Library Planning Secretariat. He was coeditor of the second edition of *Anglo-American Cataloging Rules* and editor of the periodical *Catalogue and Index* during the period 1969-73.

SUSANNE HENDERSON is Librarian/Analyst, Systems Analysis Staff, Office of Central Reference of the CIA. She received an AB in mathematics from DePauw University and an MSLS from Case Western Reserve University. She previously served as librarian of the Denver Public Library. She is a member of ALA and ASIS.

STARR ROXANNE HILTZ is Associate Professor and Chairperson of the Department of Sociology and Anthropology at Upsala College, East Orange, New Jersey. She holds an AB degree from Vassar College and MA and Ph.D. degrees in sociology from Columbia University. Her interests and activities include sociology, computer science and communications, consulting and research. She has published one book and several papers and belongs to several professional organizations, including the American Association for the Advancement of Science, the International Communication Association and the Association for Computing Machinery.

ROBERT S. HOOPER is Chief of Systems Analysis Staff, Office of Central Reference of the CIA. He received a BS in physics from Seattle University, and graduate degrees in physics from the University of New Mexico and in management technology from American University. He was employed as an industrial engineer for Boeing and an engineer-physics for Sandia. He also served as information scientist for IBM, ITT and Sandia. He is the author of various papers related to information science.

WILLIAM J. KUBITZ is Associate Professor of Computer Science at the University of Illinois at Urbana-Champaign, where he received a BS in engineering physics, an MS in physics and a Ph.D. in electrical engineering. He has served as development engineer for the General Electric Company and is currently researching array design approaches for the implementation of logic and arithmetic functions in VLSI circuits. He is a member of the Association for Computing Machinery, the Institute of Electrical and Electronics Engineers and the Society for Information Display.

F. WILFRID LANCASTER is a fellow of the Library Association of Great Britain and graduate of Newcastle upon Tyne School of Librarianship. He has served as Information Systems Specialist for the National Library of Medicine, Director of Information Retrieval Services for Westat, Inc., and since 1972 Professor of Library Science at the University of Illinois at Urbana-Champaign. His fields of interest are information storage and retrieval, medical libraries and evaluation of library services. He is the author of five books and many reports and articles in the field of information science.

LEONARD G. LEVY is Manager of Advanced Systems at Combustion Engineering, Inc. at Stamford, Connecticut, where he is involved in using data processing and communications technology to improve administrative and managerial performance. His previous positions include Manager of Information Services at American Airlines, Consultant in Management Services at Touch, Ross and Co., and Director of Data Processing at St. Johnsburg Trucking Company. He earned his BA at the University of Pennsylvania and his MBA at the Wharton School of Finance and Commerce.

MARY S. MANDER is a visiting lecturer in the Department of Journalism at the University of Illinois at Urbana-Champaign, where she received her Ph.D. in communications.

ELLEN B. MARKS is a doctoral student at the University of Illinois at Urbana-Champaign. She recently served as Head of Development at the University of Cincinnati Medical Center Libraries. Her interests involve information-seeking strategies in libraries and research methodologies. She is currently investigating librarians' attitudes toward the future of libraries.

CAROLYN MARVIN is a lecturer for the Institute for Communications Research and the Department of Journalism at the University of

Illinois at Urbana-Champaign. She received an MA from the University of Texas at Austin as well as from the University of Sussex. She is currently completing her Ph.D. in communications at the University of Illinois and will be a Fulbright scholar next year.

DEREK DE SOLLA PRICE is Avalon Professor of the History of Science and curator of historic scientific instruments at Yale University. His degrees include a bachelor's in science and a Ph.D. in physics, both from the University of London, and a Ph.D. in the history of science from the University of Cambridge. He has held posts with such organizations as the National Science Foundation, the Smithsonian Institution and the National Endowment for the Humanities. He is the author of several books and approximately two hundred published papers.

RICHARD C. ROISTACHER is Research Associate for the Bureau of Social Science Research, Washington, D.C. His degrees include an MS in administrative sciences from Purdue University and a Ph.D. in psychology from the University of Michigan. His current research involves the use, interchange and archiving of large social data bases; the design of computer network-based scientific research groups; the social and organizational effects of computer networks; and social science data processing and analysis techniques. He is the author of a number of reports, papers and articles on information processing.

GERARD SALTON is Professor of Computer Science at Cornell University, Regional Editor of *Information Systems,* Associate Editor of *ACM Computing Surveys,* and a member of the advisory committee for the *Annual Review of Information Science and Technology.* He has also served as editor-in-chief of *ACM Communications* and *ACM Journal.* He received his MA in mathematics at Cornell University and his Ph.D. in applied mathematics at Harvard, and has given instruction at both universities. He has written three books and contributed more than twenty articles to various books and journals.

MURRAY TUROFF is Associate Professor of Computer Science and Director of the Computerized Conferencing and Communications Center at the New Jersey Institute of Technology at Newark. He earned his BA in mathematics and physics from the University of California, and his doctoral degree in physics at Brandeis University, Waltham, Massachusetts. Dr. Turoff has been widely published in the field of computerized conferencing and has worked with IBM, the Institute for Defense Analysis and the Office for Emergency Preparedness. He is a member of such professional organizations as the American Association for the Advancement of Science, the Association for Computing Machinery and the American Society for Information Science.

MARTHA E. WILLIAMS is Director of the Information Retrieval Research Laboratory and research professor at the Coordinated Science Laboratory of the College of Engineering, University of Illinois at Urbana-Champaign. Her previous positions include adjunct associate professor of science information at the Illinois Institute of Technology, and manager of information sciences and of the Computer Search Center of the IIT Research Institute. She is editor of the *Annual Review of Information Science and Technology*, U.S. editor of *Online Review*, contributing editor of the *Bulletin of the American Society for Information Science* and author or editor of well over one hundred scholarly books, articles and presentations.

ACRONYMS

ABI/INFORM—Abstracted Business Information
ACS—Advanced Communications System
A.D.—Anno Domini
ADSTAR—Automatic Document Storage and Retrieval
AFIPS—American Federation of Information Processing Societies
ALA—American Library Association
AOK—Automatic Organization of Knowledge
ANPA—American Newspaper Publishers Association
AP—Associated Press
ASIS—American Society for Information Science
ATMS—Automated Tracking and Monitoring System
ATOM—Automatic Transmission of Mail
AT&T—American Telephone & Telegraph
B.C.—Before Christ
BEAMOS—Beam Accessed Metal Oxide Semiconductor
BIOSIS—BioScience Information Service
BOOKS—Built-in Orderly Organized Knowledge System
BRS—Bibliographic Retrieval Services
CA—Chemical Abstracts
CACON—Chemical Abstracts Condensates
CAN/OLE—Canadian On-Line Enquiry
CAS—Chemical Abstracts Service
CASIA—Chemical Abstracts Subject Index Alert
CBS—Columbia Broadcasting System
CCD—Charge Coupled Device
CCS—Computerized Conferencing System
CDC—Control Data Corporation
C-E—Combustion Engineering
CIA—Central Intelligence Agency
CISTI—Canada Institute for Scientific and Technical Information
CMS—Computer Message System
COMPCON—Computer Conference
COMPENDEX—Computerized Engineering Index
CONIT—Connector for Networked Information Center
CPS—Characters Per Second
CRT—Cathode Ray Tube
DBI—Data Base Index
DBS—Data Base Selector
DIA—Defense Intelligence Agency
DIANE—Direct Information Access Network for Europe
DNA—Deoxyribonucleic Acid
DOCEX—Documents Expediting Project
DRAW—Direct Read After Write
EBAM—Electron Beam Accessed Memory
EIES—Electronic Information Exchange System
ENIAC—Electronic Numerical Integrator and Calculator
FCC—Federal Communications Commission
FHD—Fixed Head Disk

GNP—Gross National Product
GTE—General Telephone and Electronics
IBM—International Business Machines
ID—Identification
IEEE—Institute of Electrical and Electronics Engineers
IS&R—Information Storage & Retrieval
ITT—International Telephone & Telegraph
K-R—Knight-Ridder
LC—Library of Congress
LSI—Large-Scale Integrated
MAD—Machine-Assisted Dissemination
MEDLINE—Medical Literature Analysis and Retrieval On-line
MHD—Moving Head Disk
MIPS—Million Instructions per Second
MIT—Massachusetts Institute of Technology
MOS—Metal Oxide Semiconductor
MTS—Michigan Terminal System
NJIT—New Jersey Institute of Technology
NOS—Network Operating System
NSF—National Science Foundation
NTIS—National Technical Information Service
OCLC—Ohio College Library Center
OCR—Optical Character Reader
ORBIT—On-line Retrieval of Bibliographic Information Time-shared
RAM—Random Access Memory
RCA—Radio Corporation of America
RECON—Remote Console System
ROM—Read-Only Memory
RSM—Rapid Search Machine
SAFE—Support for the Analysts' File Environment
SAM—Serial Access Memory
SBS—Satellite Business Systems
SDC—System Development Corporation
SDI—Selective Dissemination of Information
SMA—SAFE Message Analysis
TAP—Terminal Access Point
TSO—Time-Sharing Option
TV—Television
UBC—Universal Book Code
UPI—United Press International
USGPO—United States Government Printing Office
VDT—Video Display Terminal
VLSI—Very Large-Scale Integrated
WESCON—Western Electronics Show and Convention

INDEX